I0831454

THE HISTORY OF THE PELOPONNESIAN WAR

VOLUME TWO OF TWO

The History of the Peloponnesian War
Thucydides c. 460 – c. 400 BC
Translated by Richard Crawley
Crawley, Richard 1840 – 1893

Text set in 18 point Helvetica.
Chapter headings set in Helvetica Neue.

ISBN: 978-1-83412-417-9 Volume One
ISBN: 978-1-83412-418-6 Volume Two

THE HISTORY OF THE PELOPONNESIAN WAR

VOLUME TWO OF TWO

THUCYDIDES

Translated by
Richard Crawley

GRAND TYPE CLASSICS

CONTENTS

VOLUME ONE

VOLUME TWO

BOOK FIVE

Chapter Fifteen

Tenth Year of the War–Death of Cleon and Brasidas–Peace of Nicias

THE NEXT SUMMER THE truce for a year ended, after lasting until the Pythian games. During the armistice the Athenians expelled the Delians from Delos, concluding that they must have been polluted by some old offence at the time of their consecration, and that this had been the omission in the previous purification of the island, which, as I have related, had been thought to have been duly accomplished by the removal of the graves of the dead. The Delians had Atramyttium in Asia given them by Pharnaces, and settled there as they removed from Delos.

Meanwhile Cleon prevailed on the Athenians to let him set sail at the expiration of the armistice for the towns in the direction of Thrace with twelve hundred heavy infantry and three hundred horse from Athens, a large force of the allies, and thirty ships. First touching at the still besieged Scione, and taking some heavy infantry from the army there, he next sailed into Cophos, a harbour in the territory of Torone, which is not far from the town. From thence, having learnt from deserters that Brasidas was not in Torone, and that its garrison was not strong enough to give him battle, he advanced with his army against the town, sending ten ships to sail round into the harbour. He first came to the fortification lately thrown up in front of the town by Brasidas in order to take in the suburb, to do which he had pulled down part of the original wall and made it all one city. To this point Pasitelidas, the Lacedaemonian commander, with such garrison as there was in the place, hurried to repel the Athenian assault; but finding himself hard pressed, and seeing the ships that had been sent round sailing into the harbour, Pasitelidas began to be afraid that they might get up to the city before its defenders were there and, the fortification being also carried, he might be taken prisoner, and so abandoned the outwork and ran into the town. But the Athenians from the ships had already taken Torone, and their land forces following at his heels burst in with him with a rush over the part of the old wall that had been pulled down, killing some of the Peloponnesians and Toronaeans in the melee, and making prisoners of the rest, and Pasitelidas their commander amongst them. Brasidas meanwhile had advanced to relieve Torone, and had only about four miles more to go when he heard of its fall on the road, and turned back again. Cleon and the Athenians set up two trophies, one by the harbour, the other by the fortification and, making slaves of the wives and children of the Toronaeans, sent the men with the Peloponnesians and any Chalcidians that were there, to the number of seven hundred, to Athens; whence, however, they all came home afterwards, the Peloponnesians on the conclusion of peace, and the rest by being exchanged against other prisoners with the Olynthians. About the same time Panactum, a fortress on the Athenian border, was taken by treachery by the Boeotians. Meanwhile Cleon, after placing a garrison in Torone, weighed anchor and sailed around Athos on his way to Amphipolis.

About the same time Phaeax, son of Erasistratus, set sail with two colleagues as ambassador from Athens to Italy and Sicily. The Leontines, upon the departure of the

Athenians from Sicily after the pacification, had placed a number of new citizens upon the roll, and the commons had a design for redividing the land; but the upper classes, aware of their intention, called in the Syracusans and expelled the commons. These last were scattered in various directions; but the upper classes came to an agreement with the Syracusans, abandoned and laid waste their city, and went and lived at Syracuse, where they were made citizens. Afterwards some of them were dissatisfied, and leaving Syracuse occupied Phocaeae, a quarter of the town of Leontini, and Bricinniae, a strong place in the Leontine country, and being there joined by most of the exiled commons carried on war from the fortifications. The Athenians hearing this, sent Phaeax to see if they could not by some means so convince their allies there and the rest of the Sicilians of the ambitious designs of Syracuse as to induce them to form a general coalition against her, and thus save the commons of Leontini. Arrived in Sicily, Phaeax succeeded at Camarina and Agrigentum, but meeting with a repulse at Gela did not go on to the rest, as he saw that he should not succeed with them, but returned through the country of the Sicels to Catana, and after visiting Bricinniae as he passed, and encouraging its inhabitants, sailed back to Athens.

During his voyage along the coast to and from Sicily, he treated with some cities in Italy on the subject of friendship with Athens, and also fell in with some Locrian settlers exiled from Messina, who had been sent thither when the Locrians were called in by one of the factions that divided Messina after the pacification of Sicily, and Messina came for a time into the hands of the Locrians. These being met by Phaeax on their return home received no injury at his hands, as the Locrians had agreed with him for a treaty with Athens. They were the only people of the allies who, when the reconciliation between the Sicilians took place, had not made peace with her; nor indeed would they have done so now, if they had not been pressed by a war with the Hipponians and Medmaeans who lived on their border, and were colonists of theirs. Phaeax meanwhile proceeded on his voyage, and at length arrived at Athens.

Cleon, whom we left on his voyage from Torone to Amphipolis, made Eion his base, and after an unsuccessful assault upon the Andrian colony of Stagirus, took Galepsus, a colony of Thasos, by storm. He now sent envoys to Perdiccas to command his attendance with an army, as provided by the alliance; and others to Thrace, to Polles, king of the Odomantians, who was to bring as many Thracian mercenaries as possible; and himself remained inactive in Eion, awaiting their arrival. Informed of this, Brasidas on his part took up a position of observation upon Cerdylium, a place situated in the Argilian country on high ground across the river, not far from

Amphipolis, and commanding a view on all sides, and thus made it impossible for Cleon's army to move without his seeing it; for he fully expected that Cleon, despising the scanty numbers of his opponent, would march against Amphipolis with the force that he had got with him. At the same time Brasidas made his preparations, calling to his standard fifteen hundred Thracian mercenaries and all the Edonians, horse and targeteers; he also had a thousand Myrcinian and Chalcidian targeteers, besides those in Amphipolis, and a force of heavy infantry numbering altogether about two thousand, and three hundred Hellenic horse. Fifteen hundred of these he had with him upon Cerdylium; the rest were stationed with Clearidas in Amphipolis.

After remaining quiet for some time, Cleon was at length obliged to do as Brasidas expected. His soldiers, tired of their inactivity, began also seriously to reflect on the weakness and incompetence of their commander, and the skill and valour that would be opposed to him, and on their own original unwillingness to accompany him. These murmurs coming to the ears of Cleon, he resolved not to disgust the army by keeping it in the same place, and broke up his camp and advanced. The temper of the general was what it had been at Pylos, his success on that occasion having given him confidence in his capacity. He never dreamed of any one coming out to fight him, but said that he was rather going up to view the place; and if he waited for his reinforcements, it was not in order to make victory secure in case he should be compelled to engage, but to be enabled to surround and storm the city. He accordingly came and posted his army upon a strong hill in front of Amphipolis, and proceeded to examine the lake formed by the Strymon, and how the town lay on the side of Thrace. He thought to retire at pleasure without fighting, as there was no one to be seen upon the wall or coming out of the gates, all of which were shut. Indeed, it seemed a mistake not to have brought down engines with him; he could then have taken the town, there being no one to defend it.

As soon as Brasidas saw the Athenians in motion he descended himself from Cerdylium and entered Amphipolis. He did not venture to go out in regular order against the Athenians: he mistrusted his strength, and thought it inadequate to the attempt; not in numbers–these were not so unequal–but in quality, the flower of the Athenian army being in the field, with the best of the Lemnians and Imbrians. He therefore prepared to assail them by stratagem. By showing the enemy the number of his troops, and the shifts which he had been put to to to arm them, he thought that he should have less chance of beating him than by not letting him have a sight of them, and thus learn how good a right he had to despise them. He accordingly picked out a hundred and fifty heavy infantry and, putting the rest under Clearidas, determined to attack suddenly before the Athenians retired; thinking that he should not have again such a chance of catching them alone, if their reinforcements were once allowed to come up; and so calling all his soldiers together in order to encourage them and explain his intention, spoke as follows:

"Peloponnesians, the character of the country from which we have come, one which has always owed its freedom to valour, and the fact that you are Dorians and the enemy you are about to fight Ionians, whom you are accustomed to beat, are things that do not need further comment. But the plan of attack that I propose to pursue, this it is as well to explain, in order that the fact of our adventuring with a part instead of with the whole of our forces may not damp your courage by the apparent disadvantage at which it places you. I imagine it is the poor opinion that he has of us, and the fact that he has no idea of any one coming out to engage him, that has made the enemy march up to the place and carelessly look about him as he is doing, without noticing us. But the most successful soldier will always be the man who most happily detects a blunder like this, and who carefully consulting his own means makes his attack not so much by open and regular approaches, as by seizing the opportunity of the moment; and these stratagems, which do the greatest service to our friends by most completely deceiving our enemies, have the most brilliant name in war. Therefore, while their careless confidence continues, and they are still thinking, as in my judgment they are now doing, more of retreat than of maintaining their position, while their spirit is slack and not high-strung with expectation, I with the men under my command will, if possible, take them by surprise and fall with a run upon their centre; and do you, Clearidas, afterwards, when you see me already upon them, and, as is likely, dealing terror among them, take with you the Amphipolitans, and the rest of the allies, and suddenly open the gates and dash at them, and hasten to engage as quickly as you can. That is our best chance of establishing a panic among them, as a fresh assailant has always more terrors for an enemy than the one he is immediately engaged with. Show yourself a brave man, as a Spartan should; and do you, allies, follow him like men, and remember that zeal, honour, and obedience mark the good soldier, and that this day will make you either free men and allies of Lacedaemon, or slaves of Athens; even if you escape without personal loss of liberty or life, your bondage will be on harsher terms than before, and you will also hinder the liberation of the rest of the Hellenes. No cowardice then on your part, seeing the greatness of the issues at stake, and I will show that what I preach to others I can practise myself."

After this brief speech Brasidas himself prepared for the sally, and placed the rest with Clearidas at the Thracian gates to support him as had been agreed. Meanwhile he had been seen coming down from Cerdylium and then in the city, which is overlooked from the outside, sacrificing near the temple of Athene; in short, all his movements had been observed, and word was brought to Cleon, who had at the moment gone on to look about him, that the whole of the enemy's force could be seen in the town, and that the feet of horses and men in great numbers were visible under the gates, as if a sally were intended. Upon hearing this he went up to look, and having done so, being unwilling to venture upon the decisive step of a battle before his reinforcements came up, and fancying that he would have time to retire, bid the retreat be sounded and sent orders to the men to effect it by moving on the left wing in the direction of Eion, which was indeed the only way practicable. This however not being quick enough for him, he joined the retreat in person and made the right wing wheel round, thus turning its unarmed side to the enemy. It was then that Brasidas, seeing the Athenian force in motion and his opportunity come, said to the men with him and the rest: “Those fellows will never stand before us, one can see that by the way their spears and heads are going. Troops which do as they do seldom stand a charge. Quick, someone, and open the gates I spoke of, and let us be out and at them with no fears for the result.” Accordingly issuing out by the palisade gate and by the first in the long wall then existing, he ran at the top of his speed along the straight road, where the trophy now stands as you go by the steepest part of the hill, and fell upon and routed the centre of the Athenians, panic-stricken by their own disorder and astounded at his audacity. At the same moment Clearidas in execution of his orders issued out from the Thracian gates to support him, and also attacked the enemy. The result was that the Athenians, suddenly and unexpectedly attacked on both sides, fell into confusion; and their left towards Eion, which had already got on some distance, at once broke and fled. Just as it was in full retreat and Brasidas was passing on to attack the right, he received a wound; but his fall was not perceived by the Athenians, as he was taken up by those near him and carried off the field. The Athenian right made a better stand, and though Cleon, who from the first had no thought of fighting, at once fled and was overtaken and slain by a Myrcinian targeteer, his infantry forming in close order upon the hill twice or thrice repulsed the attacks of Clearidas, and did not finally give way until they were surrounded and routed by the missiles of the Myrcinian and Chalcidian horse and the targeteers. Thus the Athenian army was all now in flight; and such as escaped being killed in the battle, or by the Chalcidian horse and the targeteers, dispersed among the hills, and with difficulty made their way to Eion. The men who had taken up and rescued Brasidas, brought him into the town with the breath still in him: he lived to hear of the victory of his troops, and not long after expired. The rest of the army returning with Clearidas from the pursuit stripped the dead and set up a trophy.

After this all the allies attended in arms and buried Brasidas at the public expense in the city, in front of what is now the marketplace, and the Amphipolitans, having enclosed his tomb, ever afterwards sacrifice to him as a hero and have given to him the honour of games and annual offerings. They constituted him the founder of their colony, and pulled down the Hagnonic erections, and obliterated everything that could be interpreted as a memorial of his having founded the place; for they considered that Brasidas had been their preserver, and courting as they did the alliance of Lacedaemon for fear of Athens, in their present hostile relations with the latter they could no longer with the same advantage or satisfaction pay Hagnon his honours. They also gave the Athenians back their dead. About six hundred of the latter had fallen and only seven of the enemy, owing to there having been no regular engagement, but the affair of accident and panic that I have described. After taking up their dead the Athenians sailed off home, while Clearidas and his troops remained to arrange matters at Amphipolis.

About the same time three Lacedaemonians–Ramphias, Autocharidas, and Epicydidas–led a reinforcement of nine hundred heavy infantry to the towns in the direction of Thrace, and arriving at Heraclea in Trachis reformed matters there as seemed good to them. While they delayed there, this battle took place and so the summer ended.

With the beginning of the winter following, Ramphias and his companions penetrated as far as Pierium in Thessaly; but as the Thessalians opposed their further advance, and Brasidas whom they came to reinforce was dead, they turned back home, thinking that the moment had gone by, the Athenians being defeated and gone, and themselves not equal to the execution of Brasidas's designs. The main cause however of their return was because they knew that when they set out Lacedaemonian opinion was really in favour of peace.

Indeed it so happened that directly after the battle of Amphipolis and the retreat of Ramphias from Thessaly, both sides ceased to prosecute the war and turned their attention to peace. Athens had suffered severely at Delium, and again shortly afterwards at Amphipolis, and had no longer that confidence in her strength which had made her before refuse to treat, in the belief of ultimate victory which her success at the moment had inspired; besides, she was afraid of her allies being tempted by her reverses to rebel more generally, and repented having let go the splendid opportunity for peace which the affair of Pylos had offered. Lacedaemon, on the other hand, found the event of the war to falsify her notion that a few years would suffice for the overthrow of the power of the Athenians by the devastation of their land. She had suffered on the island a disaster hitherto unknown at Sparta; she saw her country plundered from Pylos and Cythera; the Helots were deserting, and she was in constant apprehension that those who remained in Peloponnese would rely upon those outside and take advantage of the situation to renew their old attempts at revolution. Besides this, as chance would have it, her thirty years' truce with the Argives was upon the point of expiring; and they refused to renew it unless Cynuria were restored to them; so that it seemed impossible to fight Argos and Athens at once. She also suspected some of the cities in Peloponnese of intending to go over to the enemy and that was indeed the case.

These considerations made both sides disposed for an accommodation; the Lacedaemonians being probably the most eager, as they ardently desired to recover the men taken upon the island, the Spartans among whom belonged to the first families and were accordingly related to the governing body in Lacedaemon. Negotiations had been begun directly after their capture, but the Athenians in their hour of triumph would not consent to any reasonable terms; though after their defeat at Delium, Lacedaemon, knowing that they would be now more inclined to listen, at once concluded the armistice for a year, during which they were to confer together and see if a longer period could not be agreed upon.

Now, however, after the Athenian defeat at Amphipolis, and the death of Cleon and Brasidas, who had been the two principal opponents of peace on either side–the latter from the success and honour which war gave him, the former because he thought that, if tranquillity were restored, his crimes would be more open to detection and his slanders less credited–the foremost candidates for power in either city, Pleistoanax, son of Pausanias, king of Lacedaemon, and Nicias, son of Niceratus, the most fortunate general of his time, each desired peace more ardently than ever. Nicias, while still happy and honoured, wished to secure his good fortune, to obtain a present release from trouble for himself and his countrymen, and hand down to posterity a name as an ever-successful statesman, and thought the way to do this was to keep out of danger and commit himself as little as possible to fortune, and that peace alone made this keeping out of danger possible. Pleistoanax, again, was assailed by his enemies for his restoration, and regularly held up by them to the prejudice of his countrymen, upon every reverse that befell them, as though his unjust restoration were the cause; the accusation being that he and his brother Aristocles had bribed the prophetess of Delphi to tell the Lacedaemonian deputations which successively arrived at the temple to bring home the seed of the demigod son of Zeus from abroad, else they would have to plough with a silver share. In this way, it was insisted, in time he had induced the Lacedaemonians in the nineteenth year of his exile to Lycaeum (whither he had gone when banished on suspicion of having been bribed to retreat from Attica, and had built half his house within the consecrated precinct of Zeus for fear of the Lacedaemonians), to restore him with the same dances and sacrifices with which they had instituted their kings upon the first settlement of Lacedaemon. The smart of this accusation, and the reflection that in peace no disaster could occur, and that when Lacedaemon had recovered her men there would be nothing for his enemies to take hold of (whereas, while war lasted, the highest station must always bear the scandal of everything that went wrong), made him ardently desire a settlement. Accordingly this winter was employed in conferences; and as spring rapidly approached, the Lacedaemonians sent round orders to the cities to prepare for a fortified occupation of Attica, and held this as a sword over the heads of the Athenians to induce them to listen to their overtures; and at last, after many claims had been urged on either side at the conferences a peace was agreed on upon the following basis. Each party was to restore its conquests, but Athens was to keep Nisaea; her demand for Plataea being met by the Thebans asserting that they had acquired the place not by force or treachery, but by the voluntary adhesion upon agreement of its citizens; and the same, according to the Athenian account, being the history of her acquisition of Nisaea. This arranged, the Lacedaemonians summoned their allies, and all voting for peace except the Boeotians, Corinthians, Eleans, and Megarians, who did not approve of these proceedings, they concluded the treaty and made peace, each of the contracting parties swearing to the following articles:

The Athenians and Lacedaemonians and their allies made a treaty, and swore to it, city by city, as follows;

1. Touching the national temples, there shall be a free passage by land and by sea to all who wish it, to sacrifice, travel, consult, and attend the oracle or games, according to the customs of their countries.

2. The temple and shrine of Apollo at Delphi and the Delphians shall be governed by their own laws, taxed by their own state, and judged by their own judges, the land and the people, according to the custom of their country.

3. The treaty shall be binding for fifty years

upon the Athenians and the allies of the Athenians, and upon the Lacedaemonians and the allies of the Lacedaemonians, without fraud or hurt by land or by sea.

4. It shall not be lawful to take up arms, with intent to do hurt, either for the Lacedaemonians and their allies against the Athenians and their allies, or for the Athenians and their allies against the Lacedaemonians and their allies, in any way or means whatsoever. But should any difference arise between them they are to have recourse to law and oaths, according as may be agreed between the parties.

5. The Lacedaemonians and their allies shall give back Amphipolis to the Athenians. Nevertheless, in the case of cities given up by the Lacedaemonians to the Athenians, the inhabitants shall be allowed to go where they please and to take their property with them: and the cities shall be independent, paying only the tribute of Aristides. And it shall not be

lawful for the Athenians or their allies to carry on war against them after the treaty has been concluded, so long as the tribute is paid. The cities referred to are Argilus, Stagirus, Acanthus, Scolus, Olynthus, and Spartolus. These cities shall be neutral, allies neither of the Lacedaemonians nor of the Athenians: but if the cities consent, it shall be lawful for the Athenians to make them their allies, provided always that the cities wish it. The Mecybernaeans, Sanaeans, and Singaeans shall inhabit their own cities, as also the Olynthians and Acanthians: but the Lacedaemonians and their allies shall give back Panactum to the Athenians.

6. The Athenians shall give back Coryphasium, Cythera, Methana, Lacedaemonians that are in the prison at Athens or elsewhere in the Athenian dominions, and shall let go the Peloponnesians besieged in Scione, and all others in Scione that are allies of the

Lacedaemonians, and all whom Brasidas sent in there, and any others of the allies of the Lacedaemonians that may be in the prison at Athens or elsewhere in the Athenian dominions.

7. The Lacedaemonians and their allies shall in like manner give back any of the Athenians or their allies that they may have in their hands.

8. In the case of Scione, Torone, and Sermylium, and any other cities that the Athenians may have, the Athenians may adopt such measures as they please.

9. The Athenians shall take an oath to the Lacedaemonians and their allies, city by city. Every man shall swear by the most binding oath of his country, seventeen from each city. The oath shall be as follows; "I will abide by this agreement and treaty honestly and without deceit." In the same way an oath shall be taken by the Lacedaemonians and their allies to the Athenians: and the oath shall be renewed annually by both parties.

Pillars shall be erected at Olympia, Pythia, the Isthmus, at Athens in the Acropolis, and at Lacedaemon in the temple at Amyclae.

10. If anything be forgotten, whatever it be, and on whatever point, it shall be consistent with their oath for both parties, the Athenians and Lacedaemonians, to alter it, according to their discretion.

The treaty begins from the ephoralty of Pleistolas in Lacedaemon, on the 27th day of the month of Artemisium, and from the archonship, of Alcaeus at Athens, on the 25th day of the month of Elaphebolion. Those who took the oath and poured the libations for the Lacedaemonians were Pleistoanax, Agis, Pleistolas, Damagetis, Chionis, Metagenes, Acanthus, Daithus, Ischagoras, Philocharidas, Zeuxidas, Antippus, Tellis, Alcinadas, Empedias, Menas, and Laphilus: for the Athenians, Lampon, Isthmonicus, Nicias, Laches, Euthydemus, Procles, Pythodorus, Hagnon, Myrtilus, Thrasycles, Theagenes, Aristocrates, Iolcius, Timocrates,

Leon, Lamachus, and Demosthenes.

This treaty was made in the spring, just at the end of winter, directly after the city festival of Dionysus, just ten years, with the difference of a few days, from the first invasion of Attica and the commencement of this war. This must be calculated by the seasons rather than by trusting to the enumeration of the names of the several magistrates or offices of honour that are used to mark past events. Accuracy is impossible where an event may have occurred in the beginning, or middle, or at any period in their tenure of office. But by computing by summers and winters, the method adopted in this history, it will be found that, each of these amounting to half a year, there were ten summers and as many winters contained in this first war.

Meanwhile the Lacedaemonians, to whose lot it fell to begin the work of restitution, immediately set free all the prisoners of war in their possession, and sent Ischagoras,

Menas, and Philocharidas as envoys to the towns in the direction of Thrace, to order Clearidas to hand over Amphipolis to the Athenians, and the rest of their allies each to accept the treaty as it affected them. They, however, did not like its terms, and refused to accept it; Clearidas also, willing to oblige the Chalcidians, would not hand over the town, averring his inability to do so against their will. Meanwhile he hastened in person to Lacedaemon with envoys from the place, to defend his disobedience against the possible accusations of Ischagoras and his companions, and also to see whether it was too late for the agreement to be altered; and on finding the Lacedaemonians were bound, quickly set out back again with instructions from them to hand over the place, if possible, or at all events to bring out the Peloponnesians that were in it.

The allies happened to be present in person at Lacedaemon, and those who had not accepted the treaty were now asked by the

Lacedaemonians to adopt it. This, however, they refused to do, for the same reasons as before, unless a fairer one than the present were agreed upon; and remaining firm in their determination were dismissed by the Lacedaemonians, who now decided on forming an alliance with the Athenians, thinking that Argos, who had refused the application of Ampelidas and Lichas for a renewal of the treaty, would without Athens be no longer formidable, and that the rest of the Peloponnese would be most likely to keep quiet, if the coveted alliance of Athens were shut against them. Accordingly, after conference with the Athenian ambassadors, an alliance was agreed upon and oaths were exchanged, upon the terms following:

1. The Lacedaemonians shall be allies of the Athenians for fifty years.

2. Should any enemy invade the territory of Lacedaemon and injure the Lacedaemonians, the Athenians shall help in such way as they most effectively can,

according to their power. But if the invader be gone after plundering the country, that city shall be the enemy of Lacedaemon and Athens, and shall be chastised by both, and one shall not make peace without the other. This to be honestly, loyally, and without fraud.

3. Should any enemy invade the territory of Athens and injure the Athenians, the Lacedaemonians shall help them in such way as they most effectively can, according to their power. But if the invader be gone after plundering the country, that city shall be the enemy of Lacedaemon and Athens, and shall be chastised by both, and one shall not make peace without the other. This to be honestly, loyally, and without fraud.

4. Should the slave population rise, the Athenians shall help the Lacedaemonians with all their might, according to their power.

5. This treaty shall be sworn to by the same persons on either side that swore to the other. It shall be renewed annually by the Lacedaemonians going to Athens

for the Dionysia, and the Athenians to Lacedaemon for the Hyacinthia, and a pillar shall be set up by either party: at Lacedaemon near the statue of Apollo at Amyclae, and at Athens on the Acropolis near the statue of Athene. Should the Lacedaemonians and Athenians see to add to or take away from the alliance in any particular, it shall be consistent with their oaths for both parties to do so, according to their discretion.

Those who took the oath for the Lacedaemonians were Pleistoanax, Agis, Pleistolas, Damagetus, Chionis, Metagenes, Acanthus, Daithus, Ischagoras, Philocharidas, Zeuxidas, Antippus, Alcinadas, Tellis, Empedias, Menas, and Laphilus; for the Athenians, Lampon, Isthmionicus, Laches, Nicias, Euthydemus, Procles, Pythodorus, Hagnon, Myrtilus, Thrasycles, Theagenes, Aristocrates, Iolcius, Timocrates, Leon, Lamachus, and Demosthenes.

This alliance was made not long after the treaty; and the Athenians gave back the men from the island to the Lacedaemonians, and the summer of the eleventh year began. This completes the history of the first war, which occupied the whole of the ten years previously.

Chapter Sixteen

Feeling against Sparta in Peloponnese–League of the Mantineans, Eleans, Argives, and Athenians–Battle of Mantinea and breaking up of the League

AFTER THE TREATY AND the alliance between the Lacedaemonians and Athenians, concluded after the ten years' war, in the ephorate of Pleistolas at Lacedaemon, and the archonship of Alcaeus at Athens, the states which had accepted them were at peace; but the Corinthians and some of the cities in Peloponnese trying to disturb the settlement, a fresh agitation was instantly commenced by the allies against Lacedaemon. Further, the Lacedaemonians, as time went on, became suspected by the Athenians through their not performing some of the provisions in the treaty; and though for six years and ten months they abstained from invasion of each other's territory, yet abroad an unstable armistice did not prevent either party doing the other the most effectual injury, until they were finally obliged to break the treaty made after the ten years' war and to have recourse to open hostilities.

The history of this period has been also written by the same Thucydides, an Athenian, in the chronological order of events by summers and winters, to the time when the Lacedaemonians and their allies put an end to the Athenian empire, and took the Long Walls and Piraeus. The war had then lasted for twenty-seven years in all. Only a mistaken judgment can object to including the interval of treaty in the war. Looked at by the light of facts it cannot, it will be found, be rationally considered a state of peace, where neither party either gave or got back all that they had agreed, apart from the violations of it which occurred on both sides in the Mantinean and Epidaurian wars and other instances, and the fact that the allies in the direction of Thrace were in as open hostility as ever, while the Boeotians had only a truce renewed every ten days. So that the first ten years' war, the treacherous armistice that followed it, and the subsequent war will, calculating by the seasons, be found to make up the number of years which I have mentioned, with the difference of a few days, and to afford an instance of faith in oracles being for once justified by the event. I certainly all along remember from the beginning to the end of the war its being commonly declared that it would last thrice nine years. I lived through the whole of it, being of an age to comprehend events, and giving my attention to them in order to know the exact truth about them. It was also my fate to be an exile from my country for twenty years after my command at Amphipolis; and being present with both parties, and more especially with the Peloponnesians by reason of my exile, I had leisure to observe affairs somewhat particularly. I will accordingly now relate the differences that arose after the ten years' war, the breach of the treaty, and the hostilities that followed.

After the conclusion of the fifty years' truce and of the subsequent alliance, the embassies from Peloponnese which had been summoned for this business returned from Lacedaemon. The rest went straight home, but the Corinthians first turned aside to Argos and opened negotiations with some of the men in office there, pointing out that Lacedaemon could have no good end in view, but only the subjugation of Peloponnese, or she would never have entered into treaty and alliance with the once detested Athenians, and that the duty of consulting for the safety of Peloponnese had now fallen upon Argos, who should immediately pass a decree inviting any Hellenic state that chose, such state being independent and accustomed to meet fellow powers upon the fair and equal ground of law and justice, to make a defensive alliance with the Argives; appointing a few individuals with plenipotentiary powers, instead of making the people the medium of negotiation, in order that, in the case of an applicant being rejected, the fact of his overtures might not be made public. They said that many would come over from hatred of the Lacedaemonians. After this explanation of their views, the Corinthians returned home.

The persons with whom they had

communicated reported the proposal to their government and people, and the Argives passed the decree and chose twelve men to negotiate an alliance for any Hellenic state that wished it, except Athens and Lacedaemon, neither of which should be able to join without reference to the Argive people. Argos came into the plan the more readily because she saw that war with Lacedaemon was inevitable, the truce being on the point of expiring; and also because she hoped to gain the supremacy of Peloponnese. For at this time Lacedaemon had sunk very low in public estimation because of her disasters, while the Argives were in a most flourishing condition, having taken no part in the Attic war, but having on the contrary profited largely by their neutrality. The Argives accordingly prepared to receive into alliance any of the Hellenes that desired it.

The Mantineans and their allies were the first to come over through fear of the

Lacedaemonians. Having taken advantage of the war against Athens to reduce a large part of Arcadia into subjection, they thought that Lacedaemon would not leave them undisturbed in their conquests, now that she had leisure to interfere, and consequently gladly turned to a powerful city like Argos, the historical enemy of the Lacedaemonians, and a sister democracy. Upon the defection of Mantinea, the rest of Peloponnese at once began to agitate the propriety of following her example, conceiving that the Mantineans not have changed sides without good reason; besides which they were angry with Lacedaemon among other reasons for having inserted in the treaty with Athens that it should be consistent with their oaths for both parties, Lacedaemonians and Athenians, to add to or take away from it according to their discretion. It was this clause that was the real origin of the panic in Peloponnese, by exciting suspicions of a Lacedaemonian and Athenian combination against their liberties: any alteration should properly have been made conditional upon the consent of the whole body of the allies. With these apprehensions there was a very general desire in each state to place itself in alliance with Argos.

In the meantime the Lacedaemonians perceiving the agitation going on in Peloponnese, and that Corinth was the author of it and was herself about to enter into alliance with the Argives, sent ambassadors thither in the hope of preventing what was in contemplation. They accused her of having brought it all about, and told her that she could not desert Lacedaemon and become the ally of Argos, without adding violation of her oaths to the crime which she had already committed in not accepting the treaty with Athens, when it had been expressly agreed that the decision of the majority of the allies should be binding, unless the gods or heroes stood in the way. Corinth in her answer, delivered before those of her allies who had like her refused to accept the treaty, and whom she had previously invited to attend, refrained from openly stating the injuries she complained of, such as the non-recovery of Sollium or Anactorium from the Athenians, or any other point in which she thought she had been prejudiced, but took shelter under the pretext that she could not give up her Thracian allies, to whom her separate individual security had been given, when they first rebelled with Potidaea, as well as upon subsequent occasions. She denied, therefore, that she committed any violation of her oaths to the allies in not entering into the treaty with Athens; having sworn upon the faith of the gods to her Thracian friends, she could not honestly give them up. Besides, the expression was, "unless the gods or heroes stand in the way." Now here, as it appeared to her, the gods stood in the way. This was what she said on the subject of her former oaths. As to the Argive alliance, she would confer with her friends and do whatever was right. The Lacedaemonian envoys returning home, some Argive ambassadors who happened to be in Corinth pressed her to conclude the alliance without further delay, but were told to attend at the next congress to be held at Corinth.

Immediately afterwards an Elean embassy arrived, and first making an alliance with Corinth went on from thence to Argos, according to their instructions, and became allies of the Argives, their country being just then at enmity with Lacedaemon and Lepreum. Some time back there had been a war between the Lepreans and some of the Arcadians; and the Eleans being called in by the former with the offer of half their lands, had put an end to the war, and leaving the land in the hands of its Leprean occupiers had imposed upon them the tribute of a talent to the Olympian Zeus. Till the Attic war this tribute was paid by the Lepreans, who then took the war as an excuse for no longer doing so, and upon the Eleans using force appealed to Lacedaemon. The case was thus submitted to her arbitrament; but the Eleans, suspecting the fairness of the tribunal, renounced the reference and laid waste the Leprean territory. The Lacedaemonians nevertheless decided that the Lepreans were independent and the Eleans aggressors, and as the latter did not abide by the arbitration, sent a garrison of heavy infantry into Lepreum. Upon this the Eleans, holding that Lacedaemon had received one of their rebel subjects, put forward the convention providing that each confederate should come out of the Attic war in possession of what he had when he went into it, and considering that justice had not been done them went over to the Argives, and now made the alliance through their ambassadors, who had been instructed for that purpose. Immediately after them the Corinthians and the Thracian Chalcidians became allies of Argos. Meanwhile the

Boeotians and Megarians, who acted together, remained quiet, being left to do as they pleased by Lacedaemon, and thinking that the Argive democracy would not suit so well with their aristocratic government as the Lacedaemonian constitution.

About the same time in this summer Athens succeeded in reducing Scione, put the adult males to death, and, making slaves of the women and children, gave the land for the Plataeans to live in. She also brought back the Delians to Delos, moved by her misfortunes in the field and by the commands of the god at Delphi. Meanwhile the Phocians and Locrians commenced hostilities. The Corinthians and Argives, being now in alliance, went to Tegea to bring about its defection from Lacedaemon, seeing that, if so considerable a state could be persuaded to join, all Peloponnese would be with them. But when the Tegeans said that they would do nothing against Lacedaemon, the hitherto zealous Corinthians relaxed their activity, and began to fear that none of the rest would now come over. Still they went to the Boeotians and tried to persuade them to alliance and a common action generally with Argos and themselves, and also begged them to go with them to Athens and obtain for them a ten days' truce similar to that made between the Athenians and Boeotians not long after the fifty years' treaty, and, in the event of the Athenians refusing, to throw up the armistice, and not make any truce in future without Corinth. These were the requests of the Corinthians. The Boeotians stopped them on the subject of the Argive alliance, but went with them to Athens, where however they failed to obtain the ten days' truce; the Athenian answer being that the Corinthians had truce already, as being allies of Lacedaemon. Nevertheless the Boeotians did not throw up their ten days' truce, in spite of the prayers and reproaches of the Corinthians for their breach of faith; and these last had to content themselves with a de facto armistice with Athens.

The same summer the Lacedaemonians marched into Arcadia with their whole levy under Pleistoanax, son of Pausanias, king of Lacedaemon, against the Parrhasians, who were subjects of Mantinea, and a faction of whom had invited their aid. They also meant to demolish, if possible, the fort of Cypsela which the Mantineans had built and garrisoned in the Parrhasian territory, to annoy the district of Sciritis in Laconia. The Lacedaemonians accordingly laid waste the Parrhasian country, and the Mantineans, placing their town in the hands of an Argive garrison, addressed themselves to the defence of their confederacy, but being unable to save Cypsela or the Parrhasian towns went back to Mantinea. Meanwhile the Lacedaemonians made the Parrhasians independent, razed the fortress, and returned home.

The same summer the soldiers from Thrace who had gone out with Brasidas came back, having been brought from thence after the treaty by Clearidas; and the Lacedaemonians decreed that the Helots who had fought with Brasidas should be free and allowed to live where they liked, and not long afterwards settled them with the Neodamodes at Lepreum, which is situated on the Laconian and Elean border; Lacedaemon being at this time at enmity with Elis. Those however of the Spartans who had been taken prisoners on the island and had surrendered their arms might, it was feared, suppose that they were to be subjected to some degradation in consequence of their misfortune, and so make some attempt at revolution, if left in possession of their franchise. These were therefore at once disfranchised, although some of them were in office at the time, and thus placed under a disability to take office, or buy and sell anything. After some time, however, the franchise was restored to them.

The same summer the Dians took Thyssus, a town on Acte by Athos in alliance with Athens. During the whole of this summer intercourse between the Athenians and Peloponnesians continued, although each party began to suspect the other directly after the treaty, because of the places specified in it not being restored. Lacedaemon, to whose lot it had fallen to begin by restoring Amphipolis and the other towns, had not done so. She had equally failed to get the treaty accepted by her Thracian allies, or by the Boeotians or the Corinthians; although she was continually promising to unite with Athens in compelling their compliance, if it were longer refused. She also kept fixing a time at which those who still refused to come in were to be declared enemies to both parties, but took care not to bind herself by any written agreement. Meanwhile the Athenians, seeing none of these professions performed in fact, began to suspect the honesty of her intentions, and consequently not only refused to comply with her demands for Pylos, but also repented having given up the prisoners from the island, and kept tight hold of the other places, until Lacedaemon's part of the treaty should be fulfilled. Lacedaemon, on the other hand, said she had done what she could, having given up the Athenian prisoners of war in her possession, evacuated Thrace, and performed everything else in her power. Amphipolis it was out of her ability to restore; but she would endeavour to bring the Boeotians and Corinthians into the treaty, to recover Panactum, and send home all the Athenian prisoners of war in Boeotia. Meanwhile she required that Pylos should be restored, or at all events that the Messenians and Helots should be withdrawn, as her troops had been from Thrace, and the place garrisoned, if necessary, by the Athenians themselves. After a number of different conferences held during the summer, she succeeded in persuading Athens to withdraw from Pylos the Messenians and the rest of the Helots and deserters from Laconia, who were accordingly settled by her at Cranii in Cephallenia. Thus during this summer there was peace and intercourse between the two peoples.

Next winter, however, the ephors under whom the treaty had been made were no longer in office, and some of their successors were directly opposed to it. Embassies now arrived from the Lacedaemonian confederacy, and the Athenians, Boeotians, and Corinthians also presented themselves at Lacedaemon, and after much discussion and no agreement between them, separated for their several homes; when Cleobulus and Xenares, the two ephors who were the most anxious to break off the treaty, took advantage of this opportunity to communicate privately with the Boeotians and Corinthians, and, advising them to act as much as possible together, instructed the former first to enter into alliance with Argos, and then try and bring themselves and the

Argives into alliance with Lacedaemon. The Boeotians would so be least likely to be compelled to come into the Attic treaty; and the Lacedaemonians would prefer gaining the friendship and alliance of Argos even at the price of the hostility of Athens and the rupture of the treaty. The Boeotians knew that an honourable friendship with Argos had been long the desire of Lacedaemon; for the Lacedaemonians believed that this would considerably facilitate the conduct of the war outside Peloponnese. Meanwhile they begged the Boeotians to place Panactum in her hands in order that she might, if possible, obtain Pylos in exchange for it, and so be more in a position to resume hostilities with Athens.

After receiving these instructions for their governments from Xenares and Cleobulus and their friends at Lacedaemon, the Boeotians and Corinthians departed. On their way home they were joined by two persons high in office at Argos, who had waited for them on the road, and who now sounded them upon the possibility of the Boeotians joining the Corinthians, Eleans, and Mantineans in becoming the allies of Argos, in the idea that if this could be effected they would be able, thus united, to make peace or war as they pleased either against Lacedaemon or any other power. The Boeotian envoys were were pleased at thus hearing themselves accidentally asked to do what their friends at Lacedaemon had told them; and the two Argives perceiving that their proposal was agreeable, departed with a promise to send ambassadors to the Boeotians. On their arrival the Boeotians reported to the Boeotarchs what had been said to them at Lacedaemon and also by the Argives who had met them, and the Boeotarchs, pleased with the idea, embraced it with the more eagerness from the lucky coincidence of Argos soliciting the very thing wanted by their friends at Lacedaemon. Shortly afterwards ambassadors appeared from Argos with the proposals indicated; and the Boeotarchs approved of the terms and dismissed the ambassadors with a promise to send envoys to Argos to negotiate the alliance.

In the meantime it was decided by the Boeotarchs, the Corinthians, the Megarians, and the envoys from Thrace first to interchange oaths together to give help to each other whenever it was required and not to make war or peace except in common; after which the Boeotians and Megarians, who acted together, should make the alliance with Argos. But before the oaths were taken the Boeotarchs communicated these proposals to the four councils of the Boeotians, in whom the supreme power resides, and advised them to interchange oaths with all such cities as should be willing to enter into a defensive league with the Boeotians. But the members of the Boeotian councils refused their assent to the proposal, being afraid of offending Lacedaemon by entering into a league with the deserter Corinth; the Boeotarchs not having acquainted them with what had passed at Lacedaemon and with the advice given by Cleobulus and Xenares and the Boeotian partisans there, namely, that they should become allies of Corinth and Argos as a preliminary to a junction with Lacedaemon; fancying that, even if they should say nothing about this, the councils would not vote against what had been decided and advised by the Boeotarchs. This difficulty arising, the Corinthians and the envoys from Thrace departed without anything having been concluded; and the Boeotarchs, who had previously intended after carrying this to try and effect the alliance with Argos, now omitted to bring the Argive question before the councils, or to send to Argos the envoys whom they had promised; and a general coldness and delay ensued in the matter.

In this same winter Mecyberna was assaulted and taken by the Olynthians, having an Athenian garrison inside it.

All this while negotiations had been going on between the Athenians and Lacedaemonians about the conquests still retained by each, and Lacedaemon, hoping that if Athens were to get back Panactum from the Boeotians she might herself recover Pylos, now sent an embassy to the Boeotians, and begged them to place Panactum and their Athenian prisoners in her hands, in order that she might exchange them for Pylos. This the Boeotians refused to do, unless Lacedaemon made a separate alliance with them as she had done with Athens. Lacedaemon knew that this would be a breach of faith to Athens, as it had been agreed that neither of them should make peace or war without the other; yet wishing to obtain Panactum which she hoped to exchange for Pylos, and the party who pressed for the dissolution of the treaty strongly affecting the Boeotian connection, she at length concluded the alliance just as winter gave way to spring; and Panactum was instantly razed. And so the eleventh year of the war ended.

In the first days of the summer following, the Argives, seeing that the promised ambassadors from Boeotia did not arrive, and that Panactum was being demolished, and that a separate alliance had been concluded between the Boeotians and Lacedaemonians, began to be afraid that Argos might be left alone, and all the confederacy go over to Lacedaemon. They fancied that the Boeotians had been persuaded by the Lacedaemonians to raze Panactum and to enter into the treaty with the Athenians, and that Athens was privy to this arrangement, and even her alliance, therefore, no longer open to them–a resource which they had always counted upon, by reason of the dissensions existing, in the event of the noncontinuance of their treaty with Lacedaemon. In this strait the Argives, afraid that, as the result of refusing to renew the treaty with Lacedaemon and of aspiring to the supremacy in Peloponnese, they would have the Lacedaemonians, Tegeans, Boeotians, and Athenians on their hands all at once, now hastily sent off Eustrophus and Aeson, who seemed the persons most likely to be acceptable, as envoys to Lacedaemon, with the view of making as good a treaty as they could with the Lacedaemonians, upon such terms as could be got, and being left in peace.

Having reached Lacedaemon, their ambassadors proceeded to negotiate the terms of the proposed treaty. What the Argives first demanded was that they might be allowed to refer to the arbitration of some state or private person the question of the Cynurian land, a piece of frontier territory about which they have always been disputing, and which contains the towns of Thyrea and Anthene, and is occupied by the Lacedaemonians. The Lacedaemonians at first said that they could not allow this point to be discussed, but were ready to conclude upon the old terms. Eventually, however, the Argive ambassadors succeeded in obtaining from them this concession: For the present there was to be a truce for fifty years, but it should be competent for either party, there being neither plague nor war in Lacedaemon or Argos, to give a formal challenge and decide the question of this territory by battle, as on a former occasion, when both sides claimed the victory; pursuit not being allowed beyond the frontier of Argos or Lacedaemon. The Lacedaemonians at first thought this mere folly; but at last, anxious at any cost to have the friendship of Argos they agreed to the terms demanded, and reduced them to writing. However, before any of this should become binding, the ambassadors were to return to Argos and communicate with their people and, in the event of their approval, to come at the feast of the Hyacinthia and take the oaths.

The envoys returned accordingly. In the meantime, while the Argives were engaged in these negotiations, the Lacedaemonian ambassadors–Andromedes, Phaedimus, and Antimenidas–who were to receive the prisoners from the Boeotians and restore them and Panactum to the Athenians, found that the Boeotians had themselves razed Panactum, upon the plea that oaths had been anciently exchanged between their people and the Athenians, after a dispute on the subject to the effect that neither should inhabit the place, but that they should graze it in common. As for the Athenian prisoners of war in the hands of the Boeotians, these were delivered over to Andromedes and his colleagues, and by them conveyed to Athens and given back. The envoys at the same time announced the razing of Panactum, which to them seemed as good as its restitution, as it would no longer lodge an enemy of Athens. This announcement was received with great indignation by the Athenians, who thought that the Lacedaemonians had played them false, both in the matter of the demolition of Panactum, which ought to have been restored to them standing, and in having, as they now heard, made a separate alliance with the Boeotians, in spite of their previous promise to join Athens in compelling the adhesion of those who refused to accede to the treaty. The Athenians also considered the other points in which Lacedaemon had failed in her compact, and thinking that they had been overreached, gave an angry answer to the ambassadors and sent them away.

The breach between the Lacedaemonians and Athenians having gone thus far, the party at Athens, also, who wished to cancel the treaty, immediately put themselves in motion. Foremost amongst these was Alcibiades, son of Clinias, a man yet young in years for any other Hellenic city, but distinguished by the splendour of his ancestry. Alcibiades thought the Argive alliance really preferable, not that personal pique had not also a great deal to do with his opposition; he being offended with the Lacedaemonians for having negotiated the treaty through Nicias and Laches, and having overlooked him on account of his youth, and also for not having shown him the respect due to the ancient connection of his family with them as their proxeni, which, renounced by his grandfather, he had lately himself thought to renew by his attentions to their prisoners taken in the island. Being thus, as he thought, slighted on all hands, he had in the first instance spoken against the treaty, saying that the Lacedaemonians were not to be trusted, but that they only treated, in order to be enabled by this means to crush Argos, and afterwards to attack Athens alone; and now, immediately upon the above occurring, he sent privately to the Argives, telling them to come as quickly as possible to Athens, accompanied by the

Mantineans and Eleans, with proposals of alliance; as the moment was propitious and he himself would do all he could to help them.

Upon receiving this message and discovering that the Athenians, far from being privy to the Boeotian alliance, were involved in a serious quarrel with the Lacedaemonians, the Argives paid no further attention to the embassy which they had just sent to Lacedaemon on the subject of the treaty, and began to incline rather towards the Athenians, reflecting that, in the event of war, they would thus have on their side a city that was not only an ancient ally of Argos, but a sister democracy and very powerful at sea. They accordingly at once sent ambassadors to Athens to treat for an alliance, accompanied by others from Elis and Mantinea.

At the same time arrived in haste from Lacedaemon an embassy consisting of persons reputed well disposed towards the Athenians–Philocharidas, Leon, and Endius–for fear that the Athenians in their irritation might conclude alliance with the Argives, and also to ask back Pylos in exchange for Panactum, and in defence of the alliance with the Boeotians to plead that it had not been made to hurt the Athenians. Upon the envoys speaking in the senate upon these points, and stating that they had come with full powers to settle all others at issue between them, Alcibiades became afraid that, if they were to repeat these statements to the popular assembly, they might gain the multitude, and the Argive alliance might be rejected, and accordingly had recourse to the following stratagem. He persuaded the Lacedaemonians by a solemn assurance that if they would say nothing of their full powers in the assembly, he would give back Pylos to them (himself, the present opponent of its restitution, engaging to obtain this from the Athenians), and would settle the other points at issue.

His plan was to detach them from Nicias and to disgrace them before the people, as being without sincerity in their intentions, or even common consistency in their language, and so to get the Argives, Eleans, and Mantineans taken into alliance. This plan proved successful. When the envoys appeared before the people, and upon the question being put to them, did not say as they had said in the senate, that they had come with full powers, the Athenians lost all patience, and carried away by Alcibiades, who thundered more loudly than ever against the Lacedaemonians, were ready instantly to introduce the Argives and their companions and to take them into alliance. An earthquake, however, occurring, before anything definite had been done, this assembly was adjourned.

In the assembly held the next day, Nicias, in spite of the Lacedaemonians having been deceived themselves, and having allowed him to be deceived also in not admitting that they had come with full powers, still maintained that it was best to be friends with the Lacedaemonians, and, letting the Argive proposals stand over, to send once more to Lacedaemon and learn her intentions. The adjournment of the war could only increase their own prestige and injure that of their rivals; the excellent state of their affairs making it their interest to preserve this prosperity as long as possible, while those of Lacedaemon were so desperate that the sooner she could try her fortune again the better. He succeeded accordingly in persuading them to send ambassadors, himself being among the number, to invite the Lacedaemonians, if they were really sincere, to restore Panactum intact with Amphipolis, and to abandon their alliance with the Boeotians (unless they consented to accede to the treaty), agreeably to the stipulation which forbade either to treat without the other. The ambassadors were also directed to say that the Athenians, had they wished to play false, might already have made alliance with the Argives, who were indeed come to Athens for that very purpose, and went off furnished with instructions as to any other complaints that the Athenians had to make. Having reached Lacedaemon, they communicated their instructions, and concluded by telling the Lacedaemonians that unless they gave up their alliance with the Boeotians, in the event of their not acceding to the treaty, the Athenians for their part would ally themselves with the Argives and their friends. The Lacedaemonians, however, refused to give up the Boeotian alliance–the party of Xenares the ephor, and such as shared their view, carrying the day upon this point–but renewed the oaths at the request of Nicias, who feared to return without having accomplished anything and to be disgraced; as was indeed his fate, he being held the author of the treaty with Lacedaemon. When he returned, and the

Athenians heard that nothing had been done at Lacedaemon, they flew into a passion, and deciding that faith had not been kept with them, took advantage of the presence of the Argives and their allies, who had been introduced by Alcibiades, and made a treaty and alliance with them upon the terms following:

The Athenians, Argives, Mantineans, and Eleans, acting for themselves and the allies in their respective empires, made a treaty for a hundred years, to be without fraud or hurt by land and by sea.

1. It shall not be lawful to carry on war, either for the Argives, Eleans, Mantineans, and their allies, against the Athenians, or the allies in the Athenian empire: or for the Athenians and their allies against the Argives, Eleans, Mantineans, or their allies, in any way or means whatsoever.

The Athenians, Argives, Eleans, and Mantineans shall be allies for a hundred years upon the terms following:

2. If an enemy invade the country of the Athenians, the Argives, Eleans, and Mantineans shall go to the relief of Athens, according as the Athenians may require by message, in such way as they most effectually can, to the best of their power. But if the invader be gone after plundering the territory, the offending state shall be the enemy of the Argives, Mantineans, Eleans, and Athenians, and war shall be made against it by all these cities: and no one of the cities shall be able to make peace with that state, except all the above cities agree to do so.

3. Likewise the Athenians shall go to the relief of Argos, Mantinea, and Elis, if an enemy invade the country of Elis, Mantinea, or Argos, according as the above cities may require by message, in such way as they most effectually can, to the best of their power. But if the invader be gone after plundering the territory, the state offending shall be the enemy of the Athenians,

Argives, Mantineans, and Eleans, and war shall be made against it by all these cities, and peace may not be made with that state except all the above cities agree to it.

4. No armed force shall be allowed to pass for hostile purposes through the country of the powers contracting, or of the allies in their respective empires, or to go by sea, except all the cities–that is to say, Athens, Argos, Mantinea, and Elis–vote for such passage.

5. The relieving troops shall be maintained by the city sending them for thirty days from their arrival in the city that has required them, and upon their return in the same way: if their services be desired for a longer period, the city that sent for them shall maintain them, at the rate of three Aeginetan obols per day for a heavy-armed soldier, archer, or light soldier, and an Aeginetan drachma for a trooper.

6. The city sending for the troops shall have the command when the war is in its own country: but in case of the cities resolving upon a joint expedition the

command shall be equally divided among all the cities.

7. The treaty shall be sworn to by the Athenians for themselves and their allies, by the Argives, Mantineans, Eleans, and their allies, by each state individually. Each shall swear the oath most binding in his country over full-grown victims: the oath being as follows:

"I STAND BY THE ALLIANCE AND ITS ARTICLES, JUSTLY, INNOCENTLY, AND SINCERELY, AND I WILL NOT TRANSGRESS THE SAME IN ANY WAY OR MEANS WHATSOEVER."

The oath shall be taken at Athens by the Senate and the magistrates, the Prytanes administering it: at Argos by the Senate, the Eighty, and the Artynae, the Eighty administering it: at Mantinea by the Demiurgi, the Senate, and the other magistrates, the Theori and Polemarchs administering it: at Elis by the Demiurgi, the magistrates, and the Six Hundred, the Demiurgi and the Thesmophylaces administering it. The oaths shall be renewed by the Athenians going to Elis, Mantinea, and Argos thirty days before the Olympic games: by the Argives, Mantineans, and Eleans going to Athens ten days before the great feast of the Panathenaea. The articles of the treaty, the oaths, and the alliance shall be inscribed on a stone pillar by the Athenians in the citadel, by the Argives in the market-place, in the temple of Apollo: by the Mantineans in the temple of Zeus, in the market-place: and a brazen pillar shall be erected jointly by them at the Olympic games now at hand. Should the above cities see good to make any addition in these articles, whatever all the above cities shall agree upon, after consulting together, shall be binding.

Although the treaty and alliances were thus concluded, still the treaty between the Lacedaemonians and Athenians was not renounced by either party. Meanwhile

Corinth, although the ally of the Argives, did not accede to the new treaty, any more than she had done to the alliance, defensive and offensive, formed before this between the Eleans, Argives, and Mantineans, when she declared herself content with the first alliance, which was defensive only, and which bound them to help each other, but not to join in attacking any. The Corinthians thus stood aloof from their allies, and again turned their thoughts towards Lacedaemon.

At the Olympic games which were held this summer, and in which the Arcadian Androsthenes was victor the first time in the wrestling and boxing, the Lacedaemonians were excluded from the temple by the Eleans, and thus prevented from sacrificing or contending, for having refused to pay the fine specified in the Olympic law imposed upon them by the Eleans, who alleged that they had attacked Fort Phyrcus, and sent heavy infantry of theirs into Lepreum during the Olympic truce. The amount of the fine was two thousand minae, two for each heavy-armed soldier, as the law prescribes. The Lacedaemonians sent envoys, and pleaded that the imposition was unjust; saying that the truce had not yet been proclaimed at Lacedaemon when the heavy infantry were sent off. But the Eleans affirmed that the armistice with them had already begun (they proclaim it first among themselves), and that the aggression of the Lacedaemonians had taken them by surprise while they were living quietly as in time of peace, and not expecting anything. Upon this the Lacedaemonians submitted, that if the Eleans really believed that they had committed an aggression, it was useless after that to proclaim the truce at Lacedaemon; but they had proclaimed it notwithstanding, as believing nothing of the kind, and from that moment the Lacedaemonians had made no attack upon their country. Nevertheless the Eleans adhered to what they had said, that nothing would persuade them that an aggression had not been committed; if, however, the Lacedaemonians would restore Lepreum, they would give up their own share of the money and pay that of the god for them.

As this proposal was not accepted, the Eleans tried a second. Instead of restoring Lepreum, if this was objected to, the Lacedaemonians should ascend the altar of the Olympian Zeus, as they were so anxious to have access to the temple, and swear before the Hellenes that they would surely pay the fine at a later day. This being also refused, the Lacedaemonians were excluded from the temple, the sacrifice, and the games, and sacrificed at home; the Lepreans being the only other Hellenes who did not attend. Still the Eleans were afraid of the Lacedaemonians sacrificing by force, and kept guard with a heavy-armed company of their young men; being also joined by a thousand Argives, the same number of Mantineans, and by some Athenian cavalry who stayed at Harpina during the feast. Great fears were felt in the assembly of the Lacedaemonians coming in arms, especially after Lichas, son of Arcesilaus, a Lacedaemonian, had been scourged on the course by the umpires; because, upon his horses being the winners, and the Boeotian people being proclaimed the victor on account of his having no right to enter, he came forward on the course and crowned the charioteer, in order to show that the chariot was his. After this incident all were more afraid than ever, and firmly looked for a disturbance: the Lacedaemonians, however, kept quiet, and let the feast pass by, as we have seen. After the Olympic games, the Argives and the allies repaired to Corinth to invite her to come over to them. There they found some Lacedaemonian envoys; and a long discussion ensued, which after all ended in nothing, as an earthquake occurred, and they dispersed to their different homes.

Summer was now over. The winter

following a battle took place between the Heracleots in Trachinia and the Aenianians, Dolopians, Malians, and certain of the Thessalians, all tribes bordering on and hostile to the town, which directly menaced their country. Accordingly, after having opposed and harassed it from its very foundation by every means in their power, they now in this battle defeated the Heracleots, Xenares, son of Cnidis, their Lacedaemonian commander, being among the slain. Thus the winter ended and the twelfth year of this war ended also. After the battle, Heraclea was so terribly reduced that in the first days of the summer following the Boeotians occupied the place and sent away the Lacedaemonian Agesippidas for misgovernment, fearing that the town might be taken by the Athenians while the Lacedaemonians were distracted with the affairs of Peloponnese. The Lacedaemonians, nevertheless, were offended with them for what they had done.

The same summer Alcibiades, son of Clinias, now one of the generals at Athens, in concert with the Argives and the allies, went into Peloponnese with a few Athenian heavy infantry and archers and some of the allies in those parts whom he took up as he passed, and with this army marched here and there through Peloponnese, and settled various matters connected with the alliance, and among other things induced the Patrians to carry their walls down to the sea, intending himself also to build a fort near the Achaean Rhium. However, the Corinthians and Sicyonians, and all others who would have suffered by its being built, came up and hindered him.

The same summer war broke out between the Epidaurians and Argives. The pretext was that the Epidaurians did not send an offering for their pasture-land to Apollo Pythaeus, as they were bound to do, the Argives having the chief management of the temple; but, apart from this pretext, Alcibiades and the Argives were determined, if possible, to gain possession of Epidaurus, and thus to ensure the neutrality of Corinth and give the Athenians a shorter passage for their reinforcements from Aegina than if they had to sail round Scyllaeum. The Argives accordingly prepared to invade Epidaurus by themselves, to exact the offering.

About the same time the Lacedaemonians marched out with all their people to Leuctra upon their frontier, opposite to Mount Lycaeum, under the command of Agis, son of Archidamus, without any one knowing their destination, not even the cities that sent the contingents. The sacrifices, however, for crossing the frontier not proving propitious, the Lacedaemonians returned home themselves, and sent word to the allies to be ready to march after the month ensuing, which happened to be the month of Carneus, a holy time for the Dorians. Upon the retreat of the Lacedaemonians the Argives marched out on the last day but three of the month before Carneus, and keeping this as the day during the whole time that they were out, invaded and plundered Epidaurus. The Epidaurians summoned their allies to their aid, some of whom pleaded the month as an excuse; others came as far as the frontier of Epidaurus and there remained inactive.

While the Argives were in Epidaurus embassies from the cities assembled at Mantinea, upon the invitation of the Athenians. The conference having begun, the Corinthian Euphamidas said that their actions did not agree with their words; while they were sitting deliberating about peace, the Epidaurians and their allies and the Argives were arrayed against each other in arms; deputies from each party should first go and separate the armies, and then the talk about peace might be resumed. In compliance with this suggestion, they went and brought back the Argives from Epidaurus, and afterwards reassembled, but without succeeding any better in coming to a conclusion; and the Argives a second time invaded Epidaurus and plundered the country. The Lacedaemonians also marched out to Caryae; but the frontier sacrifices again proving unfavourable, they went back again, and the Argives, after ravaging about a third of the Epidaurian territory, returned home. Meanwhile a thousand Athenian heavy infantry had come to their aid under the command of Alcibiades, but finding that the Lacedaemonian expedition was at an end, and that they were no longer wanted, went back again.

So passed the summer. The next winter the Lacedaemonians managed to elude the vigilance of the Athenians, and sent in a garrison of three hundred men to Epidaurus, under the command of Agesippidas. Upon this the Argives went to the Athenians and complained of their having allowed an enemy to pass by sea, in spite of the clause in the treaty by which the allies were not to allow an enemy to pass through their country. Unless, therefore, they now put the Messenians and Helots in Pylos to annoy the Lacedaemonians, they, the Argives, should consider that faith had not been kept with them. The Athenians were persuaded by Alcibiades to inscribe at the bottom of the Laconian pillar that the Lacedaemonians had not kept their oaths, and to convey the Helots at Cranii to Pylos to plunder the country; but for the rest they remained quiet as before. During this winter hostilities went on between the Argives and Epidaurians, without any pitched battle taking place, but only forays and ambuscades, in which the losses were small and fell now on one side and now on the other. At the close of the winter, towards the beginning of spring, the Argives went with scaling ladders to Epidaurus, expecting to find it left unguarded on account of the war and to be able to take it by assault, but returned unsuccessful. And the winter ended, and with it the thirteenth year of the war ended also.

In the middle of the next summer the Lacedaemonians, seeing the Epidaurians, their allies, in distress, and the rest of Peloponnese either in revolt or disaffected, concluded that it was high time for them to interfere if they wished to stop the progress of the evil, and accordingly with their full force, the Helots included, took the field against Argos, under the command of Agis, son of Archidamus, king of the Lacedaemonians. The Tegeans and the other Arcadian allies of Lacedaemon joined in the expedition. The allies from the rest of Peloponnese and from outside mustered at Phlius; the Boeotians with five thousand heavy infantry and as many light troops, and five hundred horse and the same number of dismounted troopers; the Corinthians with two thousand heavy infantry; the rest more or less as might happen; and the Phliasians with all their forces, the army being in their country.

The preparations of the Lacedaemonians

from the first had been known to the Argives, who did not, however, take the field until the enemy was on his road to join the rest at Phlius. Reinforced by the Mantineans with their allies, and by three thousand Elean heavy infantry, they advanced and fell in with the Lacedaemonians at Methydrium in Arcadia. Each party took up its position upon a hill, and the Argives prepared to engage the Lacedaemonians while they were alone; but Agis eluded them by breaking up his camp in the night, and proceeded to join the rest of the allies at Phlius. The Argives discovering this at daybreak, marched first to Argos and then to the Nemean road, by which they expected the Lacedaemonians and their allies would come down. However, Agis, instead of taking this road as they expected, gave the Lacedaemonians, Arcadians, and Epidaurians their orders, and went along another difficult road, and descended into the plain of Argos. The

Corinthians, Pellenians, and Phliasians marched by another steep road; while the Boeotians, Megarians, and Sicyonians had instructions to come down by the Nemean road where the Argives were posted, in order that, if the enemy advanced into the plain against the troops of Agis, they might fall upon his rear with their cavalry. These dispositions concluded, Agis invaded the plain and began to ravage Saminthus and other places.

Discovering this, the Argives came up from Nemea, day having now dawned. On their way they fell in with the troops of the Phliasians and Corinthians, and killed a few of the Phliasians and had perhaps a few more of their own men killed by the Corinthians. Meanwhile the Boeotians, Megarians, and Sicyonians, advancing upon Nemea according to their instructions, found the Argives no longer there, as they had gone down on seeing their property ravaged, and were now forming for battle, the Lacedaemonians imitating their example. The Argives were now completely surrounded; from the plain the Lacedaemonians and their allies shut them off from their city; above them were the Corinthians, Phliasians, and Pellenians; and on the side of Nemea the Boeotians, Sicyonians, and Megarians. Meanwhile their army was without cavalry, the Athenians alone among the allies not having yet arrived. Now the bulk of the Argives and their allies did not see the danger of their position, but thought that they could not have a fairer field, having intercepted the Lacedaemonians in their own country and close to the city. Two men, however, in the Argive army, Thrasylus, one of the five generals, and Alciphron, the Lacedaemonian proxenus, just as the armies were upon the point of engaging, went and held a parley with Agis and urged him not to bring on a battle, as the Argives were ready to refer to fair and equal arbitration whatever complaints the Lacedaemonians might have against them, and to make a treaty and live in peace in future.

The Argives who made these statements did so upon their own authority, not by order of the people, and Agis on his accepted their proposals, and without himself either consulting the majority, simply communicated the matter to a single individual, one of the high officers accompanying the expedition, and granted the Argives a truce for four months, in which to fulfil their promises; after which he immediately led off the army without giving any explanation to any of the other allies. The Lacedaemonians and allies followed their general out of respect for the law, but amongst themselves loudly blamed Agis for going away from so fair a field (the enemy being hemmed in on every side by infantry and cavalry) without having done anything worthy of their strength. Indeed this was by far the finest Hellenic army ever yet brought together; and it should have been seen while it was still united at Nemea, with the Lacedaemonians in full force, the Arcadians, Boeotians, Corinthians, Sicyonians, Pellenians, Phliasians and Megarians, and all these the flower of their respective populations, thinking themselves a match not merely for the Argive confederacy, but for another such added to it. The army thus retired blaming Agis, and returned every man to his home. The Argives however blamed still more loudly the persons who had concluded the truce without consulting the people, themselves thinking that they had let escape with the Lacedaemonians an opportunity such as they should never see again; as the struggle would have been under the walls of their city, and by the side of many and brave allies. On their return accordingly they began to stone Thrasylus in the bed of the Charadrus, where they try all military causes before entering the city.

Thrasylus fled to the altar, and so saved his life; his property however they confiscated.

After this arrived a thousand Athenian heavy infantry and three hundred horse, under the command of Laches and Nicostratus; whom the Argives, being nevertheless loath to break the truce with the Lacedaemonians, begged to depart, and refused to bring before the people, to whom they had a communication to make, until compelled to do so by the entreaties of the Mantineans and Eleans, who were still at Argos. The Athenians, by the mouth of Alcibiades their ambassador there present, told the Argives and the allies that they had no right to make a truce at all without the consent of their fellow confederates, and now that the Athenians had arrived so opportunely the war ought to be resumed. These arguments proving successful with the allies, they immediately marched upon Orchomenos, all except the Argives, who, although they had consented like the rest, stayed behind at first, but eventually joined the others. They now all sat down and besieged Orchomenos, and made assaults upon it; one of their reasons for desiring to gain this place being that hostages from Arcadia had been lodged there by the Lacedaemonians. The Orchomenians, alarmed at the weakness of their wall and the numbers of the enemy, and at the risk they ran of perishing before relief arrived, capitulated upon condition of joining the league, of giving hostages of their own to the Mantineans, and giving up those lodged with them by the Lacedaemonians. Orchomenos thus secured, the allies now consulted as to which of the remaining places they should attack next. The Eleans were urgent for Lepreum; the Mantineans for Tegea; and the Argives and Athenians giving their support to the Mantineans, the Eleans went home in a rage at their not having voted for Lepreum; while the rest of the allies made ready at Mantinea for going against Tegea, which a party inside had arranged to put into their hands.

Meanwhile the Lacedaemonians, upon their return from Argos after concluding the four months' truce, vehemently blamed Agis for not having subdued Argos, after an opportunity such as they thought they had never had before; for it was no easy matter to bring so many and so good allies together. But when the news arrived of the capture of Orchomenos, they became more angry than ever, and, departing from all precedent, in the heat of the moment had almost decided to raze his house, and to fine him ten thousand drachmae. Agis however entreated them to do none of these things, promising to atone for his fault by good service in the field, failing which they might then do to him whatever they pleased; and they accordingly abstained from razing his house or fining him as they had threatened to do, and now made a law, hitherto unknown at Lacedaemon, attaching to him ten Spartans as counsellors, without whose consent he should have no power to lead an army out of the city.

At this juncture arrived word from their friends in Tegea that, unless they speedily appeared, Tegea would go over from them to the Argives and their allies, if it had not gone over already. Upon this news a force marched out from Lacedaemon, of the Spartans and Helots and all their people, and that instantly and upon a scale never before witnessed. Advancing to Orestheum in Maenalia, they directed the Arcadians in their league to follow close after them to Tegea, and, going on themselves as far as Orestheum, from thence sent back the sixth part of the Spartans, consisting of the oldest and youngest men, to guard their homes, and with the rest of their army arrived at Tegea; where their Arcadian allies soon after joined them. Meanwhile they sent to Corinth, to the Boeotians, the Phocians, and Locrians, with orders to come up as quickly as possible to Mantinea. These had but short notice; and it was not easy except all together, and after waiting for each other, to pass through the enemy's country, which lay right across and blocked up the line of communication. Nevertheless they made what haste they could. Meanwhile the Lacedaemonians with the Arcadian allies that had joined them, entered the territory of Mantinea, and encamping near the temple of Heracles began to plunder the country.

Here they were seen by the Argives and their allies, who immediately took up a strong and difficult position, and formed in order of battle. The Lacedaemonians at once advanced against them, and came on within a stone's throw or javelin's cast, when one of the older men, seeing the enemy's position to be a strong one, hallooed to Agis that he was minded to cure one evil with another; meaning that he wished to make amends for his retreat, which had been so much blamed, from Argos, by his present untimely precipitation. Meanwhile Agis, whether in consequence of this halloo or of some sudden new idea of his own, quickly led back his army without engaging, and entering the Tegean territory, began to turn off into that of Mantinea the water about which the Mantineans and Tegeans are always fighting, on account of the extensive damage it does to whichever of the two countries it falls into. His object in this was to make the Argives and their allies come down from the hill, to resist the diversion of the water, as they would be sure to do when they knew of it, and thus to fight the battle in the plain. He accordingly stayed that day where he was, engaged in turning off the water. The Argives and their allies were at first amazed at the sudden retreat of the enemy after advancing so near, and did not know what to make of it; but when he had gone away and disappeared, without their having stirred to pursue him, they began anew to find fault with their generals, who had not only let the Lacedaemonians get off before, when they were so happily intercepted before Argos, but who now again allowed them to run away, without any one pursuing them, and to escape at their leisure while the Argive army was leisurely betrayed. The generals, half-stunned for the moment, afterwards led them down from the hill, and went forward and encamped in the plain, with the intention of attacking the enemy.

The next day the Argives and their allies formed in the order in which they meant to fight, if they chanced to encounter the enemy; and the Lacedaemonians returning from the water to their old encampment by the temple of Heracles, suddenly saw their adversaries close in front of them, all in complete order, and advanced from the hill. A shock like that of the present moment the Lacedaemonians do not ever remember to have experienced: there was scant time for preparation, as they instantly and hastily fell into their ranks, Agis, their king, directing everything, agreeably to the law. For when a king is in the field all commands proceed from him: he gives the word to the Polemarchs; they to the Lochages; these to the Pentecostyes; these again to the Enomotarchs, and these last to the Enomoties. In short all orders required pass in the same way and quickly reach the troops; as almost the whole Lacedaemonian army, save for a small part, consists of officers under officers, and the care of what is to be done falls upon many.

In this battle the left wing was composed of the Sciritae, who in a Lacedaemonian army have always that post to themselves alone; next to these were the soldiers of Brasidas from Thrace, and the Neodamodes with them; then came the Lacedaemonians themselves, company after company, with the Arcadians of Heraea at their side. After these were the Maenalians, and on the right wing the Tegeans with a few of the Lacedaemonians at the extremity; their cavalry being posted upon the two wings. Such was the Lacedaemonian formation. That of their opponents was as follows: On the right were the Mantineans, the action taking place in their country; next to them the allies from Arcadia; after whom came the thousand picked men of the Argives, to whom the state had given a long course of military training at the public expense; next to them the rest of the Argives, and after them their allies, the Cleonaeans and Orneans, and lastly the Athenians on the extreme left, and lastly the Athenians on the extreme left, and their own cavalry with them.

Such were the order and the forces of the two combatants. The Lacedaemonian army looked the largest; though as to putting down the numbers of either host, or of the contingents composing it, I could not do so with any accuracy. Owing to the secrecy of their government the number of the Lacedaemonians was not known, and men are so apt to brag about the forces of their country that the estimate of their opponents was not trusted. The following calculation, however, makes it possible to estimate the numbers of the Lacedaemonians present upon this occasion. There were seven companies in the field without counting the Sciritae, who numbered six hundred men: in each company there were four Pentecostyes, and in the Pentecosty four Enomoties. The first rank of the Enomoty was composed of four soldiers: as to the depth, although they had not been all drawn up alike, but as each captain chose, they were generally ranged eight deep; the first rank along the whole line, exclusive of the Sciritae, consisted of four hundred and forty-eight men.

The armies being now on the eve of engaging, each contingent received some words of encouragement from its own commander. The Mantineans were, reminded that they were going to fight for their country and to avoid returning to the experience of servitude after having tasted that of empire; the Argives, that they would contend for their ancient supremacy, to regain their once equal share of Peloponnese of which they had been so long deprived, and to punish an enemy and a neighbour for a thousand wrongs; the Athenians, of the glory of gaining the honours of the day with so many and brave allies in arms, and that a victory over the Lacedaemonians in Peloponnese would cement and extend their empire, and would besides preserve Attica from all invasions in future. These were the incitements addressed to the Argives and their allies. The Lacedaemonians meanwhile, man to man, and with their war-songs in the ranks, exhorted each brave comrade to remember what he had learnt before; well aware that the long training of action was of more saving virtue than any brief verbal exhortation, though never so well delivered.

After this they joined battle, the Argives

and their allies advancing with haste and fury, the Lacedaemonians slowly and to the music of many flute-players–a standing institution in their army, that has nothing to do with religion, but is meant to make them advance evenly, stepping in time, without break their order, as large armies are apt to do in the moment of engaging.

Just before the battle joined, King Agis resolved upon the following manoeuvre. All armies are alike in this: on going into action they get forced out rather on their right wing, and one and the other overlap with this adversary's left; because fear makes each man do his best to shelter his unarmed side with the shield of the man next him on the right, thinking that the closer the shields are locked together the better will he be protected. The man primarily responsible for this is the first upon the right wing, who is always striving to withdraw from the enemy his unarmed side; and the same apprehension makes the rest follow him.

On the present occasion the Mantineans reached with their wing far beyond the Sciritae, and the Lacedaemonians and Tegeans still farther beyond the Athenians, as their army was the largest. Agis, afraid of his left being surrounded, and thinking that the Mantineans outflanked it too far, ordered the Sciritae and Brasideans to move out from their place in the ranks and make the line even with the Mantineans, and told the Polemarchs Hipponoidas and Aristocles to fill up the gap thus formed, by throwing themselves into it with two companies taken from the right wing; thinking that his right would still be strong enough and to spare, and that the line fronting the Mantineans would gain in solidity.

However, as he gave these orders in the moment of the onset, and at short notice, it so happened that Aristocles and Hipponoidas would not move over, for which offence they were afterwards banished from

Sparta, as having been guilty of cowardice; and the enemy meanwhile closed before the Sciritae (whom Agis on seeing that the two companies did not move over ordered to return to their place) had time to fill up the breach in question. Now it was, however, that the Lacedaemonians, utterly worsted in respect of skill, showed themselves as superior in point of courage. As soon as they came to close quarters with the enemy, the Mantinean right broke their Sciritae and Brasideans, and, bursting in with their allies and the thousand picked Argives into the unclosed breach in their line, cut up and surrounded the Lacedaemonians, and drove them in full rout to the wagons, slaying some of the older men on guard there. But the Lacedaemonians, worsted in this part of the field, with the rest of their army, and especially the centre, where the three hundred knights, as they are called, fought round King Agis, fell on the older men of the Argives and the five companies so named, and on the Cleonaeans, the Orneans, and the Athenians next them, and instantly routed them; the greater number not even waiting to strike a blow, but giving way the moment that they came on, some even being trodden under foot, in their fear of being overtaken by their assailants.

The army of the Argives and their allies, having given way in this quarter, was now completely cut in two, and the Lacedaemonian and Tegean right simultaneously closing round the Athenians with the troops that outflanked them, these last found themselves placed between two fires, being surrounded on one side and already defeated on the other. Indeed they would have suffered more severely than any other part of the army, but for the services of the cavalry which they had with them. Agis also on perceiving the distress of his left opposed to the Mantineans and the thousand Argives, ordered all the army to advance to the support of the defeated wing; and while this took place, as the enemy moved past and slanted away from them, the Athenians escaped at their leisure, and with them the beaten Argive division. Meanwhile the Mantineans and their allies and the picked body of the Argives ceased to press the enemy, and seeing their friends defeated and the Lacedaemonians in full advance upon them, took to flight. Many of the Mantineans perished; but the bulk of the picked body of the Argives made good their escape. The flight and retreat, however, were neither hurried nor long; the Lacedaemonians fighting long and stubbornly until the rout of their enemy, but that once effected, pursuing for a short time and not far.

Such was the battle, as nearly as possible as I have described it; the greatest that had occurred for a very long while among the Hellenes, and joined by the most considerable states. The Lacedaemonians took up a position in front of the enemy's dead, and immediately set up a trophy and stripped the slain; they took up their own dead and carried them back to Tegea, where they buried them, and restored those of the enemy under truce. The Argives, Orneans, and Cleonaeans had seven hundred killed; the Mantineans two hundred, and the Athenians and Aeginetans also two hundred, with both their generals. On the side of the Lacedaemonians, the allies did not suffer any loss worth speaking of: as to the Lacedaemonians themselves it was difficult to learn the truth; it is said, however, that there were slain about three hundred of them.

While the battle was impending, Pleistoanax, the other king, set out with a reinforcement composed of the oldest and youngest men, and got as far as Tegea, where he heard of the victory and went back again. The Lacedaemonians also sent and turned back the allies from Corinth and from beyond the Isthmus, and returning themselves dismissed their allies, and kept the Carnean holidays, which happened to be at that time. The imputations cast upon them by the Hellenes at the time, whether of cowardice on account of the disaster in the island, or of mismanagement and slowness generally, were all wiped out by this single action: fortune, it was thought, might have humbled them, but the men themselves were the same as ever.

The day before this battle, the Epidaurians with all their forces invaded the deserted Argive territory, and cut off many of the guards left there in the absence of the Argive army. After the battle three thousand Elean heavy infantry arriving to aid the Mantineans, and a reinforcement of one thousand Athenians, all these allies marched at once against Epidaurus, while the Lacedaemonians were keeping the Carnea, and dividing the work among them began to build a wall round the city. The rest left off; but the Athenians finished at once the part assigned to them round Cape Heraeum; and having all joined in leaving a garrison in the fortification in question, they returned to their respective cities.

Summer now came to an end. In the first days of the next winter, when the Carnean holidays were over, the Lacedaemonians took the field, and arriving at Tegea sent on to Argos proposals of accommodation. They had before had a party in the town desirous of overthrowing the democracy; and after the battle that had been fought, these were now far more in a position to persuade the people to listen to terms. Their plan was first to make a treaty with the Lacedaemonians, to be followed by an alliance, and after this to fall upon the commons. Lichas, son of Arcesilaus, the Argive proxenus, accordingly arrived at Argos with two proposals from Lacedaemon, to regulate the conditions of war or peace, according as they preferred the one or the other. After much discussion, Alcibiades happening to be in the town, the

Lacedaemonian party, who now ventured to act openly, persuaded the Argives to accept the proposal for accommodation; which ran as follows:

The assembly of the Lacedaemonians agrees to treat with the Argives upon the terms following:

1. The Argives shall restore to the Orchomenians their children, and to the Maenalians their men, and shall restore the men they have in Mantinea to the Lacedaemonians.

2. They shall evacuate Epidaurus, and raze the fortification there. If the Athenians refuse to withdraw from Epidaurus, they shall be declared enemies of the Argives and of the Lacedaemonians, and of the allies of the Lacedaemonians and the allies of the Argives.

3. If the Lacedaemonians have any children in their custody, they shall restore them every one to his city.

4. As to the offering to the god, the Argives,

if they wish, shall impose an oath upon the Epidaurians, but, if not, they shall swear it themselves.

5. All the cities in Peloponnese, both small and great, shall be independent according to the customs of their country.

6. If any of the powers outside Peloponnese invade Peloponnesian territory, the parties contracting shall unite to repel them, on such terms as they may agree upon, as being most fair for the Peloponnesians.

7. All allies of the Lacedaemonians outside Peloponnese shall be on the same footing as the Lacedaemonians, and the allies of the Argives shall be on the same footing as the Argives, being left in enjoyment of their own possessions.

8. This treaty shall be shown to the allies, and shall be concluded, if they approve; if the allies think fit, they may send the treaty to be considered at home.

The Argives began by accepting this proposal, and the Lacedaemonian army returned home from Tegea. After this intercourse was renewed between them, and not long afterwards the same party contrived that the Argives should give up the league with the Mantineans, Eleans, and Athenians, and should make a treaty and alliance with the Lacedaemonians; which was consequently done upon the terms following:

The Lacedaemonians and Argives agree to a treaty and alliance for fifty years upon the terms following:

1. All disputes shall be decided by fair and impartial arbitration, agreeably to the customs of the two countries.

2. The rest of the cities in Peloponnese may be included in this treaty and alliance, as independent and sovereign, in full enjoyment of what they possess, all disputes being decided by fair and impartial arbitration, agreeably to the customs of the said cities.

3. All allies of the Lacedaemonians outside

Peloponnese shall be upon the same footing as the Lacedaemonians themselves, and the allies of the Argives shall be upon the same footing as the Argives themselves, continuing to enjoy what they possess.

4. If it shall be anywhere necessary to make an expedition in common, the Lacedaemonians and Argives shall consult upon it and decide, as may be most fair for the allies.

5. If any of the cities, whether inside or outside Peloponnese, have a question whether of frontiers or otherwise, it must be settled, but if one allied city should have a quarrel with another allied city, it must be referred to some third city thought impartial by both parties. Private citizens shall have their disputes decided according to the laws of their several countries.

The treaty and above alliance concluded, each party at once released everything whether acquired by war or otherwise, and thenceforth acting in common voted to receive neither herald nor embassy from the Athenians unless they evacuated their forts and withdrew from Peloponnese, and also to make neither peace nor war with any, except jointly. Zeal was not wanting: both parties sent envoys to the Thracian places and to Perdiccas, and persuaded the latter to join their league. Still he did not at once break off from Athens, although minded to do so upon seeing the way shown him by Argos, the original home of his family. They also renewed their old oaths with the Chalcidians and took new ones: the Argives, besides, sent ambassadors to the Athenians, bidding them evacuate the fort at Epidaurus. The Athenians, seeing their own men outnumbered by the rest of the garrison, sent Demosthenes to bring them out. This general, under colour of a gymnastic contest which he arranged on his arrival, got the rest of the garrison out of the place, and shut the gates behind them. Afterwards the Athenians renewed their treaty with the Epidaurians, and by themselves gave up the fortress.

After the defection of Argos from the league, the Mantineans, though they held out at first, in the end finding themselves powerless without the Argives, themselves too came to terms with Lacedaemon, and gave up their sovereignty over the towns. The Lacedaemonians and Argives, each a thousand strong, now took the field together, and the former first went by themselves to Sicyon and made the government there more oligarchical than before, and then both, uniting, put down the democracy at Argos and set up an oligarchy favourable to Lacedaemon. These events occurred at the close of the winter, just before spring; and the fourteenth year of the war ended. The next summer the people of Dium, in Athos, revolted from the Athenians to the Chalcidians, and the Lacedaemonians settled affairs in Achaea in a way more agreeable to the interests of their country.

Meanwhile the popular party at Argos little by little gathered new consistency and courage, and waited for the moment of the Gymnopaedic festival at Lacedaemon, and then fell upon the oligarchs. After a fight in the city, victory declared for the commons, who slew some of their opponents and banished others. The Lacedaemonians for a long while let the messages of their friends at Argos remain without effect. At last they put off the Gymnopaediae and marched to their succour, but learning at Tegea the defeat of the oligarchs, refused to go any further in spite of the entreaties of those who had escaped, and returned home and kept the festival. Later on, envoys arrived with messages from the Argives in the town and from the exiles, when the allies were also at Sparta; and after much had been said on both sides, the Lacedaemonians decided that the party in the town had done wrong, and resolved to march against Argos, but kept delaying and putting off the matter.

Meanwhile the commons at Argos, in fear of the Lacedaemonians, began again to court the Athenian alliance, which they were convinced would be of the greatest service to them; and accordingly proceeded to build long walls to the sea, in order that in case of a blockade by land; with the help of the Athenians they might have the advantage of importing what they wanted by sea. Some of the cities in Peloponnese were also privy to the building of these walls; and the Argives with all their people, women and slaves not excepted, addressed themselves to the work, while carpenters and masons came to them from Athens.

Summer was now over. The winter following the Lacedaemonians, hearing of the walls that were building, marched against Argos with their allies, the Corinthians excepted, being also not without intelligence in the city itself; Agis, son of Archidamus, their king, was in command. The intelligence which they counted upon within the town came to nothing; they however took and razed the walls which were being built, and after capturing the Argive town Hysiae and killing all the freemen that fell into their hands, went back and dispersed every man to his city. After this the Argives marched into Phlius and plundered it for harbouring their exiles, most of whom had settled there, and so returned home. The same winter the Athenians blockaded Macedonia, on the score of the league entered into by Perdiccas with the Argives and Lacedaemonians, and also of his breach of his engagements on the occasion of the expedition prepared by Athens against the Chalcidians in the direction of Thrace and against Amphipolis, under the command of Nicias, son of Niceratus, which had to be broken up mainly because of his desertion. He was therefore proclaimed an enemy. And thus the winter ended, and the fifteenth year of the war ended with it.

Chapter Seventeen

Sixteenth Year of the War–The Melian Conference–Fate of Melos

THE NEXT SUMMER Alcibiades sailed with twenty ships to Argos and seized the suspected persons still left of the Lacedaemonian faction to the number of three hundred, whom the Athenians forthwith lodged in the neighbouring islands of their empire. The Athenians also made an expedition against the isle of Melos with thirty ships of their own, six Chian, and two Lesbian vessels, sixteen hundred heavy infantry, three hundred archers, and twenty mounted archers from Athens, and about fifteen hundred heavy infantry from the allies and the islanders. The Melians are a colony of Lacedaemon that would not submit to the Athenians like the other islanders, and at first remained neutral and took no part in the struggle, but afterwards upon the Athenians using violence and plundering their territory, assumed an attitude of open hostility. Cleomedes, son of Lycomedes, and Tisias, son of Tisimachus, the generals, encamping in their territory with the above armament, before doing any harm to their land, sent envoys to negotiate. These the Melians did not bring before the people, but bade them state the object of their mission to the magistrates and the few; upon which the Athenian envoys spoke as follows:

Athenians. Since the negotiations are not

to go on before the people, in order that we may not be able to speak straight on without interruption, and deceive the ears of the multitude by seductive arguments which would pass without refutation (for we know that this is the meaning of our being brought before the few), what if you who sit there were to pursue a method more cautious still? Make no set speech yourselves, but take us up at whatever you do not like, and settle that before going any farther. And first tell us if this proposition of ours suits you.

The Melian commissioners answered:

Melians. To the fairness of quietly instructing each other as you propose there is nothing to object; but your military preparations are too far advanced to agree with what you say, as we see you are come to be judges in your own cause, and that all we can reasonably expect from this negotiation is war, if we prove to have right on our side and refuse to submit, and in the contrary case, slavery.

Athenians. If you have met to reason about presentiments of the future, or for anything else than to consult for the safety of your state upon the facts that you see before you, we will give over; otherwise we will go on.

Melians. It is natural and excusable for men in our position to turn more ways than one both in thought and utterance. However, the question in this conference is, as you say, the safety of our country; and the discussion, if you please, can proceed in the way which you propose.

Athenians. For ourselves, we shall not trouble you with specious pretences–either of how we have a right to our empire because we overthrew the Mede, or are now attacking you because of wrong that you have done us–and make a long speech which would not be believed; and in return we hope that you, instead of thinking to influence us by saying that you did not join the Lacedaemonians, although their colonists, or that you have done us no wrong, will aim at what is feasible, holding in view the real sentiments of us both; since you know as well as we do that right, as the world goes, is only in question between equals in power, while the strong do what they can and the weak suffer what they must.

Melians. As we think, at any rate, it is expedient–we speak as we are obliged, since you enjoin us to let right alone and talk only of interest–that you should not destroy what is our common protection, the privilege of being allowed in danger to invoke what is fair and right, and even to profit by arguments not strictly valid if they can be got to pass current. And you are as much interested in this as any, as your fall would be a signal for the heaviest vengeance and an example for the world to meditate upon.

Athenians. The end of our empire, if end it should, does not frighten us: a rival empire like Lacedaemon, even if Lacedaemon was our real antagonist, is not so terrible to the vanquished as subjects who by themselves attack and overpower their rulers. This, however, is a risk that we are content to take. We will now proceed to show you that we are come here in the interest of our empire, and that we shall say what we are now going to say, for the preservation of your country; as we would fain exercise that empire over you without trouble, and see you preserved for the good of us both.

Melians. And how, pray, could it turn out as good for us to serve as for you to rule?

Athenians. Because you would have the advantage of submitting before suffering the worst, and we should gain by not destroying you.

Melians. So that you would not consent to our being neutral, friends instead of enemies, but allies of neither side.

Athenians. No; for your hostility cannot so much hurt us as your friendship will be an argument to our subjects of our weakness, and your enmity of our power.

Melians. Is that your subjects' idea of equity, to put those who have nothing to do with you in the same category with peoples that are most of them your own colonists, and some conquered rebels?

Athenians. As far as right goes they think one has as much of it as the other, and that if any maintain their independence it is because they are strong, and that if we do not molest them it is because we are afraid; so that besides extending our empire we should gain in security by your subjection; the fact that you are islanders and weaker than others rendering it all the more important that you should not succeed in baffling the masters of the sea.

Melians. But do you consider that there is no security in the policy which we indicate? For here again if you debar us from talking about justice and invite us to obey your interest, we also must explain ours, and try to persuade you, if the two happen to coincide. How can you avoid making enemies of all existing neutrals who shall look at case from it that one day or another you will attack them? And what is this but to make greater the enemies that you have already, and to force others to become so who would otherwise have never thought of it?

Athenians. Why, the fact is that continentals generally give us but little alarm; the liberty which they enjoy will long prevent their taking precautions against us; it is rather islanders like yourselves, outside our empire, and subjects smarting under the yoke, who would be the most likely to take a rash step and lead themselves and us into obvious danger.

Melians. Well then, if you risk so much to retain your empire, and your subjects to get rid of it, it were surely great baseness and cowardice in us who are still free not to try everything that can be tried, before submitting to your yoke.

Athenians. Not if you are well advised, the contest not being an equal one, with honour as the prize and shame as the penalty, but a question of self-preservation and of not resisting those who are far stronger than you are.

Melians. But we know that the fortune of war is sometimes more impartial than the disproportion of numbers might lead one to suppose; to submit is to give ourselves over to despair, while action still preserves for us a hope that we may stand erect.

Athenians. Hope, danger's comforter, may be indulged in by those who have abundant resources, if not without loss at all events without ruin; but its nature is to be extravagant, and those who go so far as to put their all upon the venture see it in its true colours only when they are ruined; but so long as the discovery would enable them to guard against it, it is never found wanting. Let not this be the case with you, who are weak and hang on a single turn of the scale; nor be like the vulgar, who, abandoning such security as human means may still afford, when visible hopes fail them in extremity, turn to invisible, to prophecies and oracles, and other such inventions that delude men with hopes to their destruction.

Melians. You may be sure that we are as well aware as you of the difficulty of contending against your power and fortune, unless the terms be equal. But we trust that the gods may grant us fortune as good as yours, since we are just men fighting against unjust, and that what we want in power will be made up by the alliance of the Lacedaemonians, who are bound, if only for very shame, to come to the aid of their kindred. Our confidence, therefore, after all is not so utterly irrational.

Athenians. When you speak of the favour of the gods, we may as fairly hope for that as yourselves; neither our pretensions nor our conduct being in any way contrary to what men believe of the gods, or practise among themselves. Of the gods we believe, and of men we know, that by a necessary law of their nature they rule wherever they can. And it is not as if we were the first to make this law, or to act upon it when made: we found it existing before us, and shall leave it to exist for ever after us; all we do is to make use of it, knowing that you and everybody else, having the same power as we have, would do the same as we do. Thus, as far as the gods are concerned, we have no fear and no reason to fear that we shall be at a disadvantage. But when we come to your notion about the Lacedaemonians, which leads you to believe that shame will make them help you, here we bless your simplicity but do not envy your folly. The Lacedaemonians, when their own interests or their country's laws are in question, are the worthiest men alive; of their conduct towards others much might be said, but no clearer idea of it could be given than by shortly saying that of all the men we know they are most conspicuous in considering what is agreeable honourable, and what is expedient just. Such a way of thinking does not promise much for the safety which you now unreasonably count upon.

Melians. But it is for this very reason that we now trust to their respect for expediency to prevent them from betraying the Melians, their colonists, and thereby losing the confidence of their friends in Hellas and helping their enemies.

Athenians. Then you do not adopt the view that expediency goes with security, while justice and honour cannot be followed without danger; and danger the Lacedaemonians generally court as little as possible.

Melians. But we believe that they would be more likely to face even danger for our sake, and with more confidence than for others, as our nearness to Peloponnese makes it easier for them to act, and our common blood ensures our fidelity.

Athenians. Yes, but what an intending ally trusts to is not the goodwill of those who ask his aid, but a decided superiority of power for action; and the Lacedaemonians look to this even more than others. At least, such is their distrust of their home resources that it is only with numerous allies that they attack a neighbour; now is it likely that while we are masters of the sea they will cross over to an island?

Melians. But they would have others to send. The Cretan Sea is a wide one, and it is more difficult for those who command it to intercept others, than for those who wish to elude them to do so safely. And should the Lacedaemonians miscarry in this, they would fall upon your land, and upon those left of your allies whom Brasidas did not reach; and instead of places which are not yours, you will have to fight for your own country and your own confederacy.

Athenians. Some diversion of the kind you speak of you may one day experience, only to learn, as others have done, that the Athenians never once yet withdrew from a siege for fear of any. But we are struck by the fact that, after saying you would consult for the safety of your country, in all this discussion you have mentioned nothing which men might trust in and think to be saved by. Your strongest arguments depend upon hope and the future, and your actual resources are too scanty, as compared with those arrayed against you, for you to come out victorious. You will therefore show great blindness of judgment, unless, after allowing us to retire, you can find some counsel more prudent than this. You will surely not be caught by that idea of disgrace, which in dangers that are disgraceful, and at the same time too plain to be mistaken, proves so fatal to mankind; since in too many cases the very men that have their eyes perfectly open to what they are rushing into, let the thing called disgrace, by the mere influence of a seductive name, lead them on to a point at which they become so enslaved by the phrase as in fact to fall wilfully into hopeless disaster, and incur disgrace more disgraceful as the companion of error, than when it comes as the result of misfortune. This, if you are well advised, you will guard against; and you will not think it dishonourable to submit to the greatest city in Hellas, when it makes you the moderate offer of becoming its tributary ally, without ceasing to enjoy the country that belongs to you; nor when you have the choice given you between war and security, will you be so blinded as to choose the worse. And it is certain that those who do not yield to their equals, who keep terms with their superiors, and are moderate towards their inferiors, on the whole succeed best. Think over the matter, therefore, after our withdrawal, and reflect once and again that it is for your country that you are consulting, that you have not more than one, and that upon this one deliberation depends its prosperity or ruin.

The Athenians now withdrew from

the conference; and the Melians, left to themselves,cametoadecisioncorresponding with what they had maintained in the discussion, and answered: "Our resolution, Athenians, is the same as it was at first. We will not in a moment deprive of freedom a city that has been inhabited these seven hundred years; but we put our trust in the fortune by which the gods have preserved it until now, and in the help of men, that is, of the Lacedaemonians; and so we will try and save ourselves. Meanwhile we invite you to allow us to be friends to you and foes to neither party, and to retire from our country after making such a treaty as shall seem fit to us both."

Such was the answer of the Melians. The Athenians now departing from the conference said: "Well, you alone, as it seems to us, judging from these resolutions, regard what is future as more certain than what is before your eyes, and what is out of sight, in your eagerness, as already coming to pass; and as you have staked most on, and trusted most in, the Lacedaemonians, your fortune, and your hopes, so will you be most completely deceived."

The Athenian envoys now returned to the army; and the Melians showing no signs of yielding, the generals at once betook themselves to hostilities, and drew a line of circumvallation round the Melians, dividing the work among the different states. Subsequently the Athenians returned with most of their army, leaving behind them a certain number of their own citizens and of the allies to keep guard by land and sea. The force thus left stayed on and besieged the place.

About the same time the Argives invaded the territory of Phlius and lost eighty men cut off in an ambush by the Phliasians and Argive exiles. Meanwhile the Athenians at Pylos took so much plunder from the Lacedaemonians that the latter, although they still refrained from breaking off the treaty and going to war with Athens, yet proclaimed that any of their people that chose might plunder the Athenians. The Corinthians also commenced hostilities with the Athenians for private quarrels of their own; but the rest of the Peloponnesians stayed quiet. Meanwhile the Melians attacked by night and took the part of the Athenian lines over against the market, and killed some of the men, and brought in corn and all else that they could find useful to them, and so returned and kept quiet, while the Athenians took measures to keep better guard in future.

Summer was now over. The next winter the Lacedaemonians intended to invade the Argive territory, but arriving at the frontier found the sacrifices for crossing unfavourable, and went back again. This intention of theirs gave the Argives suspicions of certain of their fellow citizens, some of whom they arrested; others, however, escaped them. About the same time the Melians again took another part of the Athenian lines which were but feebly garrisoned. Reinforcements afterwards arriving from Athens in consequence, under the command of Philocrates, son of Demeas, the siege was now pressed vigorously; and some treachery taking place inside, the Melians surrendered at discretion to the Athenians, who put to death all the grown men whom they took, and sold the women and children for slaves, and subsequently sent out five hundred colonists and inhabited the place themselves.

BOOK SIX

Chapter Eighteen

Seventeenth Year of the War–The Sicilian Campaign–Affair of the Hermae–Departure of the Expedition

THE SAME WINTER THE Athenians resolved to sail again to Sicily, with a greater armament than that under Laches and Eurymedon, and, if possible, to conquer the island; most of them being ignorant of its size and of the number of its inhabitants, Hellenic and barbarian, and of the fact that they were undertaking a war not much inferior to that against the Peloponnesians. For the voyage round Sicily in a merchantman is not far short of eight days; and yet, large as the island is, there are only two miles of sea to prevent its being mainland.

It was settled originally as follows, and the peoples that occupied it are these. The earliest inhabitants spoken of in any part of the country are the Cyclopes and Laestrygones; but I cannot tell of what race they were, or whence they came or whither they went, and must leave my readers to what the poets have said of them and to what may be generally known concerning them. The Sicanians appear to have been the next settlers, although they pretend to have been the first of all and aborigines; but the facts show that they were Iberians, driven by the Ligurians from the river Sicanus in Iberia. It was from them that the island, before called Trinacria, took its name of Sicania, and to the present day they inhabit the west of Sicily. On the fall of Ilium, some of the Trojans escaped from the Achaeans, came in ships to Sicily, and settled next to the Sicanians under the general name of Elymi; their towns being called Eryx and Egesta. With them settled some of the Phocians carried on their way from Troy by a storm, first to Libya, and afterwards from thence to Sicily. The Sicels crossed over to Sicily from their first home Italy, flying from the Opicans, as tradition says and as seems not unlikely, upon rafts, having watched till the wind set down the strait to effect the passage; although perhaps they may have sailed over in some other way. Even at the present day there are still Sicels in Italy; and the country got its name of Italy from Italus, a king of the Sicels, so called. These went with a great host to Sicily, defeated the Sicanians in battle and forced them to remove to the south and west of the island, which thus came to be called Sicily instead of Sicania, and after they crossed over continued to enjoy the richest parts of the country for near three hundred years before any Hellenes came to Sicily; indeed they still hold the centre and north of the island. There were also Phoenicians living all round Sicily, who had occupied promontories upon the sea coasts and the islets adjacent for the purpose of trading with the Sicels. But when the Hellenes began to arrive in considerable numbers by sea, the Phoenicians abandoned most of their stations, and drawing together took up their abode in Motye, Soloeis, and Panormus, near the Elymi, partly because they confided in their alliance, and also because these are the nearest points for the voyage between Carthage and Sicily.

These were the barbarians in Sicily, settled as I have said. Of the Hellenes, the first to arrive were Chalcidians from Euboea with Thucles, their founder. They founded Naxos and built the altar to Apollo Archegetes, which now stands outside the town, and upon which the deputies for the games sacrifice before sailing from Sicily. Syracuse was founded the year afterwards by Archias, one of the Heraclids from Corinth, who began by driving out the Sicels from the island upon which the inner city now stands, though it is no longer surrounded by water: in process of time the outer town also was taken within the walls and became populous. Meanwhile Thucles and the Chalcidians set out from Naxos in the fifth year after the foundation of Syracuse, and drove out the Sicels by arms and founded Leontini and afterwards Catana; the Catanians themselves choosing Evarchus as their founder.

About the same time Lamis arrived in Sicily with a colony from Megara, and after founding a place called Trotilus beyond the river Pantacyas, and afterwards leaving it and for a short while joining the Chalcidians at Leontini, was driven out by them and founded Thapsus. After his death his companions were driven out of Thapsus, and founded a place called the Hyblaean Megara; Hyblon, a Sicel king, having given up the place and inviting them thither. Here they lived two hundred and forty-five years; after which they were expelled from the city and the country by the Syracusan tyrant Gelo. Before their expulsion, however, a hundred years after they had settled there, they sent out Pamillus and founded Selinus; he having come from their mother country Megara to join them in its foundation. Gela was founded by Antiphemus from Rhodes and Entimus from Crete, who joined in leading a colony thither, in the forty-fifth year after the foundation of Syracuse. The town took its name from the river Gelas, the place where the citadel now stands, and which was first fortified, being called Lindii. The institutions which they adopted were Dorian. Near one hundred and eight years after the foundation of Gela, the Geloans founded Acragas (Agrigentum), so called from the river of that name, and made Aristonous and Pystilus their founders; giving their own institutions to the colony. Zancle was originally founded by pirates from Cuma, the Chalcidian town in the country of the Opicans: afterwards, however, large numbers came from Chalcis and the rest of Euboea, and helped to people the place; the founders being Perieres and Crataemenes from Cuma and Chalcis respectively. It first had the name of Zancle given it by the Sicels, because the place is shaped like a sickle, which the Sicels call zanclon; but upon the original settlers being afterwards expelled by some Samians and other Ionians who landed in Sicily flying from the Medes, and the Samians in their turn not long afterwards by Anaxilas, tyrant of Rhegium, the town was by him colonized with a mixed population, and its name changed to Messina, after his old country.

Himera was founded from Zancle by Euclides, Simus, and Sacon, most of those who went to the colony being Chalcidians; though they were joined by some exiles from Syracuse, defeated in a civil war, called the Myletidae. The language was a mixture of Chalcidian and Doric, but the institutions which prevailed were the Chalcidian. Acrae and Casmenae were founded by the Syracusans; Acrae seventy years after Syracuse, Casmenae nearly twenty after Acrae. Camarina was first founded by the Syracusans, close upon a hundred and thirty-five years after the building of Syracuse; its founders being Daxon and Menecolus. But the Camarinaeans being expelled by arms by the Syracusans for having revolted, Hippocrates, tyrant of Gela, some time later receiving their land in ransom for some Syracusan prisoners, resettled Camarina, himself acting as its founder. Lastly, it was again depopulated by Gelo, and settled once more for the third time by the Geloans.

Such is the list of the peoples, Hellenic and barbarian, inhabiting Sicily, and such the magnitude of the island which the Athenians were now bent upon invading; being ambitious in real truth of conquering the whole, although they had also the specious design of succouring their kindred and other allies in the island. But they were especially incited by envoys from Egesta, who had come to Athens and invoked their aid more urgently than ever. The Egestaeans had gone to war with their neighbours the Selinuntines upon questions of marriage and disputed territory, and the Selinuntines had procured the alliance of the Syracusans, and pressed Egesta hard by land and sea. The Egestaeans now reminded the Athenians of the alliance made in the time of Laches, during the former Leontine war, and begged them to send a fleet to their aid, and among a number of other considerations urged as a capital argument that if the Syracusans were allowed to go unpunished for their depopulation of Leontini, to ruin the allies still left to Athens in Sicily, and to get the whole power of the island into their hands, there would be a danger of their one day coming with a large force, as Dorians, to the aid of their Dorian brethren, and as colonists, to the aid of the Peloponnesians who had sent them out, and joining these in pulling down the Athenian empire. The Athenians would, therefore, do well to unite with the allies still left to them, and to make a stand against the Syracusans; especially as they, the Egestaeans, were prepared to furnish money sufficient for the war. The Athenians, hearing these arguments constantly repeated in their assemblies by the Egestaeans and their supporters, voted first to send envoys to Egesta, to see if there was really the money that they talked of in the treasury and temples, and at the same time to ascertain in what posture was the war with the Selinuntines.

The envoys of the Athenians were accordingly dispatched to Sicily. The same winter the Lacedaemonians and their allies, the Corinthians excepted, marched into the Argive territory, and ravaged a small part of the land, and took some yokes of oxen and carried off some corn. They also settled the Argive exiles at Orneae, and left them a few soldiers taken from the rest of the army; and after making a truce for a certain while, according to which neither Orneatae nor Argives were to injure each other's territory, returned home with the army. Not long afterwards the Athenians came with thirty ships and six hundred heavy infantry, and the Argives joining them with all their forces, marched out and besieged the men in Orneae for one day; but the garrison escaped by night, the besiegers having bivouacked some way off. The next day the Argives, discovering it, razed Orneae to the ground, and went back again; after which the Athenians went home in their ships. Meanwhile the Athenians took by sea to Methone on the Macedonian border some cavalry of their own and the

Macedonian exiles that were at Athens, and plundered the country of Perdiccas. Upon this the Lacedaemonians sent to the Thracian Chalcidians, who had a truce with Athens from one ten days to another, urging them to join Perdiccas in the war, which they refused to do. And the winter ended, and with it ended the sixteenth year of this war of which Thucydides is the historian.

Early in the spring of the following summer the Athenian envoys arrived from Sicily, and the Egestaeans with them, bringing sixty talents of uncoined silver, as a month's pay for sixty ships, which they were to ask to have sent them. The Athenians held an assembly and, after hearing from the Egestaeans and their own envoys a report, as attractive as it was untrue, upon the state of affairs generally, and in particular as to the money, of which, it was said, there was abundance in the temples and the treasury, voted to send sixty ships to Sicily, under the command of Alcibiades, son of Clinias,

Nicias, son of Niceratus, and Lamachus, son of Xenophanes, who were appointed with full powers; they were to help the Egestaeans against the Selinuntines, to restore Leontini upon gaining any advantage in the war, and to order all other matters in Sicily as they should deem best for the interests of Athens. Five days after this a second assembly was held, to consider the speediest means of equipping the ships, and to vote whatever else might be required by the generals for the expedition; and Nicias, who had been chosen to the command against his will, and who thought that the state was not well advised, but upon a slight aid specious pretext was aspiring to the conquest of the whole of Sicily, a great matter to achieve, came forward in the hope of diverting the Athenians from the enterprise, and gave them the following counsel:

"Although this assembly was convened to consider the preparations to be made for sailing to Sicily, I think, notwithstanding, that we have still this question to examine, whether it be better to send out the ships at all, and that we ought not to give so little consideration to a matter of such moment, or let ourselves be persuaded by foreigners into undertaking a war with which we have nothing to do. And yet, individually, I gain in honour by such a course, and fear as little as other men for my person–not that I think a man need be any the worse citizen for taking some thought for his person and estate; on the contrary, such a man would for his own sake desire the prosperity of his country more than others–nevertheless, as I have never spoken against my convictions to gain honour, I shall not begin to do so now, but shall say what I think best. Against your character any words of mine would be weak enough, if I were to advise your keeping what you have got and not risking what is actually yours for advantages which are dubious in themselves, and which you may or may not attain. I will, therefore, content myself with showing that your ardour is out of season, and your ambition not easy of accomplishment.

"I affirm, then, that you leave many enemies behind you here to go yonder and bring more back with you. You imagine, perhaps, that the treaty which you have made can be trusted; a treaty that will continue to exist nominally, as long as you keep quiet–for nominal it has become, owing to the practices of certain men here and at Sparta–but which in the event of a serious reverse in any quarter would not delay our enemies a moment in attacking us; first, because the convention was forced upon them by disaster and was less honourable to them than to us; and secondly, because in this very convention there are many points that are still disputed. Again, some of the most powerful states have never yet accepted the arrangement at all. Some of these are at open war with us; others (as the Lacedaemonians do not yet move) are restrained by truces renewed every ten days, and it is only too probable that if they found our power divided, as we are hurrying to divide it, they would attack us vigorously with the Siceliots, whose alliance they would have in the past valued as they would that of few others. A man ought, therefore, to consider these points, and not to think of running risks with a country placed so critically, or of grasping at another empire before we have secured the one we have already; for in fact the Thracian Chalcidians have been all these years in revolt from us without being yet subdued, and others on the continents yield us but a doubtful obedience. Meanwhile the Egestaeans, our allies, have been wronged, and we run to help them, while the rebels who have so long wronged us still wait for punishment.

"And yet the latter, if brought under, might be kept under; while the Sicilians, even if conquered, are too far off and too numerous to be ruled without difficulty. Now it is folly to go against men who could not be kept under even if conquered, while failure would leave us in a very different position from that which we occupied before the enterprise. The Siceliots, again, to take them as they are at present, in the event of a Syracusan conquest (the favourite bugbear of the Egestaeans), would to my thinking be even less dangerous to us than before. At present they might possibly come here as separate states for love of Lacedaemon; in the other case one empire would scarcely attack another; for after joining the Peloponnesians to overthrow ours, they could only expect to see the same hands overthrow their own in the same way. The Hellenes in Sicily would fear us most if we never went there at all, and next to this, if after displaying our power we went away again as soon as possible. We all know that that which is farthest off, and the reputation of which can least be tested, is the object of admiration; at the least reverse they would at once begin to look down upon us, and would join our enemies here against us. You have yourselves experienced this with regard to the Lacedaemonians and their allies, whom your unexpected success, as compared with what you feared at first, has made you suddenly despise, tempting you further to aspire to the conquest of Sicily. Instead, however, of being puffed up by the misfortunes of your adversaries, you ought to think of breaking their spirit before giving yourselves up to confidence, and to understand that the one thought awakened in the Lacedaemonians by their disgrace is how they may even now, if possible, overthrow us and repair their dishonour; inasmuch as military reputation is their oldest and chiefest study. Our struggle, therefore, if we are wise, will not be for the barbarian Egestaeans in Sicily, but how to defend ourselves most effectually against the oligarchical machinations of Lacedaemon.

"We should also remember that we are but now enjoying some respite from a great pestilence and from war, to the no small benefit of our estates and persons, and that it is right to employ these at home on our own behalf, instead of using them on behalf of these exiles whose interest it is to lie as fairly as they can, who do nothing but talk themselves and leave the danger to others, and who if they succeed will show no proper gratitude, and if they fail will drag down their friends with them. And if there be any man here, overjoyed at being chosen to command, who urges you to make the expedition, merely for ends of his own–specially if he be still too young to command–who seeks to be admired for his stud of horses, but on account of its heavy expenses hopes for some profit from his appointment, do not allow such a one to maintain his private splendour at his country's risk, but remember that such persons injure the public fortune while they squander their own, and that this is a matter of importance, and not for a young man to decide or hastily to take in hand.

"When I see such persons now sitting here at the side of that same individual and summoned by him, alarm seizes me; and I, in my turn, summon any of the older men that may have such a person sitting next him not to let himself be shamed down, for fear of being thought a coward if he do not vote for war, but, remembering how rarely success is got by wishing and how often by forecast, to leave to them the mad dream of conquest, and as a true lover of his country, now threatened by the greatest danger in its history, to hold up his hand on the other side; to vote that the Siceliots be left in the limits now existing between us, limits of which no one can complain (the Ionian sea for the coasting voyage, and the Sicilian across the open main), to enjoy their own possessions and to settle their own quarrels; that the Egestaeans, for their part, be told to end by themselves with the Selinuntines the war which they began without consulting the

Athenians; and that for the future we do not enter into alliance, as we have been used to do, with people whom we must help in their need, and who can never help us in ours.

"And you, Prytanis, if you think it your duty to care for the commonwealth, and if you wish to show yourself a good citizen, put the question to the vote, and take a second time the opinions of the Athenians. If you are afraid to move the question again, consider that a violation of the law cannot carry any prejudice with so many abettors, that you will be the physician of your misguided city, and that the virtue of men in office is briefly this, to do their country as much good as they can, or in any case no harm that they can avoid."

Such were the words of Nicias. Most of the Athenians that came forward spoke in favour of the expedition, and of not annulling what had been voted, although some spoke on the other side. By far the warmest advocate of the expedition was, however, Alcibiades, son of Clinias, who wished to thwart Nicias both as his political opponent and also because of the attack he had made upon him in his speech, and who was, besides, exceedingly ambitious of a command by which he hoped to reduce Sicily and Carthage, and personally to gain in wealth and reputation by means of his successes. For the position he held among the citizens led him to indulge his tastes beyond what his real means would bear, both in keeping horses and in the rest of his expenditure; and this later on had not a little to do with the ruin of the Athenian state. Alarmed at the greatness of his licence in his own life and habits, and of the ambition which he showed in all things soever that he undertook, the mass of the people set him down as a pretender to the tyranny, and became his enemies; and although publicly his conduct of the war was as good as could be desired, individually, his habits gave offence to every one, and caused them to commit affairs to other hands, and thus before long to ruin the city. Meanwhile he now came forward and gave the following advice to the Athenians:

"Athenians, I have a better right to command than others–I must begin with this as Nicias has attacked me–and at the same time I believe myself to be worthy of it. The things for which I am abused, bring fame to my ancestors and to myself, and to the country profit besides. The Hellenes, after expecting to see our city ruined by the war, concluded it to be even greater than it really is, by reason of the magnificence with which I represented it at the Olympic games, when I sent into the lists seven chariots, a number never before entered by any private person, and won the first prize, and was second and fourth, and took care to have everything else in a style worthy of my victory. Custom regards such displays as honourable, and they cannot be made without leaving behind them an impression of power. Again, any splendour that I may have exhibited at home in providing choruses or otherwise, is naturally envied by my fellow citizens, but in the eyes of foreigners has an air of strength as in the other instance. And this is no useless folly, when a man at his own private cost benefits not himself only, but his city: nor is it unfair that he who prides himself on his position should refuse to be upon an equality with the rest. He who is badly off has his misfortunes all to himself, and as we do not see men courted in adversity, on the like principle a man ought to accept the insolence of prosperity; or else, let him first mete out equal measure to all, and then demand to have it meted out to him. What I know is that persons of this kind and all others that have attained to any distinction, although they may be unpopular in their lifetime in their relations with their fellow-men and especially with their equals, leave to posterity the desire of claiming connection with them even without any ground, and are vaunted by the country to which they belonged, not as strangers or ill-doers, but as fellow-countrymen and heroes. Such are my aspirations, and however I am abused for them in private, the question is whether any one manages public affairs better than I do. Having united the most powerful states of Peloponnese, without great danger or expense to you, I compelled the Lacedaemonians to stake their all upon the issue of a single day at Mantinea; and although victorious in the battle, they have never since fully recovered confidence.

"Thus did my youth and so-called monstrous folly find fitting arguments to deal with the power of the Peloponnesians, and by its ardour win their confidence and prevail. And do not be afraid of my youth now, but while I am still in its flower, and Nicias appears fortunate, avail yourselves to the utmost of the services of us both. Neither rescind your resolution to sail to

Sicily, on the ground that you would be going to attack a great power. The cities in Sicily are peopled by motley rabbles, and easily change their institutions and adopt new ones in their stead; and consequently the inhabitants, being without any feeling of patriotism, are not provided with arms for their persons, and have not regularly established themselves on the land; every man thinks that either by fair words or by party strife he can obtain something at the public expense, and then in the event of a catastrophe settle in some other country, and makes his preparations accordingly. From a mob like this you need not look for either unanimity in counsel or concert in action; but they will probably one by one come in as they get a fair offer, especially if they are torn by civil strife as we are told. Moreover, the Siceliots have not so many heavy infantry as they boast; just as the Hellenes generally did not prove so numerous as each state reckoned itself, but Hellas greatly over-estimated their numbers, and has hardly had an adequate force of heavy infantry throughout this war. The states in Sicily, therefore, from all that I can hear, will be found as I say, and I have not pointed out all our advantages, for we shall have the help of many barbarians, who from their hatred of the Syracusans will join us in attacking them; nor will the powers at home prove any hindrance, if you judge rightly. Our fathers with these very adversaries, which it is said we shall now leave behind us when we sail, and the Mede as their enemy as well, were able to win the empire, depending solely on their superiority at sea. The Peloponnesians had never so little hope against us as at present; and let them be ever so sanguine, although strong enough to invade our country even if we stay at home, they can never hurt us with their navy, as we leave one of our own behind us that is a match for them.

"In this state of things what reason can

we give to ourselves for holding back, or what excuse can we offer to our allies in Sicily for not helping them? They are our confederates, and we are bound to assist them, without objecting that they have not assisted us. We did not take them into alliance to have them to help us in Hellas, but that they might so annoy our enemies in Sicily as to prevent them from coming over here and attacking us. It is thus that empire has been won, both by us and by all others that have held it, by a constant readiness to support all, whether barbarians or Hellenes, that invite assistance; since if all were to keep quiet or to pick and choose whom they ought to assist, we should make but few new conquests, and should imperil those we have already won. Men do not rest content with parrying the attacks of a superior, but often strike the first blow to prevent the attack being made. And we cannot fix the exact point at which our empire shall stop; we have reached a position in which we must not be content with retaining but must scheme to extend it, for, if we cease to rule others, we are in danger of being ruled ourselves. Nor can you look at inaction from the same point of view as others, unless you are prepared to change your habits and make them like theirs.

"Be convinced, then, that we shall augment our power at home by this adventure abroad, and let us make the expedition, and so humble the pride of the Peloponnesians by sailing off to Sicily, and letting them see how little we care for the peace that we are now enjoying; and at the same time we shall either become masters, as we very easily may, of the whole of Hellas through the accession of the Sicilian Hellenes, or in any case ruin the Syracusans, to the no small advantage of ourselves and our allies. The faculty of staying if successful, or of returning, will be secured to us by our navy, as we shall be superior at sea to all the Siceliots put together. And do not let the do-nothing policy which Nicias advocates, or his setting of the young against the old, turn you from your purpose, but in the good old fashion by which our fathers, old and young together, by their united counsels brought our affairs to their present height, do you endeavour still to advance them; understanding that neither youth nor old age can do anything the one without the other, but that levity, sobriety, and deliberate judgment are strongest when united, and that, by sinking into inaction, the city, like everything else, will wear itself out, and its skill in everything decay; while each fresh struggle will give it fresh experience, and make it more used to defend itself not in word but in deed. In short, my conviction is that a city not inactive by nature could not choose a quicker way to ruin itself than by suddenly adopting such a policy, and that the safest rule of life is to take one's character and institutions for better and for worse, and to live up to them as closely as one can."

Such were the words of Alcibiades. After hearing him and the Egestaeans and some Leontine exiles, who came forward reminding them of their oaths and imploring their assistance, the Athenians became more eager for the expedition than before. Nicias, perceiving that it would be now useless to try to deter them by the old line of argument, but thinking that he might perhaps alter their resolution by the extravagance of his estimates, came forward a second time and spoke as follows:

"I see, Athenians, that you are thoroughly bent upon the expedition, and therefore hope that all will turn out as we wish, and proceed to give you my opinion at the present juncture. From all that I hear we are going against cities that are great and not subject to one another, or in need of change, so as to be glad to pass from enforced servitude to an easier condition, or in the least likely to accept our rule in exchange for freedom; and, to take only the Hellenic towns, they are very numerous for one island. Besides Naxos and Catana, which I expect to join us from their connection with Leontini, there are seven others armed at all points just like our own power, particularly Selinus and Syracuse, the chief objects of our expedition. These are full of heavy infantry, archers, and darters, have galleys in abundance and crowds to man them; they have also money, partly in the hands of private persons, partly in the temples at Selinus, and at Syracuse first-fruits from some of the barbarians as well. But their chief advantage over us lies in the number of their horses, and in the fact that they grow their corn at home instead of importing it.

"Against a power of this kind it will not do to have merely a weak naval armament, but we shall want also a large land army to sail with us, if we are to do anything worthy of our ambition, and are not to be shut out from the country by a numerous cavalry; especially if the cities should take alarm and combine, and we should be left without friends (except the Egestaeans) to furnish us with horse to defend ourselves with. It would be disgraceful to have to retire under compulsion, or to send back for reinforcements, owing to want of reflection at first: we must therefore start from home with a competent force, seeing that we are going to sail far from our country, and upon an expedition not like any which you may undertaken undertaken the quality of allies, among your subject states here in Hellas, where any additional supplies needed were easily drawn from the friendly territory; but we are cutting ourselves off, and going to a land entirely strange, from which during four months in winter it is not even easy for a messenger get to Athens.

"I think, therefore, that we ought to take great numbers of heavy infantry, both from Athens and from our allies, and not merely from our subjects, but also any we may be able to get for love or for money in Peloponnese, and great numbers also of archers and slingers, to make head against the Sicilian horse. Meanwhile we must have an overwhelming superiority at sea, to enable us the more easily to carry in what we want; and we must take our own corn in merchant vessels, that is to say, wheat and parched barley, and bakers from the mills compelled to serve for pay in the proper proportion; in order that in case of our being weather-bound the armament may not want provisions, as it is not every city that will be able to entertain numbers like ours. We must also provide ourselves with everything else as far as we can, so as not to be dependent upon others; and above all we must take with us from home as much money as possible, as the sums talked of as ready at Egesta are readier, you may be sure, in talk than in any other way.

"Indeed, even if we leave Athens with a force not only equal to that of the enemy except in the number of heavy infantry in the field, but even at all points superior to him, we shall still find it difficult to conquer Sicily or save ourselves. We must not disguise from ourselves that we go to found a city among strangers and enemies, and that he who undertakes such an enterprise should be prepared to become master of the country the first day he lands, or failing in this to find everything hostile to him. Fearing this, and knowing that we shall have need of much good counsel and more good fortune–a hard matter for mortal man to aspire to–I wish as far as may be to make myself independent of fortune before sailing, and when I do sail, to be as safe as a strong force can make me. This I believe to be surest for the country at large, and safest for us who are to go on the expedition. If any one thinks differently I resign to him my command."

With this Nicias concluded, thinking that he should either disgust the Athenians by the magnitude of the undertaking, or, if obliged to sail on the expedition, would thus do so in the safest way possible. The Athenians, however, far from having their taste for the voyage taken away by the burdensomeness of the preparations, became more eager for it than ever; and just the contrary took place of what Nicias had thought, as it was held that he had given good advice, and that the expedition would be the safest in the world. All alike fell in love with the enterprise. The older men thought that they would either subdue the places against which they were to sail, or at all events, with so large a force, meet with no disaster; those in the prime of life felt a longing for foreign sights and spectacles, and had no doubt that they should come safe home again; while the idea of the common people and the soldiery was to earn wages at the moment, and make conquests that would supply a never-ending fund of pay for the future. With this enthusiasm of the majority, the few that liked it not, feared to appear unpatriotic by holding up their hands against it, and so kept quiet.

At last one of the Athenians came forward and called upon Nicias and told him that he ought not to make excuses or put them off, but say at once before them all what forces the Athenians should vote him. Upon this he said, not without reluctance, that he would advise upon that matter more at leisure with his colleagues; as far however as he could see at present, they must sail with at least one hundred galleys–the Athenians providing as many transports as they might determine, and sending for others from the allies–not less than five thousand heavy infantry in all, Athenian and allied, and if possible more; and the rest of the armament in proportion; archers from home and from Crete, and slingers, and whatever else might seem desirable, being got ready by the generals and taken with them.

Upon hearing this the Athenians at once

voted that the generals should have full powers in the matter of the numbers of the army and of the expedition generally, to do as they judged best for the interests of Athens. After this the preparations began; messages being sent to the allies and the rolls drawn up at home. And as the city had just recovered from the plague and the long war, and a number of young men had grown up and capital had accumulated by reason of the truce, everything was the more easily provided.

In the midst of these preparations all the stone Hermae in the city of Athens, that is to say the customary square figures, so common in the doorways of private houses and temples, had in one night most of them their fares mutilated. No one knew who had done it, but large public rewards were offered to find the authors; and it was further voted that any one who knew of any other act of impiety having been committed should come and give information without fear of consequences, whether he were citizen, alien, or slave. The matter was taken up the more seriously, as it was thought to be ominous for the expedition, and part of a conspiracy to bring about a revolution and to upset the democracy.

Information was given accordingly by some resident aliens and body servants, not about the Hermae but about some previous mutilations of other images perpetrated by young men in a drunken frolic, and of mock celebrations of the mysteries, averred to take place in private houses. Alcibiades being implicated in this charge, it was taken hold of by those who could least endure him, because he stood in the way of their obtaining the undisturbed direction of the people, and who thought that if he were once removed the first place would be theirs. These accordingly magnified the matter and loudly proclaimed that the affair of the mysteries and the mutilation of the Hermae were part and parcel of a scheme to overthrow the democracy, and that nothing of all this had been done without Alcibiades; the proofs alleged being the general and undemocratic licence of his life and habits.

Alcibiades repelled on the spot the charges in question, and also before going on the expedition, the preparations for which were now complete, offered to stand his trial, that it might be seen whether he was guilty of the acts imputed to him; desiring to be punished if found guilty, but, if acquitted, to take the command. Meanwhile he protested against their receiving slanders against him in his absence, and begged them rather to put him to death at once if he were guilty, and pointed out the imprudence of sending him out at the head of so large an army, with so serious a charge still undecided. But his enemies feared that he would have the army for him if he were tried immediately, and that the people might relent in favour of the man whom they already caressed as the cause of the Argives and some of the Mantineans joining in the expedition, and did their utmost to get this proposition rejected, putting forward other orators who said that he ought at present to sail and not delay the departure of the army, and be tried on his return within a fixed number of days; their plan being to have him sent for and brought home for trial upon some graver charge, which they would the more easily get up in his absence. Accordingly it was decreed that he should sail.

After this the departure for Sicily took place, it being now about midsummer. Most of the allies, with the corn transports and the smaller craft and the rest of the expedition, had already received orders to muster at Corcyra, to cross the Ionian Sea from thence in a body to the Iapygian promontory. But the Athenians themselves, and such of their allies as happened to be with them, went down to Piraeus upon a day appointed at daybreak, and began to man the ships for putting out to sea. With them also went down the whole population, one may say, of the city, both citizens and foreigners; the inhabitants of the country each escorting those that belonged to them, their friends, their relatives, or their sons, with hope and lamentation upon their way, as they thought of the conquests which they hoped to make, or of the friends whom they might never see again, considering the long voyage which they were going to make from their country. Indeed, at this moment, when they were now upon the point of parting from one another, the danger came more home to them than when they voted for the expedition; although the strength of the armament, and the profuse provision which they remarked in every department, was a sight that could not but comfort them. As for the foreigners and the rest of the crowd, they simply went to see a sight worth looking at and passing all belief.

Indeed this armament that first sailed out was by far the most costly and splendid

Hellenic force that had ever been sent out by a single city up to that time. In mere number of ships and heavy infantry that against Epidaurus under Pericles, and the same when going against Potidaea under Hagnon, was not inferior; containing as it did four thousand Athenian heavy infantry, three hundred horse, and one hundred galleys accompanied by fifty Lesbian and Chian vessels and many allies besides. But these were sent upon a short voyage and with a scanty equipment. The present expedition was formed in contemplation of a long term of service by land and sea alike, and was furnished with ships and troops so as to be ready for either as required. The fleet had been elaborately equipped at great cost to the captains and the state; the treasury giving a drachma a day to each seaman, and providing empty ships, sixty men-of-war and forty transports, and manning these with the best crews obtainable; while the captains gave a bounty in addition to the pay from the treasury to the thranitae and crews generally, besides spending lavishly upon figure-heads and equipments, and one and all making the utmost exertions to enable their own ships to excel in beauty and fast sailing. Meanwhile the land forces had been picked from the best muster-rolls, and vied with each other in paying great attention to their arms and personal accoutrements. From this resulted not only a rivalry among themselves in their different departments, but an idea among the rest of the Hellenes that it was more a display of power and resources than an armament against an enemy. For if any one had counted up the public expenditure of the state, and the private outlay of individuals–that is to say, the sums which the state had already spent upon the expedition and was sending out in the hands of the generals, and those which individuals had expended upon their personal outfit, or as captains of galleys had laid out and were still to lay out upon their vessels; and if he had added to this the journey money which each was likely to have provided himself with, independently of the pay from the treasury, for a voyage of such length, and what the soldiers or traders took with them for the purpose of exchange–it would have been found that many talents in all were being taken out of the city. Indeed the expedition became not less famous for its wonderful boldness and for the splendour of its appearance, than for its overwhelming strength as compared with the peoples against whom it was directed, and for the fact that this was the longest passage from home hitherto attempted, and the most ambitious in its objects considering the resources of those who undertook it.

The ships being now manned, and everything put on board with which they meant to sail, the trumpet commanded silence, and the prayers customary before putting out to sea were offered, not in each ship by itself, but by all together to the voice of a herald; and bowls of wine were mixed through all the armament, and libations made by the soldiers and their officers in gold and silver goblets. In their prayers joined also the crowds on shore, the citizens and all others that wished them well. The hymn sung and the libations finished, they put out to sea, and first out in column then raced each other as far as Aegina, and so hastened to reach Corcyra, where the rest of the allied forces were also assembling.

Chapter Nineteen

Seventeenth Year of the War–Parties at Syracuse–Story of Harmodius and Aristogiton–Disgrace of Alcibiades

MEANWHILE AT SYRACUSE NEWS came in from many quarters of the expedition, but for a long while met with no credence whatever. Indeed, an assembly was held in which speeches, as will be seen, were delivered by different orators, believing or contradicting the report of the Athenian expedition; among whom Hermocrates, son of Hermon, came forward, being persuaded that he knew the truth of the matter, and gave the following counsel:

"Although I shall perhaps be no better believed than others have been when I speak upon the reality of the expedition, and although I know that those who either make or repeat statements thought not worthy of belief not only gain no converts but are thought fools for their pains, I shall certainly not be frightened into holding my tongue when the state is in danger, and when I am persuaded that I can speak with more authority on the matter than other persons. Much as you wonder at it, the Athenians nevertheless have set out against us with a large force, naval and military, professedly to help the Egestaeans and to restore Leontini, but really to conquer Sicily, and above all our city, which once gained, the rest, they think, will easily follow. Make up your minds, therefore, to see them speedily here, and see how you can best repel them with the means under your hand, and do be taken off your guard through despising the news, or neglect the common weal through disbelieving it. Meanwhile those who believe me need not be dismayed at the force or daring of the enemy. They will not be able to do us more hurt than we shall do them; nor is the greatness of their armament altogether without advantage to us. Indeed, the greater it is the better, with regard to the rest of the Siceliots, whom dismay will make more ready to join us; and if we defeat or drive them away, disappointed of the objects of their ambition (for I do not fear for a moment that they will get what they want), it will be a most glorious exploit for us, and in my judgment by no means an unlikely one. Few indeed have been the large armaments, either Hellenic or barbarian, that have gone far from home and been successful. They cannot be more numerous than the people of the country and their neighbours, all of whom fear leagues together; and if they miscarry for want of supplies in a foreign land, to those against whom their plans were laid none the less they leave renown, although they may themselves have been the main cause of their own discomfort. Thus these very Athenians rose by the defeat of the Mede, in a great measure due to accidental causes, from the mere fact that Athens had been the object of his attack; and this may very well be the case with us also.

"Let us, therefore, confidently begin preparations here; let us send and confirm some of the Sicels, and obtain the friendship and alliance of others, and dispatch envoys to the rest of Sicily to show that the danger is common to all, and to Italy to get them to become our allies, or at all events to refuse to receive the Athenians. I also think that it would be best to send to Carthage as well; they are by no means there without apprehension, but it is their constant fear that the Athenians may one day attack their city, and they may perhaps think that they might themselves suffer by letting Sicily be sacrificed, and be willing to help us secretly if not openly, in one way if not in another. They are the best able to do so, if they will, of any of the present day, as they possess most gold and silver, by which war, like everything else, flourishes. Let us also send to Lacedaemon and Corinth, and ask them to come here and help us as soon as possible, and to keep alive the war in Hellas. But the true thing of all others, in my opinion, to do at the present moment, is what you, with your constitutional love of quiet, will be slow to see, and what I must nevertheless mention. If we Siceliots, all together, or at least as many as possible besides ourselves, would only launch the whole of our actual navy with two months' provisions, and meet the Athenians at Tarentum and the Iapygian promontory, and show them that before fighting for Sicily they must first fight for their passage across the Ionian Sea, we should strike dismay into their army, and set them on thinking that we have a base for our defensive–for Tarentum is ready to receive us–while they have a wide sea to cross with all their armament, which could with difficulty keep its order through so long a voyage, and would be easy for us to attack as it came on slowly and in small detachments. On the other hand, if they were to lighten their vessels, and draw together their fast sailers and with these attack us, we could either fall upon them when they were wearied with rowing, or if we did not choose to do so, we could retire to Tarentum; while they, having crossed with few provisions just to give battle, would be hard put to it in desolate places, and would either have to remain and be blockaded, or to try to sail along the coast, abandoning the rest of their armament, and being further discouraged by not knowing for certain whether the cities would receive them. In my opinion this consideration alone would be sufficient to deter them from putting out from Corcyra; and what with deliberating and reconnoitring our numbers and whereabouts, they would let the season go on until winter was upon them, or, confounded by so unexpected a circumstance, would break up the expedition, especially as their most experienced general has, as I hear, taken the command against his will, and would grasp at the first excuse offered by any serious demonstration of ours. We should also be reported, I am certain, as more numerous than we really are, and men's minds are affected by what they hear, and besides the first to attack, or to show that they mean to defend themselves against an attack, inspire greater fear because men see that they are ready for the emergency. This would just be the case with the Athenians at present. They are now attacking us in the belief that we shall not resist, having a right to judge us severely because we did not help the Lacedaemonians in crushing them; but if they were to see us showing a courage for which they are not prepared, they would be more dismayed by the surprise than they could ever be by our actual power. I could wish to persuade you to show this courage; but if this cannot be, at all events lose not a moment in preparing generally for the war; and remember all of you that contempt for an assailant is best shown by bravery in action, but that for the present the best course is to accept the preparations which fear inspires as giving the surest promise of safety, and to act as if the danger was real. That the Athenians are coming to attack us, and are already upon the voyage, and all but here–this is what I am sure of."

Thus far spoke Hermocrates. Meanwhile the people of Syracuse were at great strife among themselves; some contending that the Athenians had no idea of coming and that there was no truth in what he said;

some asking if they did come what harm they could do that would not be repaid them tenfold in return; while others made light of the whole affair and turned it into ridicule. In short, there were few that believed Hermocrates and feared for the future. Meanwhile Athenagoras, the leader of the people and very powerful at that time with the masses, came forward and spoke as follows:

"For the Athenians, he who does not wish that they may be as misguided as they are supposed to be, and that they may come here to become our subjects, is either a coward or a traitor to his country; while as for those who carry such tidings and fill you with so much alarm, I wonder less at their audacity than at their folly if they flatter themselves that we do not see through them. The fact is that they have their private reasons to be afraid, and wish to throw the city into consternation to have their own terrors cast into the shade by the public alarm. In short, this is what these reports are worth; they do not arise of themselves, but are concocted by men who are always causing agitation here in Sicily. However, if you are well advised, you will not be guided in your calculation of probabilities by what these persons tell you, but by what shrewd men and of large experience, as I esteem the Athenians to be, would be likely to do. Now it is not likely that they would leave the Peloponnesians behind them, and before they have well ended the war in Hellas wantonly come in quest of a new war quite as arduous in Sicily; indeed, in my judgment, they are only too glad that we do not go and attack them, being so many and so great cities as we are.

"However, if they should come as is reported, I consider Sicily better able to go through with the war than Peloponnese, as being at all points better prepared, and our city by itself far more than a match for this pretended army of invasion, even were it twice as large again. I know that they will not have horses with them, or get any here, except a few perhaps from the Egestaeans; or be able to bring a force of heavy infantry equal in number to our own, in ships which will already have enough to do to come all this distance, however lightly laden, not to speak of the transport of the other stores required against a city of this magnitude, which will be no slight quantity. In fact, so strong is my opinion upon the subject, that I do not well see how they could avoid annihilation if they brought with them another city as large as Syracuse, and settled down and carried on war from our frontier; much less can they hope to succeed with all Sicily hostile to them, as all Sicily will be, and with only a camp pitched from the ships, and composed of tents and bare necessaries, from which they would not be able to stir far for fear of our cavalry.

"But the Athenians see this as I tell you, and as I have reason to know are looking after their possessions at home, while persons here invent stories that neither are true nor ever will be. Nor is this the first time that I see these persons, when they cannot resort to deeds, trying by such stories and by others even more abominable to frighten your people and get into their hands the government: it is what I see always. And I cannot help fearing that trying so often they may one day succeed, and that we, as long as we do not feel the smart, may prove too weak for the task of prevention, or, when the offenders are known, of pursuit. The result is that our city is rarely at rest, but is subject to constant troubles and to contests as frequent against herself as against the enemy, not to speak of occasional tyrannies and infamous cabals. However, I will try, if you will support me, to let nothing of this happen in our time, by gaining you, the many, and by chastising the authors of such machinations, not merely when they are caught in the act–a difficult feat to accomplish–but also for what they have the wish though not the power to do; as it is necessary to punish an enemy not only for what he does, but also beforehand for what he intends to do, if the first to relax precaution would not be also the first to suffer. I shall also reprove, watch, and on occasion warn the few–the most effectual way, in my opinion, of turning them from their evil courses. And after all, as I have often asked, what would you have, young men? Would you hold office at once? The law forbids it, a law enacted rather because you are not competent than to disgrace you when competent. Meanwhile you would not be on a legal equality with the many! But how can it be right that citizens of the same state should be held unworthy of the same privileges?

"It will be said, perhaps, that democracy is neither wise nor equitable, but that the holders of property are also the best fitted to rule. I say, on the contrary, first, that the word demos, or people, includes the whole state, oligarchy only a part; next, that if the best guardians of property are the rich, and the best counsellors the wise, none can hear and decide so well as the many; and that all these talents, severally and collectively, have their just place in a democracy. But an oligarchy gives the many their share of the danger, and not content with the largest part takes and keeps the whole of the profit; and this is what the powerful and young among you aspire to, but in a great city cannot possibly obtain.

"But even now, foolish men, most senseless of all the Hellenes that I know, if you have no sense of the wickedness of your designs, or most criminal if you have that sense and still dare to pursue them–even now, if it is not a case for repentance, you may still learn wisdom, and thus advance the interest of the country, the common interest of us all. Reflect that in the country's prosperity the men of merit in your ranks will have a share and a larger share than the great mass of your fellow countrymen, but that if you have other designs you run a risk of being deprived of all; and desist from reports like these, as the people know your object and will not put up with it. If the Athenians arrive, this city will repulse them in a manner worthy of itself; we have moreover, generals who will see to this matter. And if nothing of this be true, as I incline to believe, the city will not be thrown into a panic by your intelligence, or impose upon itself a self-chosen servitude by choosing you for its rulers; the city itself will look into the matter, and will judge your words as if they were acts, and, instead of allowing itself to be deprived of its liberty by listening to you, will strive to preserve that liberty, by taking care to have always at hand the means of making itself respected."

Such were the words of Athenagoras. One of the generals now stood up and stopped any other speakers coming forward, adding these words of his own with reference to the matter in hand: "It is not well for speakers to utter calumnies against one another, or for their hearers to entertain them; we ought rather to look to the intelligence that we have received, and see how each man by himself and the city as a whole may best prepare to repel the invaders. Even if there be no need, there is no harm in the state being furnished with horses and arms and all other insignia of war; and we will undertake to see to and order this, and to send round to the cities to reconnoitre and do all else that may appear desirable. Part of this we have seen to already, and whatever we discover shall be laid before you." After these words from the general, the Syracusans departed from the assembly.

In the meantime the Athenians with all their allies had now arrived at Corcyra. Here the generals began by again reviewing the armament, and made arrangements as to the order in which they were to anchor and encamp, and dividing the whole fleet into three divisions, allotted one to each of their number, to avoid sailing all together and being thus embarrassed for water, harbourage, or provisions at the stations which they might touch at, and at the same time to be generally better ordered and easier to handle, by each squadron having its own commander. Next they sent on three ships to Italy and Sicily to find out which of the cities would receive them, with instructions to meet them on the way and let them know before they put in to land.

After this the Athenians weighed from Corcyra, and proceeded to cross to Sicily with an armament now consisting of one hundred and thirty-four galleys in all (besides two Rhodian fifty-oars), of which one hundred were Athenian vessels–sixty men-of-war, and forty troopships–and the remainder from Chios and the other allies; five thousand and one hundred heavy infantry in all, that is to say, fifteen hundred Athenian citizens from the rolls at Athens and seven hundred Thetes shipped as marines, and the rest allied troops, some of them Athenian subjects, and besides these five hundred Argives, and two hundred and fifty Mantineans serving for hire; four hundred and eighty archers in all, eighty of whom were Cretans, seven hundred slingers from Rhodes, one hundred and twenty light-armed exiles from Megara, and one horse-transport carrying thirty horses.

Such was the strength of the first armament that sailed over for the war. The supplies for this force were carried by thirty ships of burden laden with corn, which conveyed the bakers, stone-masons, and carpenters, and the tools for raising fortifications, accompanied by one hundred boats, like the former pressed into the service, besides many other boats and ships of burden which followed the armament voluntarily for purposes of trade; all of which now left Corcyra and struck across the Ionian Sea together. The whole force making land at the Iapygian promontory and Tarentum, with more or less good fortune, coasted along the shores of Italy, the cities shutting their markets and gates against them, and according them nothing but water and liberty to anchor, and Tarentum and Locri not even that, until they arrived at Rhegium, the extreme point of Italy. Here at length they reunited, and not gaining admission within the walls pitched a camp outside the city in the precinct of Artemis, where a market was also provided for them, and drew their ships on shore and kept quiet. Meanwhile they opened negotiations with the Rhegians, and called upon them as Chalcidians to assist their Leontine kinsmen; to which the Rhegians replied that they would not side with either party, but should await the decision of the rest of the Italiots, and do as they did. Upon this the Athenians now began to consider what would be the best action to take in the affairs of Sicily, and meanwhile waited for the ships sent on to come back from Egesta, in order to know whether there was really there the money mentioned by the messengers at Athens.

In the meantime came in from all quarters to the Syracusans, as well as from their own officers sent to reconnoitre, the positive tidings that the fleet was at Rhegium; upon which they laid aside their incredulity and threw themselves heart and soul into the work of preparation. Guards or envoys, as the case might be, were sent round to the Sicels, garrisons put into the posts of the Peripoli in the country, horses and arms reviewed in the city to see that nothing was wanting, and all other steps taken to prepare for a war which might be upon them at any moment.

Meanwhile the three ships that had been sent on came from Egesta to the Athenians at Rhegium, with the news that so far from there being the sums promised, all that could be produced was thirty talents. The generals were not a little disheartened at being thus disappointed at the outset, and by the refusal to join in the expedition of the Rhegians, the people they had first tried to gain and had had had most reason to count upon, from their relationship to the Leontines and constant friendship for Athens. If Nicias was prepared for the news from Egesta, his two colleagues were taken completely by surprise. The Egestaeans had had recourse to the following stratagem, when the first envoys from Athens came to inspect their resources. They took the envoys in question to the temple of Aphrodite at Eryx and showed them the treasures deposited there: bowls, wine-ladles, censers, and a large number of other pieces of plate, which from being in silver gave an impression of wealth quite out of proportion to their really small value. They also privately entertained the ships' crews, and collected all the cups of gold and silver that they could find in Egesta itself or could borrow in the neighbouring Phoenician and Hellenic towns, and each brought them to the banquets as their own; and as all used pretty nearly the same, and everywhere a great quantity of plate was shown, the effect was most dazzling upon the Athenian sailors, and made them talk loudly of the riches they had seen when they got back to Athens. The dupes in question–who had in their turn persuaded the rest–when the news got abroad that there was not the money supposed at Egesta, were much blamed by the soldiers.

Meanwhile the generals consulted upon what was to be done. The opinion of Nicias was to sail with all the armament to Selinus, the main object of the expedition, and if the Egestaeans could provide money for the whole force, to advise accordingly; but if they could not, to require them to supply provisions for the sixty ships that they had asked for, to stay and settle matters between them and the Selinuntines either by force or by agreement, and then to coast past the other cities, and after displaying the power of Athens and proving their zeal for their friends and allies, to sail home again (unless they should have some sudden and unexpected opportunity of serving the Leontines, or of bringing over some of the other cities), and not to endanger the state by wasting its home resources.

Alcibiades said that a great expedition like the present must not disgrace itself by going away without having done anything; heralds must be sent to all the cities except Selinus and Syracuse, and efforts be made to make some of the Sicels revolt from the Syracusans, and to obtain the friendship of others, in order to have corn and troops; and first of all to gain the Messinese, who lay right in the passage and entrance to Sicily, and would afford an excellent harbour and base for the army. Thus, after bringing over the towns and knowing who would be their allies in the war, they might at length attack Syracuse and Selinus; unless the latter came to terms with Egesta and the former ceased to oppose the restoration of Leontini.

Lamachus, on the other hand, said that

they ought to sail straight to Syracuse, and fight their battle at once under the walls of the town while the people were still unprepared, and the panic at its height. Every armament was most terrible at first; if it allowed time to run on without showing itself, men's courage revived, and they saw it appear at last almost with indifference. By attacking suddenly, while Syracuse still trembled at their coming, they would have the best chance of gaining a victory for themselves and of striking a complete panic into the enemy by the aspect of their numbers–which would never appear so considerable as at present–by the anticipation of coming disaster, and above all by the immediate danger of the engagement. They might also count upon surprising many in the fields outside, incredulous of their coming; and at the moment that the enemy was carrying in his property the army would not want for booty if it sat down in force before the city. The rest of the Siceliots would thus be immediately less disposed to enter into alliance with the Syracusans, and would join the Athenians, without waiting to see which were the strongest. They must make Megara their naval station as a place to retreat to and a base from which to attack: it was an uninhabited place at no great distance from Syracuse either by land or by sea.

After speaking to this effect, Lamachus nevertheless gave his support to the opinion of Alcibiades. After this Alcibiades sailed in his own vessel across to Messina with proposals of alliance, but met with no success, the inhabitants answering that they could not receive him within their walls, though they would provide him with a market outside. Upon this he sailed back to Rhegium. Immediately upon his return the generals manned and victualled sixty ships out of the whole fleet and coasted along to Naxos, leaving the rest of the armament behind them at Rhegium with one of their number.

Received by the Naxians, they then coasted on to Catana, and being refused admittance by the inhabitants, there being a Syracusan party in the town, went on to the river Terias. Here they bivouacked, and the next day sailed in single file to Syracuse with all their ships except ten which they sent on in front to sail into the great harbour and see if there was any fleet launched, and to proclaim by herald from shipboard that the Athenians were come to restore the Leontines to their country, as being their allies and kinsmen, and that such of them, therefore, as were in Syracuse should leave it without fear and join their friends and benefactors the Athenians. After making this proclamation and reconnoitring the city and the harbours, and the features of the country which they would have to make their base of operations in the war, they sailed back to Catana.

An assembly being held here, the inhabitants refused to receive the armament, but invited the generals to come in and say what they desired; and while Alcibiades was speaking and the citizens were intent on the assembly, the soldiers broke down an ill-walled-up postern gate without being observed, and getting inside the town, flocked into the marketplace. The Syracusan party in the town no sooner saw the army inside than they became frightened and withdrew, not being at all numerous; while the rest voted for an alliance with the Athenians and invited them to fetch the rest of their forces from Rhegium. After this the Athenians sailed to Rhegium, and put off, this time with all the armament, for Catana, and fell to work at their camp immediately upon their arrival.

Meanwhile word was brought them from Camarina that if they went there the town would go over to them, and also that the Syracusans were manning a fleet. The Athenians accordingly sailed alongshore with all their armament, first to Syracuse, where they found no fleet manning, and so always along the coast to Camarina, where they brought to at the beach, and sent a herald to the people, who, however, refused to receive them, saying that their oaths bound them to receive the Athenians only with a single vessel, unless they themselves sent for more. Disappointed here, the Athenians now sailed back again, and after landing and plundering on Syracusan territory and losing some stragglers from their light infantry through the coming up of the Syracusan horse, so got back to Catana.

There they found the Salaminia come from Athens for Alcibiades, with orders for him to sail home to answer the charges which the state brought against him, and for certain others of the soldiers who with him were accused of sacrilege in the matter of the mysteries and of the Hermae. For the Athenians, after the departure of the expedition, had continued as active as ever in investigating the facts of the mysteries and of the Hermae, and, instead of testing the informers, in their suspicious temper welcomed all indifferently, arresting and imprisoning the best citizens upon the evidence of rascals, and preferring to sift the matter to the bottom sooner than to let an accused person of good character pass unquestioned, owing to the rascality of the informer. The commons had heard how oppressive the tyranny of Pisistratus and his sons had become before it ended, and further that that had been put down at last, not by themselves and Harmodius, but by the Lacedaemonians, and so were always in fear and took everything suspiciously.

Indeed, the daring action of Aristogiton and Harmodius was undertaken in consequence of a love affair, which I shall relate at some length, to show that the Athenians are not more accurate than the rest of the world in their accounts of their own tyrants and of the facts of their own history. Pisistratus dying at an advanced age in possession of the tyranny, was succeeded by his eldest son, Hippias, and not Hipparchus, as is vulgarly believed. Harmodius was then in the flower of youthful beauty, and Aristogiton, a citizen in the middle rank of life, was his lover and possessed him. Solicited without success by Hipparchus, son of Pisistratus, Harmodius told Aristogiton, and the enraged lover, afraid that the powerful Hipparchus might take Harmodius by force, immediately formed a design, such as his condition in life permitted, for overthrowing the tyranny. In the meantime Hipparchus, after a second solicitation of Harmodius, attended with no better success, unwilling to use violence, arranged to insult him in some covert way. Indeed, generally their government was not grievous to the multitude, or in any way odious in practice; and these tyrants cultivated wisdom and virtue as much as any, and without exacting from the Athenians more than a twentieth of their income, splendidly adorned their city, and carried on their wars, and provided sacrifices for the temples. For the rest, the city was left in full enjoyment of its existing laws, except that care was always taken to have the offices in the hands of some one of the family. Among those of them that held the yearly archonship at Athens was Pisistratus, son of the tyrant Hippias, and named after his grandfather, who dedicated during his term of office the altar to the twelve gods in the market-place, and that of Apollo in the Pythian precinct. The Athenian people afterwards built on to and lengthened the altar in the market-place, and obliterated the inscription; but that in the Pythian precinct can still be seen, though in faded letters, and is to the following effect:

Pisistratus, the son of Hippias, Sent up this record of his archonship In precinct of Apollo Pythias.

That Hippias was the eldest son and succeeded to the government, is what I positively assert as a fact upon which I have had more exact accounts than others, and may be also ascertained by the following circumstance. He is the only one of the legitimate brothers that appears to have had children; as the altar shows, and the pillar placed in the Athenian Acropolis, commemorating the crime of the tyrants, which mentions no child of Thessalus or of Hipparchus, but five of Hippias, which he had by Myrrhine, daughter of Callias, son of Hyperechides; and naturally the eldest would have married first. Again, his name comes first on the pillar after that of his father; and this too is quite natural, as he was the eldest after him, and the reigning tyrant. Nor can I ever believe that Hippias would have obtained the tyranny so easily, if Hipparchus had been in power when he was killed, and he, Hippias, had had to establish himself upon the same day; but he had no doubt been long accustomed to overawe the citizens, and to be obeyed by his mercenaries, and thus not only conquered, but conquered with ease, without experiencing any of the embarrassment of a younger brother unused to the exercise of authority. It was the sad fate which made Hipparchus famous that got him also the credit with posterity of having been tyrant.

To return to Harmodius; Hipparchus having been repulsed in his solicitations insulted him as he had resolved, by first inviting a sister of his, a young girl, to come and bear a basket in a certain procession, and then rejecting her, on the plea that she had never been invited at all owing to her unworthiness. If Harmodius was indignant at this, Aristogiton for his sake now became more exasperated than ever; and having arranged everything with those who were to join them in the enterprise, they only waited for the great feast of the Panathenaea, the sole day upon which the citizens forming part of the procession could meet together in arms without suspicion. Aristogiton and Harmodius were to begin, but were to be supported immediately by their accomplices against the bodyguard. The conspirators were not many, for better security, besides which they hoped that those not in the plot would be carried away by the example of a few daring spirits, and use the arms in their hands to recover their liberty.

At last the festival arrived; and Hippias with his bodyguard was outside the city in the Ceramicus, arranging how the different parts of the procession were to proceed. Harmodius and Aristogiton had already their daggers and were getting ready to act, when seeing one of their accomplices talking familiarly with Hippias, who was easy of access to every one, they took fright, and concluded that they were discovered and on the point of being taken; and eager if possible to be revenged first upon the man who had wronged them and for whom they had undertaken all this risk, they rushed, as they were, within the gates, and meeting with Hipparchus by the Leocorium recklessly fell upon him at once, infuriated, Aristogiton by love, and Harmodius by insult, and smote him and slew him. Aristogiton escaped the guards at the moment, through the crowd running up, but was afterwards taken and dispatched in no merciful way: Harmodius was killed on the spot.

When the news was brought to Hippias in the Ceramicus, he at once proceeded not to the scene of action, but to the armed men in the procession, before they, being some distance away, knew anything of the matter, and composing his features for the occasion, so as not to betray himself, pointed to a certain spot, and bade them repair thither without their arms. They withdrew accordingly, fancying he had something to say; upon which he told the mercenaries to remove the arms, and there and then picked out the men he thought guilty and all found with daggers, the shield and spear being the usual weapons for a procession.

In this way offended love first led Harmodius and Aristogiton to conspire, and the alarm of the moment to commit the rash action recounted. After this the tyranny pressed harder on the Athenians, and Hippias, now grown more fearful, put to death many of the citizens, and at the same time began to turn his eyes abroad for a refuge in case of revolution. Thus, although an Athenian, he gave his daughter, Archedice, to a Lampsacene, Aeantides, son of the tyrant of Lampsacus, seeing that they had great influence with Darius. And there is her tomb in Lampsacus with this inscription:

Archedice lies buried in this earth, Hippias her sire, and Athens gave her birth; Unto her bosom pride was never known, Though daughter, wife, and sister to the throne.

Hippias, after reigning three years longer over the Athenians, was deposed in the fourth by the Lacedaemonians and the banished Alcmaeonidae, and went with a safe conduct to Sigeum, and to Aeantides at Lampsacus, and from thence to King Darius; from whose court he set out twenty years after, in his old age, and came with the Medes to Marathon.

With these events in their minds, and recalling everything they knew by hearsay on the subject, the Athenian people grow difficult of humour and suspicious of the persons charged in the affair of the mysteries, and persuaded that all that had taken place was part of an oligarchical and monarchical conspiracy. In the state of irritation thus produced, many persons of consideration had been already thrown into prison, and far from showing any signs of abating, public feeling grew daily more savage, and more arrests were made; until at last one of those in custody, thought to be the most guilty of all, was induced by a fellow prisoner to make a revelation, whether true or not is a matter on which there are two opinions, no one having been able, either then or since, to say for certain who did the deed. However this may be, the other found arguments to persuade him, that even if he had not done it, he ought to save himself by gaining a promise of impunity, and free the state of its present suspicions; as he would be surer of safety if he confessed after promise of impunity than if he denied and were brought to trial. He accordingly made a revelation, affecting himself and others in the affair of the Hermae; and the Athenian people, glad at last, as they supposed, to get at the truth, and furious until then at not being able to discover those who had conspired against the commons, at once let go the informer and all the rest whom he had not denounced, and bringing the accused to trial executed as many as were apprehended, and condemned to death such as had fled and set a price upon their heads. In this it was, after all, not clear whether the sufferers had been punished unjustly, while in any case the rest of the city received immediate and manifest relief.

To return to Alcibiades: public feeling was very hostile to him, being worked on by the same enemies who had attacked him before he went out; and now that the Athenians fancied that they had got at the truth of the matter of the Hermae, they believed more firmly than ever that the affair of the mysteries also, in which he was implicated, had been contrived by him in the same intention and was connected with the plot against the democracy. Meanwhile it so happened that, just at the time of this agitation, a small force of Lacedaemonians had advanced as far as the Isthmus, in pursuance of some scheme with the Boeotians. It was now thought that this had come by appointment, at his instigation, and not on account of the Boeotians, and that, if the citizens had not acted on the information received, and forestalled them by arresting the prisoners, the city would have been betrayed. The citizens went so far as to sleep one night armed in the temple of Theseus within the walls. The friends also of Alcibiades at Argos were just at this time suspected of a design to attack the commons; and the Argive hostages deposited in the islands were given up by the Athenians to the Argive people to be put to death upon that account: in short, everywhere something was found to create suspicion against Alcibiades. It was therefore decided to bring him to trial and execute him, and the Salaminia was sent to Sicily for him and the others named in the information, with instructions to order him to come and answer the charges against him, but not to arrest him, because they wished to avoid causing any agitation in the army or among the enemy in Sicily, and above all to retain the services of the Mantineans and Argives, who, it was thought, had been induced to join by his influence. Alcibiades, with his own ship and his fellow accused, accordingly sailed off with the Salaminia from Sicily, as though to return to Athens, and went with her as far as Thurii, and there they left the ship and disappeared, being afraid to go home for trial with such a prejudice existing against them. The crew of the Salaminia stayed some time looking for Alcibiades and his companions, and at length, as they were nowhere to be found, set sail and departed. Alcibiades, now an outlaw, crossed in a boat not long after from Thurii to Peloponnese; and the Athenians passed sentence of death by default upon him and those in his company.

Chapter Twenty

Seventeenth and Eighteenth Years of the War–Inaction of the Athenian Army–Alcibiades at Sparta–Investment of Syracuse

THE ATHENIAN GENERALS LEFT in Sicily now divided the armament into two parts, and, each taking one by lot, sailed with the whole for Selinus and Egesta, wishing to know whether the Egestaeans would give the money, and to look into the question of Selinus and ascertain the state of the quarrel between her and Egesta. Coasting along Sicily, with the shore on their left, on the side towards the Tyrrhene Gulf they touched at Himera, the only Hellenic city in that part of the island, and being refused admission resumed their voyage. On their way they took Hyccara, a petty Sicanian seaport, nevertheless at war with Egesta, and making slaves of the inhabitants gave up the town to the Egestaeans, some of whose horse had joined them; after which the army proceeded through the territory of the Sicels until it reached Catana, while the fleet sailed along the coast with the slaves on board. Meanwhile Nicias sailed straight from Hyccara along the coast and went to Egesta and, after transacting his other business and receiving thirty talents, rejoined the forces. They now sold their slaves for the sum of one hundred and twenty talents, and sailed round to their Sicel allies to urge them to send troops;

and meanwhile went with half their own force to the hostile town of Hybla in the territory of Gela, but did not succeed in taking it.

Summer was now over. The winter following, the Athenians at once began to prepare for moving on Syracuse, and the Syracusans on their side for marching against them. From the moment when the Athenians failed to attack them instantly as they at first feared and expected, every day that passed did something to revive their courage; and when they saw them sailing far away from them on the other side of Sicily, and going to Hybla only to fail in their attempts to storm it, they thought less of them than ever, and called upon their generals, as the multitude is apt to do in its moments of confidence, to lead them to Catana, since the enemy would not come to them. Parties also of the Syracusan horse employed in reconnoitring constantly rode up to the Athenian armament, and among other insults asked them whether they had not really come to settle with the Syracusans in a foreign country rather than to resettle the Leontines in their own.

Aware of this, the Athenian generals determined to draw them out in mass as far as possible from the city, and themselves in the meantime to sail by night alongshore, and take up at their leisure a convenient position. This they knew they could not so well do, if they had to disembark from their ships in front of a force prepared for them, or to go by land openly. The numerous cavalry of the Syracusans (a force which they were themselves without) would then be able to do the greatest mischief to their light troops and the crowd that followed them; but this plan would enable them to take up a position in which the horse could do them no hurt worth speaking of, some Syracusan exiles with the army having told them of the spot near the Olympieum, which they afterwards occupied. In pursuance of their idea, the generals imagined the following stratagem. They sent to Syracuse a man devoted to them, and by the Syracusan generals thought to be no less in their interest; he was a native of Catana, and said he came from persons in that place, whose names the Syracusan generals were acquainted with, and whom they knew to be among the members of their party still left in the city. He told them that the Athenians passed the night in the town, at some distance from their arms, and that if the Syracusans would name a day and come with all their people at daybreak to attack the armament, they, their friends, would close the gates upon the troops in the city, and set fire to the vessels, while the Syracusans would easily take the camp by an attack upon the stockade. In this they would be aided by many of the Catanians, who were already prepared to act, and from whom he himself came.

The generals of the Syracusans, who did not want confidence, and who had intended even without this to march on Catana, believed the man without any sufficient inquiry, fixed at once a day upon which they would be there, and dismissed him, and the Selinuntines and others of their allies having now arrived, gave orders for all the Syracusans to march out in mass. Their preparations completed, and the time fixed for their arrival being at hand, they set out for Catana, and passed the night upon the river Symaethus, in the Leontine territory. Meanwhile the Athenians no sooner knew of their approach than they took all their forces and such of the Sicels or others as had joined them, put them on board their ships and boats, and sailed by night to Syracuse. Thus, when morning broke the Athenians were landing opposite the Olympieum ready to seize their camping ground, and the Syracusan horse having ridden up first to Catana and found that all the armament had put to sea, turned back and told the infantry, and then all turned back together, and went to the relief of the city.

In the meantime, as the march before the Syracusans was a long one, the Athenians quietly sat down their army in a convenient position, where they could begin an engagement when they pleased, and where the Syracusan cavalry would have least opportunity of annoying them, either before or during the action, being fenced off on one side by walls, houses, trees, and by a marsh, and on the other by cliffs. They also felled the neighbouring trees and carried them down to the sea, and formed a palisade alongside of their ships, and with stones which they picked up and wood hastily raised a fort at Daskon, the most vulnerable point of their position, and broke down the bridge over the Anapus. These preparations were allowed to go on without any interruption from the city, the first hostile force to appear being the Syracusan cavalry, followed afterwards by all the foot together. At first they came close up to the Athenian army, and then, finding that they did not offer to engage, crossed the Helorine road and encamped for the night.

The next day the Athenians and their allies prepared for battle, their dispositions being as follows: Their right wing was occupied by the Argives and Mantineans, the centre by the Athenians, and the rest of the field by the other allies. Half their army was drawn up eight deep in advance, half close to their tents in a hollow square, formed also eight deep, which had orders to look out and be ready to go to the support of the troops hardest pressed. The camp followers were placed inside this reserve. The Syracusans, meanwhile, formed their heavy infantry sixteen deep, consisting of the mass levy of their own people, and such allies as had joined them, the strongest contingent being that of the Selinuntines; next to them the cavalry of the Geloans, numbering two hundred in all, with about twenty horse and fifty archers from Camarina. The cavalry was posted on their right, full twelve hundred strong, and next to it the darters. As the Athenians were about to begin the attack, Nicias went along the lines, and addressed these words of encouragement to the army and the nations composing it:

"Soldiers, a long exhortation is little needed by men like ourselves, who are here to fight in the same battle, the force itself being, to my thinking, more fit to inspire confidence than a fine speech with a weak army. Where we have Argives, Mantineans, Athenians, and the first of the islanders in the ranks together, it were strange indeed, with so many and so brave companions in arms, if we did not feel confident of victory; especially when we have mass levies opposed to our picked troops, and what is more, Siceliots, who may disdain us but will not stand against us, their skill not being at all commensurate to their rashness. You may also remember that we are far from home and have no friendly land near, except what your own swords shall win you; and here I put before you a motive just the reverse of that which the enemy are appealing to; their cry being that they shall fight for their country, mine that we shall fight for a country that is not ours, where we must conquer or hardly get away, as we shall have their horse upon us in great numbers. Remember, therefore, your renown, and go boldly against the enemy, thinking the present strait and necessity more terrible than they."

After this address Nicias at once led on the army. The Syracusans were not at that moment expecting an immediate engagement, and some had even gone away to the town, which was close by; these now ran up as hard as they could and, though behind time, took their places here or there in the main body as fast as they joined it. Want of zeal or daring was certainly not the fault of the Syracusans, either in this or the other battles, but although not inferior in courage, so far as their military science might carry them, when this failed them they were compelled to give up their resolution also. On the present occasion, although they had not supposed that the Athenians would begin the attack, and although constrained to stand upon their defence at short notice, they at once took up their arms and advanced to meet them. First, the stone-throwers, slingers, and archers of either army began skirmishing, and routed or were routed by one another, as might be expected between light troops; next, soothsayers brought forward the usual victims, and trumpeters urged on the heavy infantry to the charge; and thus they advanced, the Syracusans to fight for their country, and each individual for his safety that day and liberty hereafter; in the enemy's army, the Athenians to make another's country theirs and to save their own from suffering by their defeat; the Argives and independent allies to help them in getting what they came for, and to earn by victory another sight of the country they had left behind; while the subject allies owed most of their ardour to the desire of self-preservation, which they could only hope for if victorious; next to which, as a secondary motive, came the chance of serving on easier terms, after helping the Athenians to a fresh conquest.

The armies now came to close quarters, and for a long while fought without either giving ground. Meanwhile there occurred some claps of thunder with lightning and heavy rain, which did not fail to add to the fears of the party fighting for the first time, and very little acquainted with war; while to their more experienced adversaries these phenomena appeared to be produced by the time of year, and much more alarm was felt at the continued resistance of the enemy. At last the Argives drove in the Syracusan left, and after them the Athenians routed the troops opposed to them, and the Syracusan army was thus cut in two and betook itself to flight. The

Athenians did not pursue far, being held in check by the numerous and undefeated Syracusan horse, who attacked and drove back any of their heavy infantry whom they saw pursuing in advance of the rest; in spite of which the victors followed so far as was safe in a body, and then went back and set up a trophy. Meanwhile the Syracusans rallied at the Helorine road, where they re-formed as well as they could under the circumstances, and even sent a garrison of their own citizens to the Olympieum, fearing that the Athenians might lay hands on some of the treasures there. The rest returned to the town.

The Athenians, however, did not go to the temple, but collected their dead and laid them upon a pyre, and passed the night upon the field. The next day they gave the enemy back their dead under truce, to the number of about two hundred and sixty, Syracusans and allies, and gathered together the bones of their own, some fifty, Athenians and allies, and taking the spoils of the enemy, sailed back to Catana. It was now winter; and it did not seem possible for the moment to carry on the war before Syracuse, until horse should have been sent for from Athens and levied among the allies in Sicily–to do away with their utter inferiority in cavalry–and money should have been collected in the country and received from Athens, and until some of the cities, which they hoped would be now more disposed to listen to them after the battle, should have been brought over, and corn and all other necessaries provided, for a campaign in the spring against Syracuse.

With this intention they sailed off to Naxos and Catana for the winter. Meanwhile the Syracusans burned their dead and then held an assembly, in which Hermocrates, son of Hermon, a man who with a general ability of the first order had given proofs of military capacity and brilliant courage in the war, came forward and encouraged them, and told them not to let what had occurred make them give way, since their spirit had not been conquered, but their want of discipline had done the mischief. Still they had not been beaten by so much as might have been expected, especially as they were, one might say, novices in the art of war, an army of artisans opposed to the most practised soldiers in Hellas. What had also done great mischief was the number of the generals (there were fifteen of them) and the quantity of orders given, combined with the disorder and insubordination of the troops. But if they were to have a few skilful generals, and used this winter in preparing their heavy infantry, finding arms for such as had not got any, so as to make them as numerous as possible, and forcing them to attend to their training generally, they would have every chance of beating their adversaries, courage being already theirs and discipline in the field having thus been added to it. Indeed, both these qualities would improve, since danger would exercise them in discipline, while their courage would be led to surpass itself by the confidence which skill inspires. The generals should be few and elected with full powers, and an oath should be taken to leave them entire discretion in their command: if they adopted this plan, their secrets would be better kept, all preparations would be properly made, and there would be no room for excuses.

The Syracusans heard him, and voted everything as he advised, and elected three generals, Hermocrates himself, Heraclides, son of Lysimachus, and Sicanus, son of Execestes. They also sent envoys to Corinth and Lacedaemon to procure a force of allies to join them, and to induce the Lacedaemonians for their sakes openly to address themselves in real earnest to the war against the Athenians, that they might either have to leave Sicily or be less able to send reinforcements to their army there.

The Athenian forces at Catana now at once sailed against Messina, in the expectation of its being betrayed to them. The intrigue, however, after all came to nothing: Alcibiades, who was in the secret, when he left his command upon the summons from home, foreseeing that he would be outlawed, gave information of the plot to the friends of the Syracusans in Messina, who had at once put to death its authors, and now rose in arms against the opposite faction with those of their way of thinking, and succeeded in preventing the admission of the Athenians. The latter waited for thirteen days, and then, as they were exposed to the weather and without provisions, and met with no success, went back to Naxos, where they made places for their ships to lie in, erected a palisade round their camp, and retired into winter quarters; meanwhile they sent a galley to Athens for money and cavalry to join them in the spring. During the winter the

Syracusans built a wall on to the city, so as to take in the statue of Apollo Temenites, all along the side looking towards Epipolae, to make the task of circumvallation longer and more difficult, in case of their being defeated, and also erected a fort at Megara and another in the Olympieum, and stuck palisades along the sea wherever there was a landing Place. Meanwhile, as they knew that the Athenians were wintering at Naxos, they marched with all their people to Catana, and ravaged the land and set fire to the tents and encampment of the Athenians, and so returned home. Learning also that the Athenians were sending an embassy to Camarina, on the strength of the alliance concluded in the time of Laches, to gain, if possible, that city, they sent another from Syracuse to oppose them. They had a shrewd suspicion that the Camarinaeans had not sent what they did send for the first battle very willingly; and they now feared that they would refuse to assist them at all in future, after seeing the success of the Athenians in the action, and would join the latter on the strength of their old friendship. Hermocrates, with some others, accordingly arrived at Camarina from Syracuse, and Euphemus and others from the Athenians; and an assembly of the Camarinaeans having been convened, Hermocrates spoke as follows, in the hope of prejudicing them against the Athenians:

"Camarinaeans, we did not come on this embassy because we were afraid of your being frightened by the actual forces of the Athenians, but rather of your being gained by what they would say to you before you heard anything from us. They are come to Sicily with the pretext that you know, and the intention which we all suspect, in my opinion less to restore the Leontines to their homes than to oust us from ours; as it is out of all reason that they should restore in Sicily the cities that they lay waste in Hellas, or should cherish the Leontine Chalcidians because of their Ionian blood and keep in servitude the Euboean Chalcidians, of whom the Leontines are a colony. No; but the same policy which has proved so successful in Hellas is now being tried in Sicily. After being chosen as the leaders of the Ionians and of the other allies of Athenian origin, to punish the Mede, the Athenians accused some of failure in military service, some of fighting against each other, and others, as the case might be, upon any colourable pretext that could be found, until they thus subdued them all. In fine, in the struggle against the Medes, the Athenians did not fight for the liberty of the Hellenes, or the Hellenes for their own liberty, but the former to make their countrymen serve them instead of him, the latter to change one master for another, wiser indeed than the first, but wiser for evil.

"But we are not now come to declare to an audience familiar with them the misdeeds of a state so open to accusation as is the Athenian, but much rather to blame ourselves, who, with the warnings we possess in the Hellenes in those parts that have been enslaved through not supporting each other, and seeing the same sophisms being now tried upon ourselves–such as restorations of Leontine kinsfolk and support of Egestaean allies–do not stand together and resolutely show them that here are no Ionians, or Hellespontines, or islanders, who change continually, but always serve a master, sometimes the Mede and sometimes some other, but free Dorians from independent Peloponnese, dwelling in Sicily. Or, are we waiting until we be taken in detail, one city after another; knowing as we do that in no other way can we be conquered, and seeing that they turn to this plan, so as to divide some of us by words, to draw some by the bait of an alliance into open war with each other, and to ruin others by such flattery as different circumstances may render acceptable? And do we fancy when destruction first overtakes a distant fellow countryman that the danger will not come to each of us also, or that he who suffers before us will suffer in himself alone?

"As for the Camarinaean who says that it is the Syracusan, not he, that is the enemy of the Athenian, and who thinks it hard to have to encounter risk in behalf of my country, I would have him bear in mind that he will fight in my country, not more for mine than for his own, and by so much the more safely in that he will enter on the struggle not alone, after the way has been cleared by my ruin, but with me as his ally, and that the object of the Athenian is not so much to punish the enmity of the Syracusan as to use me as a blind to secure the friendship of the Camarinaean. As for him who envies or even fears us (and envied and feared great powers must always be), and who on this account wishes Syracuse to be humbled to teach us a lesson, but would still have her survive, in the interest of his own security the wish that he indulges is not humanly possible. A man can control his own desires, but he cannot likewise control circumstances; and in the event of his calculations proving mistaken, he may live to bewail his own misfortune, and wish to be again envying my prosperity. An idle wish, if he now sacrifice us and refuse to take his share of perils which are the same, in reality though not in name, for him as for us; what is nominally the preservation of our power being really his own salvation. It was to be expected that you, of all people in the world, Camarinaeans, being our immediate neighbours and the next in danger, would have foreseen this, and instead of supporting us in the lukewarm way that you are now doing, would rather come to us of your own accord, and be now offering at Syracuse the aid which you would have asked for at Camarina, if to Camarina the Athenians had first come, to encourage us to resist the invader. Neither you, however, nor the rest have as yet bestirred yourselves in this direction.

"Fear perhaps will make you study to do right both by us and by the invaders, and plead that you have an alliance with the Athenians. But you made that alliance, not against your friends, but against the enemies that might attack you, and to help the Athenians when they were wronged by others, not when as now they are wronging their neighbours. Even the Rhegians, Chalcidians though they be, refuse to help to restore the Chalcidian Leontines; and it would be strange if, while they suspect the gist of this fine pretence and are wise without reason, you, with every reason on your side, should yet choose to assist your natural enemies, and should join with their direst foes in undoing those whom nature has made your own kinsfolk. This is not to do right; but you should help us without fear of their armament, which has no terrors if we hold together, but only if we let them succeed in their endeavours to separate us; since even after attacking us by ourselves and being victorious in battle, they had to go off without effecting their purpose.

"United, therefore, we have no cause to despair, but rather new encouragement to league together; especially as succour will come to us from the Peloponnesians, in military matters the undoubted superiors of the Athenians. And you need not think that your prudent policy of taking sides with neither, because allies of both, is either safe for you or fair to us. Practically it is not as fair as it pretends to be. If the vanquished be defeated, and the victor conquer, through your refusing to join, what is the effect of your abstention but to leave the former to perish unaided, and to allow the latter to offend unhindered? And yet it were more honourable to join those who are not only the injured party, but your own kindred, and by so doing to defend the common interests of Sicily and save your friends the Athenians from doing wrong.

"In conclusion, we Syracusans say that it is

useless for us to demonstrate either to you or to the rest what you know already as well as we do; but we entreat, and if our entreaty fail, we protest that we are menaced by our eternal enemies the Ionians, and are betrayed by you our fellow Dorians. If the Athenians reduce us, they will owe their victory to your decision, but in their own name will reap the honour, and will receive as the prize of their triumph the very men who enabled them to gain it. On the other hand, if we are the conquerors, you will have to pay for having been the cause of our danger. Consider, therefore; and now make your choice between the security which present servitude offers and the prospect of conquering with us and so escaping disgraceful submission to an Athenian master and avoiding the lasting enmity of Syracuse."

Such were the words of Hermocrates; after whom Euphemus, the Athenian ambassador, spoke as follows:

"Although we came here only to renew the

former alliance, the attack of the Syracusans compels us to speak of our empire and of the good right we have to it. The best proof of this the speaker himself furnished, when he called the Ionians eternal enemies of the Dorians. It is the fact; and the Peloponnesian Dorians being our superiors in numbers and next neighbours, we Ionians looked out for the best means of escaping their domination. After the Median War we had a fleet, and so got rid of the empire and supremacy of the Lacedaemonians, who had no right to give orders to us more than we to them, except that of being the strongest at that moment; and being appointed leaders of the King's former subjects, we continue to be so, thinking that we are least likely to fall under the dominion of the Peloponnesians, if we have a force to defend ourselves with, and in strict truth having done nothing unfair in reducing to subjection the Ionians and islanders, the kinsfolk whom the Syracusans say we have enslaved. They, our kinsfolk, came against their mother country, that is to say against us, together with the Mede, and, instead of having the courage to revolt and sacrifice their property as we did when we abandoned our city, chose to be slaves themselves, and to try to make us so.

"We, therefore, deserve to rule because we placed the largest fleet and an unflinching patriotism at the service of the Hellenes, and because these, our subjects, did us mischief by their ready subservience to the Medes; and, desert apart, we seek to strengthen ourselves against the Peloponnesians. We make no fine profession of having a right to rule because we overthrew the barbarian single-handed, or because we risked what we did risk for the freedom of the subjects in question any more than for that of all, and for our own: no one can be quarrelled with for providing for his proper safety. If we are now here in Sicily, it is equally in the interest of our security, with which we perceive that your interest also coincides. We prove this from the conduct which the Syracusans cast against us and which you somewhat too timorously suspect; knowing that those whom fear has made suspicious may be carried away by the charm of eloquence for the moment, but when they come to act follow their interests.

"Now, as we have said, fear makes us hold our empire in Hellas, and fear makes us now come, with the help of our friends, to order safely matters in Sicily, and not to enslave any but rather to prevent any from being enslaved. Meanwhile, let no one imagine that we are interesting ourselves in you without your having anything to do with us, seeing that, if you are preserved and able to make head against the Syracusans, they will be less likely to harm us by sending troops to the Peloponnesians. In this way you have everything to do with us, and on this account it is perfectly reasonable for us to restore the Leontines, and to make them, not subjects like their kinsmen in Euboea, but as powerful as possible, to help us by annoying the Syracusans from their frontier. In Hellas we are alone a match for our enemies; and as for the assertion that it is out of all reason that we should free the Sicilian, while we enslave the Chalcidian, the fact is that the latter is useful to us by being without arms and contributing money only; while the former, the Leontines and our other friends, cannot be too independent.

"Besides, for tyrants and imperial cities nothing is unreasonable if expedient, no one a kinsman unless sure; but friendship or enmity is everywhere an affair of time and circumstance. Here, in Sicily, our interest is not to weaken our friends, but by means of their strength to cripple our enemies. Why doubt this? In Hellas we treat our allies as we find them useful. The Chians and Methymnians govern themselves and furnish ships; most of the rest have harder terms and pay tribute in money; while others, although islanders and easy for us to take, are free altogether, because they occupy convenient positions round Peloponnese. In our settlement of the states here in Sicily, we should therefore; naturally be guided by our interest, and by fear, as we say, of the Syracusans. Their ambition is to rule you, their object to use the suspicions that we excite to unite you, and then, when we have gone away without effecting anything, by force or through your isolation, to become the masters of Sicily. And masters they must become, if you unite with them; as a force of that magnitude would be no longer easy for us to deal with united, and they would be more than a match for you as soon as we were away.

"Any other view of the case is condemned by the facts. When you first asked us over, the fear which you held out was that of danger to Athens if we let you come under the dominion of Syracuse; and it is not right now to mistrust the very same argument by which you claimed to convince us, or to give way to suspicion because we are come with a larger force against the power of that city. Those whom you should really distrust are the Syracusans. We are not able to stay here without you, and if we proved perfidious enough to bring you into subjection, we should be unable to keep you in bondage, owing to the length of the voyage and the difficulty of guarding large, and in a military sense continental, towns: they, the Syracusans, live close to you, not in a camp, but in a city greater than the force we have with us, plot always against you, never let slip an opportunity once offered, as they have shown in the case of the Leontines and others, and now have the face, just as if you were fools, to invite you to aid them against the power that hinders this, and that has thus far maintained Sicily independent. We, as against them, invite you to a much more real safety, when we beg you not to betray that common safety which we each have in the other, and to reflect that they, even without allies, will, by their numbers, have always the way open to you, while you will not often have the opportunity of defending yourselves with such numerous auxiliaries; if, through your suspicions, you once let these go away unsuccessful or defeated, you will wish to see if only a handful of them back again, when the day is past in which their presence could do anything for you.

"But we hope, Camarinaeans, that the calumnies of the Syracusans will not be allowed to succeed either with you or with the rest: we have told you the whole truth upon the things we are suspected of, and will now briefly recapitulate, in the hope of convincing you. We assert that we are rulers in Hellas in order not to be subjects; liberators in Sicily that we may not be harmed by the Sicilians; that we are compelled to interfere in many things, because we have many things to guard against; and that now, as before, we are come as allies to those of you who suffer wrong in this island, not without invitation but upon invitation. Accordingly, instead of making yourselves judges or censors of our conduct, and trying to turn us, which it were now difficult to do, so far as there is anything in our interfering policy or in our character that chimes in with your interest, this take and make use of; and be sure that, far from being injurious to all alike, to most of the Hellenes that policy is even beneficial. Thanks to it, all men in all places, even where we are not, who either apprehend or meditate aggression, from the near prospect before them, in the one case, of obtaining our intervention in their favour, in the other, of our arrival making the venture dangerous, find themselves constrained, respectively, to be moderate against their will, and to be preserved without trouble of their own. Do not you reject this security that is open to all who desire it, and is now offered to you; but do like others, and instead of being always on the defensive against the Syracusans, unite with us, and in your turn at last threaten them."

Such were the words of Euphemus. What the Camarinaeans felt was this. Sympathizing with the Athenians, except in so far as they might be afraid of their subjugating Sicily, they had always been at enmity with their neighbour Syracuse. From the very fact, however, that they were their neighbours, they feared the Syracusans most of the two, and being apprehensive of their conquering even without them, both sent them in the first instance the few horsemen mentioned, and for the future determined to support them most in fact, although as sparingly as possible; but for the moment in order not to seem to slight the Athenians, especially as they had been successful in the engagement, to answer both alike. Agreeably to this resolution they answered that as both the contending parties happened to be allies of theirs, they thought it most consistent with their oaths at present to side with neither; with which answer the ambassadors of either party departed.

In the meantime, while Syracuse pursued her preparations for war, the Athenians were encamped at Naxos, and tried by negotiation to gain as many of the Sicels as possible. Those more in the low lands, and subjects of Syracuse, mostly held aloof; but the peoples of the interior who had never been otherwise than independent, with few exceptions, at once joined the Athenians, and brought down corn to the army, and in some cases even money. The Athenians marched against those who refused to join, and forced some of them to do so; in the case of others they were stopped by the Syracusans sending garrisons and reinforcements. Meanwhile the Athenians moved their winter quarters from Naxos to Catana, and reconstructed the camp burnt by the Syracusans, and stayed there the rest of the winter. They also sent a galley to Carthage, with proffers of friendship, on the chance of obtaining assistance, and another to Tyrrhenia; some of the cities there having spontaneously offered to join them in the war. They also sent round to the Sicels and to Egesta, desiring them to send them as many horses as possible, and meanwhile prepared bricks, iron, and all other things necessary for the work of circumvallation, intending by the spring to begin hostilities.

In the meantime the Syracusan envoys dispatched to Corinth and Lacedaemon tried as they passed along the coast to persuade the Italiots to interfere with the proceedings of the Athenians, which threatened Italy quite as much as Syracuse, and having arrived at Corinth made a speech calling on the Corinthians to assist them on the ground of their common origin. The Corinthians voted at once to aid them heart and soul themselves, and then sent on envoys with them to Lacedaemon, to help them to persuade her also to prosecute the war with the Athenians more openly at home and to send succours to Sicily. The envoys from Corinth having reached Lacedaemon found there Alcibiades with his fellow refugees, who had at once crossed over in a trading vessel from Thurii, first to Cyllene in Elis, and afterwards from thence to Lacedaemon; upon the Lacedaemonians' own invitation, after first obtaining a safe conduct, as he feared them for the part he had taken in the affair of Mantinea. The result was that the Corinthians, Syracusans, and Alcibiades, pressing all the same request in the assembly of the Lacedaemonians, succeeded in persuading them; but as the ephors and the authorities, although resolved to send envoys to Syracuse to prevent their surrendering to the Athenians, showed no disposition to send them any assistance, Alcibiades now came forward and inflamed and stirred the Lacedaemonians by speaking as follows:

"I am forced first to speak to you of the prejudice with which I am regarded, in order that suspicion may not make you disinclined to listen to me upon public matters. The connection, with you as your proxeni, which the ancestors of our family by reason of some discontent renounced, I personally tried to renew by my good offices towards you, in particular upon the occasion of the disaster at Pylos. But although I maintained this friendly attitude, you yet chose to negotiate the peace with the Athenians through my enemies, and thus to strengthen them and to discredit me. You had therefore no right to complain if I turned to the Mantineans and Argives, and seized other occasions of thwarting and injuring you; and the time has now come when those among you, who in the bitterness of the moment may have been then unfairly angry with me, should look at the matter in its true light, and take a different view. Those again who judged me unfavourably, because I leaned rather to the side of the commons, must not think that their dislike is any better founded. We have always been hostile to tyrants, and all who oppose arbitrary power are called commons; hence we continued to act as leaders of the multitude; besides which, as democracy was the government of the city, it was necessary in most things to conform to established conditions. However, we endeavoured to be more moderate than the licentious temper of the times; and while there were others, formerly as now, who tried to lead the multitude astray–the same who banished me–our party was that of the whole people, our creed being to do our part in preserving the form of government under which the city enjoyed the utmost greatness and freedom, and which we had found existing. As for democracy, the men of sense among us knew what it was, and I perhaps as well as any, as I have the more cause to complain of it; but there is nothing new to be said of a patent absurdity; meanwhile we did not think it safe to alter it under the pressure of your hostility.

"So much then for the prejudices with which

I am regarded: I now can call your attention to the questions you must consider, and upon which superior knowledge perhaps permits me to speak. We sailed to Sicily first to conquer, if possible, the Siceliots, and after them the Italiots also, and finally to assail the empire and city of Carthage. In the event of all or most of these schemes succeeding, we were then to attack Peloponnese, bringing with us the entire force of the Hellenes lately acquired in those parts, and taking a number of barbarians into our pay, such as the Iberians and others in those countries, confessedly the most warlike known, and building numerous galleys in addition to those which we had already, timber being plentiful in Italy; and with this fleet blockading Peloponnese from the sea and assailing it with our armies by land, taking some of the cities by storm, drawing works of circumvallation round others, we hoped without difficulty to effect its reduction, and after this to rule the whole of the Hellenic name. Money and corn meanwhile for the better execution of these plans were to be supplied in sufficient quantities by the newly acquired places in those countries, independently of our revenues here at home.

"You have thus heard the history of the present expedition from the man who most exactly knows what our objects were; and the remaining generals will, if they can, carry these out just the same. But that the states in Sicily must succumb if you do not help them, I will now show. Although the Siceliots, with all their inexperience, might even now be saved if their forces were united, the Syracusans alone, beaten already in one battle with all their people and blockaded from the sea, will be unable to withstand the Athenian armament that is now there. But if Syracuse falls, all Sicily falls also, and Italy immediately afterwards; and the danger which I just now spoke of from that quarter will before long be upon you. None need therefore fancy that Sicily only is in question; Peloponnese will be so also, unless you speedily do as I tell you, and send on board ship to Syracuse troops that shall able to row their ships themselves, and serve as heavy infantry the moment that they land; and what I consider even more important than the troops, a Spartan as commanding officer to discipline the forces already on foot and to compel recusants to serve. The friends that you have already will thus become more confident, and the waverers will be encouraged to join you. Meanwhile you must carry on the war here more openly, that the Syracusans, seeing that you do not forget them, may put heart into their resistance, and that the Athenians may be less able to reinforce their armament. You must fortify Decelea in Attica, the blow of which the Athenians are always most afraid and the only one that they think they have not experienced in the present war; the surest method of harming an enemy being to find out what he most fears, and to choose this means of attacking him, since every one naturally knows best his own weak points and fears accordingly. The fortification in question, while it benefits you, will create difficulties for your adversaries, of which I shall pass over many, and shall only mention the chief. Whatever property there is in the country will most of it become yours, either by capture or surrender; and the Athenians will at once be deprived of their revenues from the silver mines at Laurium, of their present gains from their land and from the law courts, and above all of the revenue from their allies, which will be paid less regularly, as they lose their awe of Athens and see you addressing yourselves with vigour to the war. The zeal and speed with which all this shall be done depends, Lacedaemonians, upon yourselves; as to its possibility, I am quite confident, and I have little fear of being mistaken.

"Meanwhile I hope that none of you will think any the worse of me if, after having hitherto passed as a lover of my country, I now actively join its worst enemies in attacking it, or will suspect what I say as the fruit of an outlaw's enthusiasm. I am an outlaw from the iniquity of those who drove me forth, not, if you will be guided by me, from your service; my worst enemies are not you who only harmed your foes, but they who forced their friends to become enemies; and love of country is what I do not feel when I am wronged, but what I felt when secure in my rights as a citizen. Indeed I do not consider that I am now attacking a country that is still mine; I am rather trying to recover one that is mine no longer; and the true lover of his country is not he who consents to lose it unjustly rather than attack it, but he who longs for it so much that he will go all lengths to recover it. For myself, therefore, Lacedaemonians, I beg you to use me without scruple for danger and trouble of every kind, and to remember the argument in every one's mouth, that if I did you great harm as an enemy, I could likewise do you good service as a friend, inasmuch as I know the plans of the Athenians, while I only guessed yours. For yourselves I entreat you to believe that your most capital interests are now under deliberation; and I urge you to send without hesitation the expeditions to Sicily and Attica; by the presence of a small part of your forces you will save important cities in that island, and you will destroy the power of Athens both present and prospective; after this you will dwell in security and enjoy the supremacy over all Hellas, resting not on force but upon consent and affection."

Such were the words of Alcibiades. The Lacedaemonians, who had themselves before intended to march against Athens, but were still waiting and looking about them, at once became much more in earnest when they received this particular information from Alcibiades, and considered that they had heard it from the man who best knew the truth of the matter. Accordingly they now turned their attention to the fortifying of Decelea and sending immediate aid to the Sicilians; and naming Gylippus, son of Cleandridas, to the command of the Syracusans, bade him consult with that people and with the Corinthians and arrange for succours reaching the island, in the best and speediest way possible under the circumstances. Gylippus desired the Corinthians to send him at once two ships to Asine, and to prepare the rest that they intended to send, and to have them ready to sail at the proper time. Having settled this, the envoys departed from Lacedaemon.

In the meantime arrived the Athenian galley from Sicily sent by the generals for money and cavalry; and the Athenians, after hearing what they wanted, voted to send the supplies for the armament and the cavalry. And the winter ended, and with it ended the seventeenth year of the present war of which Thucydides is the historian.

The next summer, at the very beginning of the season, the Athenians in Sicily put out from Catana, and sailed along shore to Megara in Sicily, from which, as I have mentioned above, the Syracusans expelled the inhabitants in the time of their tyrant Gelo, themselves occupying the territory. Here the Athenians landed and laid waste the country, and after an unsuccessful attack upon a fort of the Syracusans, went on with the fleet and army to the river Terias, and advancing inland laid waste the plain and set fire to the corn; and after killing some of a small Syracusan party which they encountered, and setting up a trophy, went back again to their ships. They now sailed to Catana and took in provisions there, and going with their whole force against Centoripa, a town of the Sicels, acquired it by capitulation, and departed, after also burning the corn of the Inessaeans and Hybleans. Upon their return to Catana they found the horsemen arrived from Athens, to the number of two hundred and fifty (with their equipments, but without their horses which were to be procured upon the spot), and thirty mounted archers and three hundred talents of silver.

The same spring the Lacedaemonians marched against Argos, and went as far as Cleonae, when an earthquake occurred and caused them to return. After this the Argives invaded the Thyreatid, which is on their border, and took much booty from the Lacedaemonians, which was sold for no less than twenty-five talents. The same summer, not long after, the Thespian commons made an attack upon the party in office, which was not successful, but succours arrived from Thebes, and some were caught, while others took refuge at Athens.

The same summer the Syracusans learned that the Athenians had been joined by their cavalry, and were on the point of marching against them; and seeing that without becoming masters of Epipolae, a precipitous spot situated exactly over the town, the Athenians could not, even if victorious in battle, easily invest them, they determined to guard its approaches, in order that the enemy might not ascend unobserved by this, the sole way by which ascent was possible, as the remainder is lofty ground, and falls right down to the city, and can all be seen from inside; and as it lies above the rest the place is called by the Syracusans Epipolae or Overtown. They accordingly went out in mass at daybreak into the meadow along the river Anapus, their new generals, Hermocrates and his colleagues, having just come into office, and held a review of their heavy infantry, from whom they first selected a picked body of six hundred, under the command of Diomilus, an exile from Andros, to guard Epipolae, and to be ready to muster at a moment's notice to help wherever help should be required.

Meanwhile the Athenians, the very same morning, were holding a review, having already made land unobserved with all the armament from Catana, opposite a place called Leon, not much more than half a mile from Epipolae, where they disembarked their army, bringing the fleet to anchor at Thapsus, a peninsula running out into the sea, with a narrow isthmus, and not far from the city of Syracuse either by land or water. While the naval force of the Athenians threw a stockade across the isthmus and remained quiet at Thapsus, the land army immediately went on at a run to Epipolae, and succeeded in getting up by Euryelus before the Syracusans perceived them, or could come up from the meadow and the review. Diomilus with his six hundred and the rest advanced as quickly as they could, but they had nearly three miles to go from the meadow before reaching them. Attacking in this way in considerable disorder, the Syracusans were defeated in battle at Epipolae and retired to the town, with a loss of about three hundred killed, and Diomilus among the number. After this the Athenians set up a trophy and restored to the Syracusans their dead under truce, and next day descended to Syracuse itself; and no one coming out to meet them, reascended and built a fort at Labdalum, upon the edge of the cliffs of Epipolae, looking towards Megara, to serve as a magazine for their baggage and money, whenever they advanced to battle or to work at the lines.

Not long afterwards three hundred cavalry came to them from Egesta, and about a hundred from the Sicels, Naxians, and others; and thus, with the two hundred and fifty from Athens, for whom they had got horses from the Egestaeans and Catanians, besides others that they bought, they now mustered six hundred and fifty cavalry in all. After posting a garrison in Labdalum, they advanced to Syca, where they sat down and quickly built the Circle or centre of their wall of circumvallation. The Syracusans, appalled at the rapidity with which the work advanced, determined to go out against them and give battle and interrupt it; and the two armies were already in battle array, when the Syracusan generals observed that their troops found such difficulty in getting into line, and were in such disorder, that they led them back into the town, except part of the cavalry. These remained and hindered the Athenians from carrying stones or dispersing to any great distance, until a tribe of the Athenian heavy infantry, with all the cavalry, charged and routed the Syracusan horse with some loss; after which they set up a trophy for the cavalry action.

The next day the Athenians began building the wall to the north of the Circle, at the same time collecting stone and timber, which they kept laying down towards Trogilus along the shortest line for their works from the great harbour to the sea; while the Syracusans, guided by their generals, and above all by Hermocrates, instead of risking any more general engagements, determined to build a counterwork in the direction in which the Athenians were going to carry their wall. If this could be completed in time, the enemy's lines would be cut; and meanwhile, if he were to attempt to interrupt them by an attack, they would send a part of their forces against him, and would secure the approaches beforehand with their stockade, while the Athenians would have to leave off working with their whole force in order to attend to them. They accordingly sallied forth and began to build, starting from their city, running a cross wall below the Athenian Circle, cutting down the olives and erecting wooden towers. As the Athenian fleet had not yet sailed round into the great harbour, the Syracusans still commanded the seacoast, and the Athenians brought their provisions by land from Thapsus.

The Syracusans now thought the stockades and stonework of their counterwall sufficiently far advanced; and as the Athenians, afraid of being divided and so fighting at a disadvantage, and intent upon their own wall, did not come out to interrupt them, they left one tribe to guard the new work and went back into the city. Meanwhile the Athenians destroyed their pipes of drinking-water carried underground into the city; and watching until the rest of the Syracusans were in their tents at midday, and some even gone away into the city, and those in the stockade keeping but indifferent guard, appointed three hundred picked men of their own, and some men picked from the light troops and armed for the purpose, to run suddenly as fast as they could to the counterwork, while the rest of the army advanced in two divisions, the one with one of the generals to the city in case of a sortie, the other with the other general to the stockade by the postern gate. The three hundred attacked and took the stockade, abandoned by its garrison, who took refuge in the outworks round the statue of Apollo

Temenites. Here the pursuers burst in with them, and after getting in were beaten out by the Syracusans, and some few of the Argives and Athenians slain; after which the whole army retired, and having demolished the counterwork and pulled up the stockade, carried away the stakes to their own lines, and set up a trophy.

The next day the Athenians from the Circle proceeded to fortify the cliff above the marsh which on this side of Epipolae looks towards the great harbour; this being also the shortest line for their work to go down across the plain and the marsh to the harbour. Meanwhile the Syracusans marched out and began a second stockade, starting from the city, across the middle of the marsh, digging a trench alongside to make it impossible for the Athenians to carry their wall down to the sea. As soon as the Athenians had finished their work at the cliff they again attacked the stockade and ditch of the Syracusans. Ordering the fleet to sail round from Thapsus into the great harbour of Syracuse, they descended at about dawn from Epipolae into the plain, and laying doors and planks over the marsh, where it was muddy and firmest, crossed over on these, and by daybreak took the ditch and the stockade, except a small portion which they captured afterwards. A battle now ensued, in which the Athenians were victorious, the right wing of the Syracusans flying to the town and the left to the river. The three hundred picked Athenians, wishing to cut off their passage, pressed on at a run to the bridge, when the alarmed Syracusans, who had with them most of their cavalry, closed and routed them, hurling them back upon the Athenian right wing, the first tribe of which was thrown into a panic by the shock. Seeing this, Lamachus came to their aid from the Athenian left with a few archers and with the Argives, and crossing a ditch, was left alone with a few that had crossed with him, and was killed with five or six of his men. These the Syracusans managed immediately to snatch up in haste and get across the river into a place of security, themselves retreating as the rest of the Athenian army now came up.

Meanwhile those who had at first fled for refuge to the city, seeing the turn affairs were taking, now rallied from the town and formed against the Athenians in front of them, sending also a part of their number to the Circle on Epipolae, which they hoped to take while denuded of its defenders. These took and destroyed the Athenian outwork of a thousand feet, the Circle itself being saved by Nicias, who happened to have been left in it through illness, and who now ordered the servants to set fire to the engines and timber thrown down before the wall; want of men, as he was aware, rendering all other means of escape impossible. This step was justified by the result, the Syracusans not coming any further on account of the fire, but retreating. Meanwhile succours were coming up from the Athenians below, who had put to flight the troops opposed to them; and the fleet also, according to orders, was sailing from Thapsus into the great harbour. Seeing this, the troops on the heights retired in haste, and the whole army of the Syracusans re-entered the city, thinking that with their present force they would no longer be able to hinder the wall reaching the sea.

After this the Athenians set up a trophy and restored to the Syracusans their dead under truce, receiving in return Lamachus and those who had fallen with him. The whole of their forces, naval and military, being now with them, they began from Epipolae and the cliffs and enclosed the Syracusans with a double wall down to the sea. Provisions were now brought in for the armament from all parts of Italy; and many of the Sicels, who had hitherto been looking to see how things went, came as allies to the Athenians: there also arrived three ships of fifty oars from Tyrrhenia. Meanwhile everything else progressed favourably for their hopes. The Syracusans began to despair of finding safety in arms, no relief having reached them from Peloponnese, and were now proposing terms of capitulation among themselves and to Nicias, who after the death of Lamachus was left sole commander. No decision was come to, but, as was natural with men in difficulties and besieged more straitly than before, there was much discussion with Nicias and still more in the town. Their present misfortunes had also made them suspicious of one another; and the blame of their disasters was thrown upon the ill-fortune or treachery of the generals under whose command they had happened; and these were deposed and others, Heraclides, Eucles, and Tellias, elected in their stead.

Meanwhile the Lacedaemonian, Gylippus, and the ships from Corinth were now off Leucas, intent upon going with all haste to the relief of Sicily. The reports that reached them being of an alarming kind, and all agreeing in the falsehood that Syracuse was already completely invested, Gylippus abandoned all hope of Sicily, and wishing to save Italy, rapidly crossed the Ionian Sea to Tarentum with the Corinthian, Pythen, two Laconian, and two Corinthian vessels, leaving the Corinthians to follow him after manning, in addition to their own ten, two Leucadian and two Ambraciot ships. From Tarentum Gylippus first went on an embassy to Thurii, and claimed anew the rights of citizenship which his father had enjoyed; failing to bring over the townspeople, he weighed anchor and coasted along Italy. Opposite the Terinaean Gulf he was caught by the wind which blows violently and steadily from the north in that quarter, and was carried out to sea; and after experiencing very rough weather, remade Tarentum, where he hauled ashore and refitted such of his ships as had suffered most from the tempest. Nicias heard of his approach, but, like the

Thurians, despised the scanty number of his ships, and set down piracy as the only probable object of the voyage, and so took no precautions for the present.

About the same time in this summer, the Lacedaemonians invaded Argos with their allies, and laid waste most of the country. The Athenians went with thirty ships to the relief of the Argives, thus breaking their treaty with the Lacedaemonians in the most overt manner. Up to this time incursions from Pylos, descents on the coast of the rest of Peloponnese, instead of on the Laconian, had been the extent of their co-operation with the Argives and Mantineans; and although the Argives had often begged them to land, if only for a moment, with their heavy infantry in Laconia, lay waste ever so little of it with them, and depart, they had always refused to do so. Now, however, under the command of Phytodorus, Laespodius, and Demaratus, they landed at Epidaurus Limera, Prasiae, and other places, and plundered the country; and thus furnished the Lacedaemonians with a better pretext for hostilities against Athens. After the Athenians had retired from Argos with their fleet, and the Lacedaemonians also, the Argives made an incursion into the Phlisaid, and returned home after ravaging their land and killing some of the inhabitants.

BOOK SEVEN

Chapter Twenty One

Eighteenth and Nineteenth Years of the War–Arrival of Gylippus at Syracuse–Fortification of Decelea–Successes of the Syracusans

AFTER REFITTING THEIR SHIPS, Gylippus and Pythen coasted along from Tarentum to Epizephyrian Locris. They now received the more correct information that Syracuse was not yet completely invested, but that it was still possible for an army arriving at Epipolae to effect an entrance; and they consulted, accordingly, whether they should keep Sicily on their right and risk sailing in by sea, or, leaving it on their left, should first sail to Himera and, taking with them the Himeraeans and any others that might agree to join them, go to Syracuse by land. Finally they determined to sail for Himera, especially as the four Athenian ships which Nicias had at length sent off, on hearing that they were at Locris, had not yet arrived at Rhegium. Accordingly, before these reached their post, the Peloponnesians crossed the strait and, after touching at Rhegium and Messina, came to Himera. Arrived there, they persuaded the Himeraeans to join in the war, and not only to go with them themselves but to provide arms for the seamen from their vessels which they had drawn ashore at Himera; and they sent and appointed a place for the Selinuntines to meet them with all their forces. A few troops were also promised by the Geloans and some of the Sicels, who were now ready to join them with much greater alacrity, owing to the recent death of Archonidas, a powerful Sicel king in that neighbourhood and friendly to Athens, and owing also to the vigour shown by Gylippus in coming from Lacedaemon. Gylippus now took with him about seven hundred of his sailors and marines, that number only having arms, a thousand heavy infantry and light troops from Himera with a body of a hundred horse, some light troops and cavalry from Selinus, a few Geloans, and Sicels numbering a thousand in all, and set out on his march for Syracuse.

Meanwhile the Corinthian fleet from Leucas made all haste to arrive; and one of their commanders, Gongylus, starting last with a single ship, was the first to reach Syracuse, a little before Gylippus. Gongylus found the Syracusans on the point of holding an assembly to consider whether they should put an end to the war. This he prevented, and reassured them by telling them that more vessels were still to arrive, and that Gylippus, son of Cleandridas, had been dispatched by the Lacedaemonians to take the command. Upon this the Syracusans took courage, and immediately marched out with all their forces to meet Gylippus, who they found was now close at hand. Meanwhile Gylippus, after taking letae, a fort of the Sicels, on his way, formed his army in order of battle, and so arrived at Epipolae, and ascending by Euryelus, as the Athenians had done at first, now advanced with the Syracusans against the Athenian lines. His arrival chanced at a critical moment. The Athenians had already finished a double wall of six or seven furlongs to the great harbour, with the exception of a small portion next the sea, which they were still engaged upon; and in the remainder of the circle towards Trogilus on the other sea, stones had been laid ready for building for the greater part of the distance, and some points had been left half finished, while others were entirely completed. The danger of Syracuse had indeed been great.

Meanwhile the Athenians, recovering from the confusion into which they had been first thrown by the sudden approach of Gylippus and the Syracusans, formed in order of battle. Gylippus halted at a short distance off and sent on a herald to tell them that, if they would evacuate Sicily with bag and baggage within five days' time, he was willing to make a truce accordingly. The Athenians treated this proposition with contempt, and dismissed the herald without an answer. After this both sides began to prepare for action. Gylippus, observing that the Syracusans were in disorder and did not easily fall into line, drew off his troops more into the open ground, while Nicias did not lead on the Athenians but lay still by his own wall. When Gylippus saw that they did not come on, he led off his army to the citadel of the quarter of Apollo Temenites, and passed the night there. On the following day he led out the main body of his army, and, drawing them up in order of battle before the walls of the Athenians to prevent their going to the relief of any other quarter, dispatched a strong force against Fort Labdalum, and took it, and put all whom he found in it to the sword, the place not being within sight of the Athenians. On the same day an Athenian galley that lay moored off the harbour was captured by the Syracusans.

After this the Syracusans and their allies began to carry a single wall, starting from the city, in a slanting direction up Epipolae, in order that the Athenians, unless they could hinder the work, might be no longer able to invest them. Meanwhile the Athenians, having now finished their wall down to the sea, had come up to the heights; and part of their wall being weak, Gylippus drew out his army by night and attacked it. However, the Athenians who happened to be bivouacking outside took the alarm and came out to meet him, upon seeing which he quickly led his men back again. The Athenians now built their wall higher, and in future kept guard at this point themselves, disposing their confederates along the remainder of the works, at the stations assigned to them. Nicias also determined to fortify Plemmyrium, a promontory over against the city, which juts out and narrows the mouth of the Great Harbour. He thought that the fortification of this place would make it easier to bring in supplies, as they would be able to carry on their blockade from a less distance, near to the port occupied by the Syracusans; instead of being obliged, upon every movement of the enemy's navy, to put out against them from the bottom of the great harbour. Besides this, he now began to pay more attention to the war by sea, seeing that the coming of Gylippus had diminished their hopes by land. Accordingly, he conveyed over his ships and some troops, and built three forts in which he placed most of his baggage, and moored there for the future the larger craft and men-of-war. This was the first and chief occasion of the losses which the crews experienced. The water which they used was scarce and had to be fetched from far, and the sailors could not go out for firewood without being cut off by the Syracusan horse, who were masters of the country; a third of the enemy's cavalry being stationed at the little town of Olympieum, to prevent plundering incursions on the part of the Athenians at Plemmyrium. Meanwhile Nicias learned that the rest of the Corinthian fleet was approaching, and sent twenty ships to watch for them, with orders to be on the look-out for them about Locris and Rhegium and the approach to Sicily.

Gylippus, meanwhile, went on with the wall across Epipolae, using the stones which the Athenians had laid down for their own wall, and at the same time constantly led out the Syracusans and their allies, and formed them in order of battle in front of the lines, the Athenians forming against him. At last he thought that the moment was come, and began the attack; and a hand-to-hand fight ensued between the lines, where the Syracusan cavalry could be of no use; and the Syracusans and their allies were defeated and took up their dead under truce, while the Athenians erected a trophy. After this Gylippus called the soldiers together, and said that the fault was not theirs but his; he had kept their lines too much within the works, and had thus deprived them of the services of their cavalry and darters. He would now, therefore, lead them on a second time. He begged them to remember that in material force they would be fully a match for their opponents, while, with respect to moral advantages, it were intolerable if Peloponnesians and Dorians should not feel confident of overcoming Ionians and islanders with the motley rabble that accompanied them, and of driving them out of the country.

After this he embraced the first opportunity that offered of again leading them against the enemy. Now Nicias and the Athenians held the opinion that even if the Syracusans should not wish to offer battle, it was necessary for them to prevent the building of the cross wall, as it already almost overlapped the extreme point of their own, and if it went any further it would from that moment make no difference whether they fought ever so many successful actions, or never fought at all. They accordingly came out to meet the Syracusans. Gylippus led out his heavy infantry further from the fortifications than on the former occasion, and so joined battle; posting his horse and darters upon the flank of the Athenians in the open space, where the works of the two walls terminated. During the engagement the cavalry attacked and routed the left wing of the Athenians, which was opposed to them; and the rest of the Athenian army was in consequence defeated by the Syracusans and driven headlong within their lines. The night following the Syracusans carried their wall up to the Athenian works and passed them, thus putting it out of their power any longer to stop them, and depriving them, even if victorious in the field, of all chance of investing the city for the future.

After this the remaining twelve vessels of the Corinthians, Ambraciots, and Leucadians sailed into the harbour under the command of Erasinides, a Corinthian, having eluded the Athenian ships on guard, and helped the Syracusans in completing the remainder of the cross wall. Meanwhile Gylippus went into the rest of Sicily to raise land and naval forces, and also to bring over any of the cities that either were lukewarm in the cause or had hitherto kept out of the war altogether. Syracusan and Corinthian envoys were also dispatched to Lacedaemon and Corinth to get a fresh force sent over, in any way that might offer, either in merchant vessels or transports, or in any other manner likely to prove successful, as the Athenians too were sending for reinforcements; while the Syracusans proceeded to man a fleet and to exercise, meaning to try their fortune in this way also, and generally became exceedingly confident.

Nicias perceiving this, and seeing the strength of the enemy and his own difficulties daily increasing, himself also sent to Athens. He had before sent frequent reports of events as they occurred, and felt it especially incumbent upon him to do so now, as he thought that they were in a critical position, and that, unless speedily recalled or strongly reinforced from home, they had no hope of safety. He feared, however, that the messengers, either through inability to speak, or through failure of memory, or from a wish to please the multitude, might not report the truth, and so thought it best to write a letter, to ensure that the Athenians should know his own opinion without its being lost in transmission, and be able to decide upon the real facts of the case.

His emissaries, accordingly, departed with the letter and the requisite verbal instructions; and he attended to the affairs of the army, making it his aim now to keep on the defensive and to avoid any unnecessary danger.

At the close of the same summer the Athenian general Euetion marched in concert with Perdiccas with a large body of Thracians against Amphipolis, and failing to take it brought some galleys round into the Strymon, and blockaded the town from the river, having his base at Himeraeum.

Summer was now over. The winter ensuing, the persons sent by Nicias, reaching Athens, gave the verbal messages which had been entrusted to them, and answered any questions that were asked them, and delivered the letter. The clerk of the city now came forward and read out to the Athenians the letter, which was as follows:

"Our past operations, Athenians, have been made known to you by many other letters; it is now time for you to become equally familiar with our present condition, and to take your measures accordingly. We had defeated in most of our engagements with them the Syracusans, against whom we were sent, and we had built the works which we now occupy, when Gylippus arrived from Lacedaemon with an army obtained from Peloponnese and from some of the cities in Sicily. In our first battle with him we were victorious; in the battle on the following day we were overpowered by a multitude of cavalry and darters, and compelled to retire within our lines. We have now, therefore, been forced by the numbers of those opposed to us to discontinue the work of circumvallation, and to remain inactive; being unable to make use even of all the force we have, since a large portion of our heavy infantry is absorbed in the defence of our lines. Meanwhile the enemy have carried a single wall past our lines, thus making it impossible for us to invest them in future, until this cross wall be attacked by a strong force and captured. So that the besieger in name has become, at least from the land side, the besieged in reality; as we are prevented by their cavalry from even going for any distance into the country.

"Besides this, an embassy has been dispatched to Peloponnese to procure reinforcements, and Gylippus has gone to the cities in Sicily, partly in the hope of inducing those that are at present neutral to join him in the war, partly of bringing from his allies additional contingents for the land forces and material for the navy. For I understand that they contemplate a combined attack, upon our lines with their land forces and with their fleet by sea. You must none of you be surprised that I say by sea also. They have discovered that the length of the time we have now been in commission has rotted our ships and wasted our crews, and that with the entireness of our crews and the soundness of our ships the pristine efficiency of our navy has departed. For it is impossible for us to haul our ships ashore and careen them, because, the enemy's vessels being as many or more than our own, we are constantly anticipating an attack. Indeed, they may be seen exercising, and it lies with them to take the initiative; and not having to maintain a blockade, they have greater facilities for drying their ships.

"This we should scarcely be able to do, even if we had plenty of ships to spare, and were freed from our present necessity of exhausting all our strength upon the blockade. For it is already difficult to carry in supplies past Syracuse; and were we to relax our vigilance in the slightest degree it would become impossible. The losses which our crews have suffered and still continue to suffer arise from the following causes. Expeditions for fuel and for forage, and the distance from which water has to be fetched, cause our sailors to be cut off by the Syracusan cavalry; the loss of our previous superiority emboldens our slaves to desert; our foreign seamen are impressed by the unexpected appearance of a navy against us, and the strength of the enemy's resistance; such of them as were pressed into the service take the first opportunity of departing to their respective cities; such as were originally seduced by the temptation of high pay, and expected little fighting and large gains, leave us either by desertion to the enemy or by availing themselves of one or other of the various facilities of escape which the magnitude of Sicily affords them. Some even engage in trade themselves and prevail upon the captains to take Hyccaric slaves on board in their place; thus they have ruined the efficiency of our navy.

"Now I need not remind you that the time during which a crew is in its prime is short, and that the number of sailors who can start a ship on her way and keep the rowing in time is small. But by far my greatest trouble is, that holding the post which I do, I am prevented by the natural indocility of the Athenian seaman from putting a stop to these evils; and that meanwhile we have no source from which to recruit our crews, which the enemy can do from many quarters, but are compelled to depend both for supplying the crews in service and for making good our losses upon the men whom we brought with us. For our present confederates, Naxos and Catana, are incapable of supplying us. There is only one thing more wanting to our opponents, I mean the defection of our Italian markets. If they were to see you neglect to relieve us from our present condition, and were to go over to the enemy, famine would compel us to evacuate, and Syracuse would finish the war without a blow.

"I might, it is true, have written to you something different and more agreeable than this, but nothing certainly more useful, if it is desirable for you to know the real state of things here before taking your measures. Besides I know that it is your nature to love to be told the best side of things, and then to blame the teller if the expectations which he has raised in your minds are not answered by the result; and I therefore thought it safest to declare to you the truth.

“Now you are not to think that either your generals or your soldiers have ceased to be a match for the forces originally opposed to them. But you are to reflect that a general Sicilian coalition is being formed against us; that a fresh army is expected from Peloponnese, while the force we have here is unable to cope even with our present antagonists; and you must promptly decide either to recall us or to send out to us another fleet and army as numerous again, with a large sum of money, and someone to succeed me, as a disease in the kidneys unfits me for retaining my post. I have, I think, some claim on your indulgence, as while I was in my prime I did you much good service in my commands. But whatever you mean to do, do it at the commencement of spring and without delay, as the enemy will obtain his Sicilian reinforcements shortly, those from Peloponnese after a longer interval; and unless you attend to the matter the former will be here before you, while the latter will elude you as they have done before."

Such were the contents of Nicias's letter. When the Athenians had heard it they refused to accept his resignation, but chose him two colleagues, naming Menander and Euthydemus, two of the officers at the seat of war, to fill their places until their arrival, that Nicias might not be left alone in his sickness to bear the whole weight of affairs. They also voted to send out another army and navy, drawn partly from the Athenians on the muster-roll, partly from the allies. The colleagues chosen for Nicias were

Demosthenes, son of Alcisthenes, and Eurymedon, son of Thucles. Eurymedon was sent off at once, about the time of the winter solstice, with ten ships, a hundred and twenty talents of silver, and instructions to tell the army that reinforcements would arrive, and that care would be taken of them; but Demosthenes stayed behind to organize the expedition, meaning to start as soon as it was spring, and sent for troops to the allies, and meanwhile got together money, ships, and heavy infantry at home.

The Athenians also sent twenty vessels round Peloponnese to prevent any one crossing over to Sicily from Corinth or Peloponnese. For the Corinthians, filled with confidence by the favourable alteration in Sicilian affairs which had been reported by the envoys upon their arrival, and convinced that the fleet which they had before sent out had not been without its use, were now preparing to dispatch a force of heavy infantry in merchant vessels to Sicily, while the Lacedaemonians did the like for the rest of Peloponnese. The Corinthians also manned a fleet of twenty-five vessels, intending to try the result of a battle with the squadron on guard at Naupactus, and meanwhile to make it less easy for the Athenians there to hinder the departure of their merchantmen, by obliging them to keep an eye upon the galleys thus arrayed against them.

In the meantime the Lacedaemonians prepared for their invasion of Attica, in accordance with their own previous resolve, and at the instigation of the Syracusans and Corinthians, who wished for an invasion to arrest the reinforcements which they heard that Athens was about to send to Sicily. Alcibiades also urgently advised the fortification of Decelea, and a vigorous prosecution of the war. But the Lacedaemonians derived most encouragement from the belief that Athens, with two wars on her hands, against themselves and against the Siceliots, would be more easy to subdue, and from the conviction that she had been the first to infringe the truce. In the former war, they considered, the offence had been more on their own side, both on account of the entrance of the Thebans into Plataea in time of peace, and also of their own refusal to listen to the Athenian offer of arbitration, in spite of the clause in the former treaty that where arbitration should be offered there should be no appeal to arms. For this reason they thought that they deserved their misfortunes, and took to heart seriously the disaster at Pylos and whatever else had befallen them. But when, besides the ravages from Pylos, which went on without any intermission, the thirty Athenian ships came out from Argos and wasted part of Epidaurus, Prasiae, and other places; when upon every dispute that arose as to the interpretation of any doubtful point in the treaty, their own offers of arbitration were always rejected by the Athenians, the Lacedaemonians at length decided that Athens had now committed the very same offence as they had before done, and had become the guilty party; and they began to be full of ardour for the war. They spent this winter in sending round to their allies for iron, and in getting ready the other implements for building their fort; and meanwhile began raising at home, and also by forced requisitions in the rest of Peloponnese, a force to be sent out in the merchantmen to their allies in Sicily. Winter thus ended, and with it the eighteenth year of this war of which Thucydides is the historian.

In the first days of the spring following, at an earlier period than usual, the Lacedaemonians and their allies invaded Attica, under the command of Agis, son of Archidamus, king of the Lacedaemonians. They began by devastating the parts bordering upon the plain, and next proceeded to fortify Decelea, dividing the work among the different cities. Decelea is about thirteen or fourteen miles from the city of Athens, and the same distance or not much further from Boeotia; and the fort was meant to annoy the plain and the richest parts of the country, being in sight of Athens. While the Peloponnesians and their allies in Attica were engaged in the work of fortification, their countrymen at home sent off, at about the same time, the heavy infantry in the merchant vessels to Sicily; the Lacedaemonians furnishing a picked force of Helots and Neodamodes (or freedmen), six hundred heavy infantry in all, under the command of Eccritus, a Spartan; and the Boeotians three hundred heavy infantry, commanded by two Thebans, Xenon and Nicon, and by Hegesander, a Thespian. These were among the first to put out into the open sea, starting from Taenarus in Laconia. Not long after their departure the Corinthians sent off a force of five hundred heavy infantry, consisting partly of men from Corinth itself, and partly of Arcadian mercenaries, placed under the command of

Alexarchus, a Corinthian. The Sicyonians also sent off two hundred heavy infantry at same time as the Corinthians, under the command of Sargeus, a Sicyonian. Meantime the five-and-twenty vessels manned by Corinth during the winter lay confronting the twenty Athenian ships at Naupactus until the heavy infantry in the merchantmen were fairly on their way from Peloponnese; thus fulfilling the object for which they had been manned originally, which was to divert the attention of the Athenians from the merchantmen to the galleys.

During this time the Athenians were not idle. Simultaneously with the fortification of Decelea, at the very beginning of spring, they sent thirty ships round Peloponnese, under Charicles, son of Apollodorus, with instructions to call at Argos and demand a force of their heavy infantry for the fleet, agreeably to the alliance. At the same time they dispatched Demosthenes to Sicily, as they had intended, with sixty Athenian and five Chian vessels, twelve hundred Athenian heavy infantry from the muster-roll, and as many of the islanders as could be raised in the different quarters, drawing upon the other subject allies for whatever they could supply that would be of use for the war. Demosthenes was instructed first to sail round with Charicles and to operate with him upon the coasts of Laconia, and accordingly sailed to Aegina and there waited for the remainder of his armament, and for Charicles to fetch the Argive troops.

In Sicily, about the same time in this spring, Gylippus came to Syracuse with as many troops as he could bring from the cities which he had persuaded to join. Calling the Syracusans together, he told them that they must man as many ships as possible, and try their hand at a sea-fight, by which he hoped to achieve an advantage in the war not unworthy of the risk. With him Hermocrates actively joined in trying to encourage his countrymen to attack the Athenians at sea, saying that the latter had not inherited their naval prowess nor would they retain it for ever; they had been landsmen even to a greater degree than the Syracusans, and had only become a maritime power when obliged by the Mede. Besides, to daring spirits like the Athenians, a daring adversary would seem the most formidable; and the Athenian plan of paralysing by the boldness of their attack a neighbour often not their inferior in strength could now be used against them with as good effect by the Syracusans. He was convinced also that the unlooked-for spectacle of Syracusans daring to face the Athenian navy would cause a terror to the enemy, the advantages of which would far outweigh any loss that Athenian science might inflict upon their inexperience. He accordingly urged them to throw aside their fears and to try their fortune at sea; and the Syracusans, under the influence of

Gylippus and Hermocrates, and perhaps some others, made up their minds for the sea-fight and began to man their vessels.

When the fleet was ready, Gylippus led out the whole army by night; his plan being to assault in person the forts on Plemmyrium by land, while thirty-five Syracusan galleys sailed according to appointment against the enemy from the great harbour, and the forty-five remaining came round from the lesser harbour, where they had their arsenal, in order to effect a junction with those inside and simultaneously to attack Plemmyrium, and thus to distract the Athenians by assaulting them on two sides at once. The Athenians quickly manned sixty ships, and with twenty-five of these engaged the thirty-five of the Syracusans in the great harbour, sending the rest to meet those sailing round from the arsenal; and an action now ensued directly in front of the mouth of the great harbour, maintained with equal tenacity on both sides; the one wishing to force the passage, the other to prevent them.

In the meantime, while the Athenians in Plemmyrium were down at the sea, attending to the engagement, Gylippus made a sudden attack on the forts in the early morning and took the largest first, and afterwards the two smaller, whose garrisons did not wait for him, seeing the largest so easily taken. At the fall of the first fort, the men from it who succeeded in taking refuge in their boats and merchantmen, found great difficulty in reaching the camp, as the Syracusans were having the best of it in the engagement in the great harbour, and sent a fast-sailing galley to pursue them. But when the two others fell, the Syracusans were now being defeated; and the fugitives from these sailed alongshore with more ease. The Syracusan ships fighting off the mouth of the harbour forced their way through the Athenian vessels and sailing in without any order fell foul of one another, and transferred the victory to the Athenians; who not only routed the squadron in question, but also that by which they were at first being defeated in the harbour, sinking eleven of the Syracusan vessels and killing most of the men, except the crews of three ships whom they made prisoners. Their own loss was confined to three vessels; and after hauling ashore the Syracusan wrecks and setting up a trophy upon the islet in front of Plemmyrium, they retired to their own camp.

Unsuccessful at sea, the Syracusans had nevertheless the forts in Plemmyrium, for which they set up three trophies. One of the two last taken they razed, but put in order and garrisoned the two others. In the capture of the forts a great many men were killed and made prisoners, and a great quantity of property was taken in all. As the Athenians had used them as a magazine, there was a large stock of goods and corn of the merchants inside, and also a large stock belonging to the captains; the masts and other furniture of forty galleys being taken, besides three galleys which had been drawn up on shore. Indeed the first and chiefest cause of the ruin of the Athenian army was the capture of Plemmyrium; even the entrance of the harbour being now no longer safe for carrying in provisions, as the Syracusan vessels were stationed there to prevent it, and nothing could be brought in without fighting; besides the general impression of dismay and discouragement produced upon the army.

After this the Syracusans sent out twelve ships under the command of Agatharchus, a Syracusan. One of these went to Peloponnese with ambassadors to describe the hopeful state of their affairs, and to incite the Peloponnesians to prosecute the war there even more actively than they were now doing, while the eleven others sailed to Italy, hearing that vessels laden with stores were on their way to the Athenians. After falling in with and destroying most of the vessels in question, and burning in the Caulonian territory a quantity of timber for shipbuilding, which had been got ready for the Athenians, the Syracusan squadron went to Locri, and one of the merchantmen from Peloponnese coming in, while they were at anchor there, carrying Thespian heavy infantry, took these on board and sailed alongshore towards home. The Athenians were on the look-out for them with twenty ships at Megara, but were only able to take one vessel with its crew; the rest getting clear off to Syracuse. There was also some skirmishing in the harbour about the piles which the Syracusans had driven in the sea in front of the old docks, to allow their ships to lie at anchor inside, without being hurt by the Athenians sailing up and running them down. The Athenians brought up to them a ship of ten thousand talents burden furnished with wooden turrets and screens, and fastened ropes round the piles from their boats, wrenched them up and broke them, or dived down and sawed them in two. Meanwhile the Syracusans plied them with missiles from the docks, to which they replied from their large vessel; until at last most of the piles were removed by the Athenians. But the most awkward part of the stockade was the part out of sight: some of the piles which had been driven in did not appear above water, so that it was dangerous to sail up, for fear of running the ships upon them, just as upon a reef, through not seeing them. However divers went down and sawed off even these for reward; although the Syracusans drove in others. Indeed there was no end to the contrivances to which they resorted against each other, as might be expected between two hostile armies confronting each other at such a short distance: and skirmishes and all kinds of other attempts were of constant occurrence. Meanwhile the Syracusans sent embassies to the cities, composed of Corinthians, Ambraciots, and

Lacedaemonians, to tell them of the capture of Plemmyrium, and that their defeat in the sea-fight was due less to the strength of the enemy than to their own disorder; and generally, to let them know that they were full of hope, and to desire them to come to their help with ships and troops, as the Athenians were expected with a fresh army, and if the one already there could be destroyed before the other arrived, the war would be at an end.

While the contending parties in Sicily were thus engaged, Demosthenes, having now got together the armament with which he was to go to the island, put out from Aegina, and making sail for Peloponnese, joined Charicles and the thirty ships of the Athenians. Taking on board the heavy infantry from Argos they sailed to Laconia, and, after first plundering part of Epidaurus Limera, landed on the coast of Laconia, opposite Cythera, where the temple of Apollo stands, and, laying waste part of the country, fortified a sort of isthmus, to which the Helots of the Lacedaemonians might desert, and from whence plundering incursions might be made as from Pylos. Demosthenes helped to occupy this place, and then immediately sailed on to Corcyra to take up some of the allies in that island, and so to proceed without delay to Sicily; while Charicles waited until he had completed the fortification of the place and, leaving a garrison there, returned home subsequently with his thirty ships and the Argives also.

This same summer arrived at Athens thirteen hundred targeteers, Thracian swordsmen of the tribe of the Dii, who were to have sailed to Sicily with Demosthenes. Since they had come too late, the Athenians determined to send them back to Thrace, whence they had come; to keep them for the Decelean war appearing too expensive, as the pay of each man was a drachma a day. Indeed since Decelea had been first fortified by the whole Peloponnesian army during this summer, and then occupied for the annoyance of the country by the garrisons from the cities relieving each other at stated intervals, it had been doing great mischief to the Athenians; in fact this occupation, by the destruction of property and loss of men which resulted from it, was one of the principal causes of their ruin. Previously the invasions were short, and did not prevent their enjoying their land during the rest of the time: the enemy was now permanently fixed in Attica; at one time it was an attack in force, at another it was the regular garrison overrunning the country and making forays for its subsistence, and the Lacedaemonian king, Agis, was in the field and diligently prosecuting the war; great mischief was therefore done to the Athenians. They were deprived of their whole country: more than twenty thousand slaves had deserted, a great part of them artisans, and all their sheep and beasts of burden were lost; and as the cavalry rode out daily upon excursions to Decelea and to guard the country, their horses were either lamed by being constantly worked upon rocky ground, or wounded by the enemy.

Besides, the transport of provisions from Euboea, which had before been carried on so much more quickly overland by Decelea from Oropus, was now effected at great cost by sea round Sunium; everything the city required had to be imported from abroad, and instead of a city it became a fortress. Summer and winter the Athenians were worn out by having to keep guard on the fortifications, during the day by turns, by night all together, the cavalry excepted, at the different military posts or upon the wall. But what most oppressed them was that they had two wars at once, and had thus reached a pitch of frenzy which no one would have believed possible if he had heard of it before it had come to pass. For could any one have imagined that even when besieged by the

Peloponnesians entrenched in Attica, they would still, instead of withdrawing from Sicily, stay on there besieging in like manner Syracuse, a town (taken as a town) in no way inferior to Athens, or would so thoroughly upset the Hellenic estimate of their strength and audacity, as to give the spectacle of a people which, at the beginning of the war, some thought might hold out one year, some two, none more than three, if the Peloponnesians invaded their country, now seventeen years after the first invasion, after having already suffered from all the evils of war, going to Sicily and undertaking a new war nothing inferior to that which they already had with the Peloponnesians? These causes, the great losses from Decelea, and the other heavy charges that fell upon them, produced their financial embarrassment; and it was at this time that they imposed upon their subjects, instead of the tribute, the tax of a twentieth upon all imports and exports by sea, which they thought would bring them in more money; their expenditure being now not the same as at first, but having grown with the war while their revenues decayed.

Accordingly, not wishing to incur expense in their present want of money, they sent back at once the Thracians who came too late for Demosthenes, under the conduct of Diitrephes, who was instructed, as they were to pass through the Euripus, to make use of them if possible in the voyage alongshore to injure the enemy. Diitrephes first landed them at Tanagra and hastily snatched some booty; he then sailed across the Euripus in the evening from Chalcis in Euboea and disembarking in Boeotia led them against Mycalessus. The night he passed unobserved near the temple of Hermes, not quite two miles from Mycalessus, and at daybreak assaulted and took the town, which is not a large one; the inhabitants being off their guard and not expecting that any one would ever come up so far from the sea to molest them, the wall too being weak, and in some places having tumbled down, while in others it had not been built to any height, and the gates also being left open through their feeling of security. The Thracians bursting into Mycalessus sacked the houses and temples, and butchered the inhabitants, sparing neither youth nor age, but killing all they fell in with, one after the other, children and women, and even beasts of burden, and whatever other living creatures they saw; the Thracian race, like the bloodiest of the barbarians, being even more so when it has nothing to fear. Everywhere confusion reigned and death in all its shapes; and in particular they attacked a boys' school, the largest that there was in the place, into which the children had just gone, and massacred them all. In short, the disaster falling upon the whole town was unsurpassed in magnitude, and unapproached by any in suddenness and in horror.

Meanwhile the Thebans heard of it and marched to the rescue, and overtaking the Thracians before they had gone far, recovered the plunder and drove them in panic to the Euripus and the sea, where the vessels which brought them were lying. The greatest slaughter took place while they were embarking, as they did not know how to swim, and those in the vessels on seeing what was going on on on shore moored them out of bowshot: in the rest of the retreat the Thracians made a very respectable defence against the Theban horse, by which they were first attacked, dashing out and closing their ranks according to the tactics of their country, and lost only a few men in that part of the affair. A good number who were after plunder were actually caught in the town and put to death. Altogether the Thracians had two hundred and fifty killed out of thirteen hundred, the Thebans and the rest who came to the rescue about twenty, troopers and heavy infantry, with Scirphondas, one of the Boeotarchs. The Mycalessians lost a large proportion of their population.

While Mycalessus thus experienced a calamity for its extent as lamentable as any that happened in the war, Demosthenes, whom we left sailing to Corcyra, after the building of the fort in Laconia, found a merchantman lying at Phea in Elis, in which the Corinthian heavy infantry were to cross to Sicily. The ship he destroyed, but the men escaped, and subsequently got another in which they pursued their voyage. After this, arriving at Zacynthus and Cephallenia, he took a body of heavy infantry on board, and sending for some of the Messenians from Naupactus, crossed over to the opposite coast of Acarnania, to Alyzia, and to Anactorium which was held by the Athenians. While he was in these parts he was met by Eurymedon returning from Sicily, where he had been sent, as has been mentioned, during the winter, with the money for the army, who told him the news, and also that he had heard, while at sea, that the

Syracusans had taken Plemmyrium. Here, also, Conon came to them, the commander at Naupactus, with news that the twenty-five Corinthian ships stationed opposite to him, far from giving over the war, were meditating an engagement; and he therefore begged them to send him some ships, as his own eighteen were not a match for the enemy's twenty-five. Demosthenes and Eurymedon, accordingly, sent ten of their best sailers with Conon to reinforce the squadron at Naupactus, and meanwhile prepared for the muster of their forces; Eurymedon, who was now the colleague of Demosthenes, and had turned back in consequence of his appointment, sailing to Corcyra to tell them to man fifteen ships and to enlist heavy infantry; while Demosthenes raised slingers and darters from the parts about Acarnania.

Meanwhile the envoys, already mentioned, who had gone from Syracuse to the cities after the capture of Plemmyrium, had succeeded in their mission, and were about to bring the army that they had collected, when Nicias got scent of it, and sent to the Centoripae and Alicyaeans and other of the friendly Sicels, who held the passes, not to let the enemy through, but to combine to prevent their passing, there being no other way by which they could even attempt it, as the Agrigentines would not give them a passage through their country. Agreeably to this request the Sicels laid a triple ambuscade for the Siceliots upon their march, and attacking them suddenly, while off their guard, killed about eight hundred of them and all the envoys, the Corinthian only excepted, by whom fifteen hundred who escaped were conducted to Syracuse.

About the same time the Camarinaeans also came to the assistance of Syracuse with five hundred heavy infantry, three hundred darters, and as many archers, while the Geloans sent crews for five ships, four hundred darters, and two hundred horse. Indeed almost the whole of Sicily, except the Agrigentines, who were neutral, now ceased merely to watch events as it had hitherto done, and actively joined Syracuse against the Athenians.

While the Syracusans after the Sicel disaster put off any immediate attack upon the Athenians, Demosthenes and Eurymedon, whose forces from Corcyra and the continent were now ready, crossed the Ionian Gulf with all their armament to the Iapygian promontory, and starting from thence touched at the Choerades Isles lying off Iapygia, where they took on board a hundred and fifty Iapygian darters of the Messapian tribe, and after renewing an old friendship with Artas the chief, who had furnished them with the darters, arrived at Metapontium in Italy. Here they persuaded their allies the Metapontines to send with them three hundred darters and two galleys, and with this reinforcement coasted on to Thurii, where they found the party hostile to Athens recently expelled by a revolution, and accordingly remained there to muster and review the whole army, to see if any had been left behind, and to prevail upon the Thurians resolutely to join them in their expedition, and in the circumstances in which they found themselves to conclude a defensive and offensive alliance with the Athenians.

About the same time the Peloponnesians in the twenty-five ships stationed opposite to the squadron at Naupactus to protect the passage of the transports to Sicily had got ready for engaging, and manning some additional vessels, so as to be numerically little inferior to the Athenians, anchored off Erineus in Achaia in the Rhypic country. The place off which they lay being in the form of a crescent, the land forces furnished by the Corinthians and their allies on the spot came up and ranged themselves upon the projecting headlands on either side, while the fleet, under the command of Polyanthes, a Corinthian, held the intervening space and blocked up the entrance. The Athenians under Diphilus now sailed out against them with thirty-three ships from Naupactus, and the Corinthians, at first not moving, at length thought they saw their opportunity, raised the signal, and advanced and engaged the Athenians. After an obstinate struggle, the Corinthians lost three ships, and without sinking any altogether, disabled seven of the enemy, which were struck prow to prow and had their foreships stove in by the Corinthian vessels, whose cheeks had been strengthened for this very purpose. After an action of this even character, in which either party could claim the victory (although the Athenians became masters of the wrecks through the wind driving them out to sea, the Corinthians not putting out again to meet them), the two combatants parted. No pursuit took place, and no prisoners were made on either side; the Corinthians and Peloponnesians who were fighting near the shore escaping with ease, and none of the Athenian vessels having been sunk. The

Athenians now sailed back to Naupactus, and the Corinthians immediately set up a trophy as victors, because they had disabled a greater number of the enemy's ships. Moreover they held that they had not been worsted, for the very same reason that their opponent held that he had not been victorious; the Corinthians considering that they were conquerors, if not decidedly conquered, and the Athenians thinking themselves vanquished, because not decidedly victorious. However, when the Peloponnesians sailed off and their land forces had dispersed, the Athenians also set up a trophy as victors in Achaia, about two miles and a quarter from Erineus, the Corinthian station.

This was the termination of the action at Naupactus. To return to Demosthenes and Eurymedon: the Thurians having now got ready to join in the expedition with seven hundred heavy infantry and three hundred darters, the two generals ordered the ships to sail along the coast to the Crotonian territory, and meanwhile held a review of all the land forces upon the river Sybaris, and then led them through the Thurian country. Arrived at the river Hylias, they here received a message from the Crotonians, saying that they would not allow the army to pass through their country; upon which the Athenians descended towards the shore, and bivouacked near the sea and the mouth of the Hylias, where the fleet also met them, and the next day embarked and sailed along the coast touching at all the cities except Locri, until they came to Petra in the Rhegian territory.

Meanwhile the Syracusans hearing of their approach resolved to make a second attempt with their fleet and their other forces on shore, which they had been collecting for this very purpose in order to do something before their arrival. In addition to other improvements suggested by the former sea-fight which they now adopted in the equipment of their navy, they cut down their prows to a smaller compass to make them more solid and made their cheeks stouter, and from these let stays into the vessels' sides for a length of six cubits within and without, in the same way as the Corinthians had altered their prows before engaging the squadron at Naupactus. The Syracusans thought that they would thus have an advantage over the Athenian vessels, which were not constructed with equal strength, but were slight in the bows, from their being more used to sail round and charge the enemy's side than to meet him prow to prow, and that the battle being in the great harbour, with a great many ships in not much room, was also a fact in their favour. Charging prow to prow, they would stave in the enemy's bows, by striking with solid and stout beaks against hollow and weak ones; and secondly, the Athenians for want of room would be unable to use their favourite manoeuvre of breaking the line or of sailing round, as the Syracusans would do their best not to let them do the one, and want of room would prevent their doing the other. This charging prow to prow, which had hitherto been thought want of skill in a helmsman, would be the Syracusans' chief manoeuvre, as being that which they should find most useful, since the Athenians, if repulsed, would not be able to back water in any direction except towards the shore, and that only for a little way, and in the little space in front of their own camp. The rest of the harbour would be commanded by the Syracusans; and the Athenians, if hard pressed, by crowding together in a small space and all to the same point, would run foul of one another and fall into disorder, which was, in fact, the thing that did the Athenians most harm in all the sea-fights, they not having, like the Syracusans, the whole harbour to retreat over. As to their sailing round into the open sea, this would be impossible, with the Syracusans in possession of the way out and in, especially as Plemmyrium would be hostile to them, and the mouth of the harbour was not large.

With these contrivances to suit their skill and ability, and now more confident after the previous sea-fight, the Syracusans attacked by land and sea at once. The town force Gylippus led out a little the first and brought them up to the wall of the Athenians, where it looked towards the city, while the force from the Olympieum, that is to say, the heavy infantry that were there with the horse and the light troops of the Syracusans, advanced against the wall from the opposite side; the ships of the Syracusans and allies sailing out immediately afterwards. The Athenians at first fancied that they were to be attacked by land only, and it was not without alarm that they saw the fleet suddenly approaching as well; and while some were forming upon the walls and in front of them against the advancing enemy, and some marching out in haste against the numbers of horse and darters coming from the Olympieum and from outside, others manned the ships or rushed down to the beach to oppose the enemy, and when the ships were manned put out with seventy-five sail against about eighty of the Syracusans.

After spending a great part of the day in advancing and retreating and skirmishing with each other, without either being able to gain any advantage worth speaking of, except that the Syracusans sank one or two of the Athenian vessels, they parted, the land force at the same time retiring from the lines. The next day the Syracusans remained quiet, and gave no signs of what they were going to do; but Nicias, seeing that the battle had been a drawn one, and expecting that they would attack again, compelled the captains to refit any of the ships that had suffered, and moored merchant vessels before the stockade which they had driven into the sea in front of their ships, to serve instead of an enclosed harbour, at about two hundred feet from each other, in order that any ship that was hard pressed might be able to retreat in safety and sail out again at leisure. These preparations occupied the Athenians all day until nightfall.

The next day the Syracusans began operations at an earlier hour, but with the same plan of attack by land and sea. A great part of the day the rivals spent as before, confronting and skirmishing with each other; until at last Ariston, son of Pyrrhicus, a Corinthian, the ablest helmsman in the Syracusan service, persuaded their naval commanders to send to the officials in the city, and tell them to move the sale market as quickly as they could down to the sea, and oblige every one to bring whatever eatables he had and sell them there, thus enabling the commanders to land the crews and dine at once close to the ships, and shortly afterwards, the selfsame day, to attack the Athenians again when they were not expecting it.

In compliance with this advice a messenger was sent and the market got ready, upon which the Syracusans suddenly backed water and withdrew to the town, and at once landed and took their dinner upon the spot; while the Athenians, supposing that they had returned to the town because they felt they were beaten, disembarked at their leisure and set about getting their dinners and about their other occupations, under the idea that they done with fighting for that day. Suddenly the Syracusans had manned their ships and again sailed against them; and the Athenians, in great confusion and most of them fasting, got on board, and with great difficulty put out to meet them. For some time both parties remained on the defensive without engaging, until the Athenians at last resolved not to let themselves be worn out by waiting where they were, but to attack without delay, and giving a cheer, went into action. The Syracusans received them, and charging prow to prow as they had intended, stove in a great part of the Athenian foreships by the strength of their beaks; the darters on the decks also did great damage to the Athenians, but still greater damage was done by the Syracusans who went about in small boats, ran in upon the oars of the Athenian galleys, and sailed against their sides, and discharged from thence their darts upon the sailors.

At last, fighting hard in this fashion, the Syracusans gained the victory, and the Athenians turned and fled between the merchantmen to their own station. The Syracusan ships pursued them as far as the merchantmen, where they were stopped by the beams armed with dolphins suspended from those vessels over the passage. Two of the Syracusan vessels went too near in the excitement of victory and were destroyed, one of them being taken with its crew. After sinking seven of the Athenian vessels and disabling many, and taking most of the men prisoners and killing others, the Syracusans retired and set up trophies for both the engagements, being now confident of having a decided superiority by sea, and by no means despairing of equal success by land.

Chapter Twenty Two

Nineteenth Year of the War–Arrival of Demosthenes–Defeat of the Athenians at Epipolae–Folly and Obstinancy of Nicias

IN THE MEANTIME, while the Syracusans were preparing for a second attack upon both elements, Demosthenes and Eurymedon arrived with the succours from Athens, consisting of about seventy-three ships, including the foreigners; nearly five thousand heavy infantry, Athenian and allied; a large number of darters, Hellenic and barbarian, and slingers and archers and everything else upon a corresponding scale. The Syracusans and their allies were for the moment not a little dismayed at the idea that there was to be no term or ending to their dangers, seeing, in spite of the fortification of Decelea, a new army arrive nearly equal to the former, and the power of Athens proving so great in every quarter. On the other hand, the first Athenian armament regained a certain confidence in the midst of its misfortunes. Demosthenes, seeing how matters stood, felt that he could not drag on and fare as Nicias had done, who by wintering in Catana instead of at once attacking Syracuse had allowed the terror of his first arrival to evaporate in contempt, and had given time to Gylippus to arrive with a force from Peloponnese, which the Syracusans would never have sent for if he had attacked immediately; for they fancied that they were a match for him by themselves, and would not have discovered their inferiority until they were already invested, and even if they then sent for succours, they would no longer have been equally able to profit by their arrival. Recollecting this, and well aware that it was now on the first day after his arrival that he like Nicias was most formidable to the enemy, Demosthenes determined to lose no time in drawing the utmost profit from the consternation at the moment inspired by his army; and seeing that the counterwall of the Syracusans, which hindered the Athenians from investing them, was a single one, and that he who should become master of the way up to Epipolae, and afterwards of the camp there, would find no difficulty in taking it, as no one would even wait for his attack, made all haste to attempt the enterprise. This he took to be the shortest way of ending the war, as he would either succeed and take Syracuse, or would lead back the armament instead of frittering away the lives of the

Athenians engaged in the expedition and the resources of the country at large.

First therefore the Athenians went out and laid waste the lands of the Syracusans about the Anapus and carried all before them as at first by land and by sea, the Syracusans not offering to oppose them upon either element, unless it were with their cavalry and darters from the Olympieum. Next Demosthenes resolved to attempt the counterwall first by means of engines. As however the engines that he brought up were burnt by the enemy fighting from the wall, and the rest of the forces repulsed after attacking at many different points, he determined to delay no longer, and having obtained the consent of Nicias and his fellow commanders, proceeded to put in execution his plan of attacking Epipolae. As by day it seemed impossible to approach and get up without being observed, he ordered provisions for five days, took all the masons and carpenters, and other things, such as arrows, and everything else that they could want for the work of fortification if successful, and, after the first watch, set out with Eurymedon and Menander and the whole army for Epipolae, Nicias being left behind in the lines. Having come up by the hill of Euryelus (where the former army had ascended at first) unobserved by the enemy's guards, they went up to the fort which the Syracusans had there, and took it, and put to the sword part of the garrison. The greater number, however, escaped at once and gave the alarm to the camps, of which there were three upon Epipolae, defended by outworks, one of the Syracusans, one of the other Siceliots, and one of the allies; and also to the six hundred Syracusans forming the original garrison for this part of Epipolae. These at once advanced against the assailants and, falling in with Demosthenes and the Athenians, were routed by them after a sharp resistance, the victors immediately pushing on, eager to achieve the objects of the attack without giving time for their ardour to cool; meanwhile others from the very beginning were taking the counterwall of the Syracusans, which was abandoned by its garrison, and pulling down the battlements. The Syracusans and the allies, and Gylippus with the troops under his command, advanced to the rescue from the outworks, but engaged in some consternation (a night attack being a piece of audacity which they had never expected), and were at first compelled to retreat. But while the Athenians, flushed with their victory, now advanced with less order, wishing to make their way as quickly as possible through the whole force of the enemy not yet engaged, without relaxing their attack or giving them time to rally, the Boeotians made the first stand against them, attacked them, routed them, and put them to flight.

The Athenians now fell into great disorder and perplexity, so that it was not easy to get from one side or the other any detailed account of the affair. By day certainly the combatants have a clearer notion, though even then by no means of all that takes place, no one knowing much of anything that does not go on in his own immediate neighbourhood; but in a night engagement (and this was the only one that occurred between great armies during the war) how could any one know anything for certain? Although there was a bright moon they saw each other only as men do by moonlight, that is to say, they could distinguish the form of the body, but could not tell for certain whether it was a friend or an enemy. Both had great numbers of heavy infantry moving about in a small space. Some of the Athenians were already defeated, while others were coming up yet unconquered for their first attack. A large part also of the rest of their forces either had only just got up, or were still ascending, so that they did not know which way to march. Owing to the rout that had taken place all in front was now in confusion, and the noise made it difficult to distinguish anything. The victorious Syracusans and allies were cheering each other on with loud cries, by night the only possible means of communication, and meanwhile receiving all who came against them; while the Athenians were seeking for one another, taking all in front of them for enemies, even although they might be some of their now flying friends; and by constantly asking for the watchword, which was their only means of recognition, not only caused great confusion among themselves by asking all at once, but also made it known to the enemy, whose own they did not so readily discover, as the Syracusans were victorious and not scattered, and thus less easily mistaken. The result was that if the Athenians fell in with a party of the enemy that was weaker than they, it escaped them through knowing their watchword; while if they themselves failed to answer they were put to the sword. But what hurt them as much, or indeed more than anything else, was the singing of the paean, from the perplexity which it caused by being nearly the same on either side; the Argives and Corcyraeans and any other Dorian peoples in the army, struck terror into the Athenians whenever they raised their paean, no less than did the enemy. Thus, after being once thrown into disorder, they ended by coming into collision with each other in many parts of the field, friends with friends, and citizens with citizens, and not only terrified one another, but even came to blows and could only be parted with difficulty. In the pursuit many perished by throwing themselves down the cliffs, the way down from Epipolae being narrow; and of those who got down safely into the plain, although many, especially those who belonged to the first armament, escaped through their better acquaintance with the locality, some of the newcomers lost their way and wandered over the country, and were cut off in the morning by the Syracusan cavalry and killed.

The next day the Syracusans set up two trophies, one upon Epipolae where the ascent had been made, and the other on the spot where the first check was given by the Boeotians; and the Athenians took back their dead under truce. A great many of the Athenians and allies were killed, although still more arms were taken than could be accounted for by the number of the dead, as some of those who were obliged to leap down from the cliffs without their shields escaped with their lives and did not perish like the rest.

After this the Syracusans, recovering their old confidence at such an unexpected stroke of good fortune, dispatched Sicanus with fifteen ships to Agrigentum where there was a revolution, to induce if possible the city to join them; while Gylippus again went by land into the rest of Sicily to bring up reinforcements, being now in hope of taking the Athenian lines by storm, after the result of the affair on Epipolae.

In the meantime the Athenian generals consulted upon the disaster which had happened, and upon the general weakness of the army. They saw themselves unsuccessful in their enterprises, and the soldiers disgusted with their stay; disease being rife among them owing to its being the sickly season of the year, and to the marshy and unhealthy nature of the spot in which they were encamped; and the state of their affairs generally being thought desperate. Accordingly, Demosthenes was of opinion that they ought not to stay any longer; but agreeably to his original idea in risking the attempt upon Epipolae, now that this had failed, he gave his vote for going away without further loss of time, while the sea might yet be crossed, and their late reinforcement might give them the superiority at all events on that element. He also said that it would be more profitable for the state to carry on the war against those who were building fortifications in Attica, than against the Syracusans whom it was no longer easy to subdue; besides which it was not right to squander large sums of money to no purpose by going on with the siege.

This was the opinion of Demosthenes. Nicias, without denying the bad state of their affairs, was unwilling to avow their weakness, or to have it reported to the enemy that the Athenians in full council were openly voting for retreat; for in that case they would be much less likely to effect it when they wanted without discovery. Moreover, his own particular information still gave him reason to hope that the affairs of the enemy would soon be in a worse state than their own, if the Athenians persevered in the siege; as they would wear out the Syracusans by want of money, especially with the more extensive command of the sea now given them by their present navy. Besides this, there was a party in Syracuse who wished to betray the city to the Athenians, and kept sending him messages and telling him not to raise the siege. Accordingly, knowing this and really waiting because he hesitated between the two courses and wished to see his way more clearly, in his public speech on this occasion he refused to lead off the army, saying he was sure the Athenians would never approve of their returning without a vote of theirs. Those who would vote upon their conduct, instead of judging the facts as eye-witnesses like themselves and not from what they might hear from hostile critics, would simply be guided by the calumnies of the first clever speaker; while many, indeed most, of the soldiers on the spot, who now so loudly proclaimed the danger of their position, when they reached Athens would proclaim just as loudly the opposite, and would say that their generals had been bribed to betray them and return. For himself, therefore, who knew the Athenian temper, sooner than perish under a dishonourable charge and by an unjust sentence at the hands of the Athenians, he would rather take his chance and die, if die he must, a soldier's death at the hand of the enemy. Besides, after all, the Syracusans were in a worse case than themselves. What with paying mercenaries, spending upon fortified posts, and now for a full year maintaining a large navy, they were already at a loss and would soon be at a standstill: they had already spent two thousand talents and incurred heavy debts besides, and could not lose even ever so small a fraction of their present force through not paying it, without ruin to their cause; depending as they did more upon mercenaries than upon soldiers obliged to serve, like their own. He therefore said that they ought to stay and carry on the siege, and not depart defeated in point of money, in which they were much superior.

Nicias spoke positively because he had exact information of the financial distress at Syracuse, and also because of the strength of the Athenian party there which kept sending him messages not to raise the siege; besides which he had more confidence than before in his fleet, and felt sure at least of its success. Demosthenes, however, would not hear for a moment of continuing the siege, but said that if they could not lead off the army without a decree from Athens, and if they were obliged to stay on, they ought to remove to Thapsus or Catana; where their land forces would have a wide extent of country to overrun, and could live by plundering the enemy, and would thus do them damage; while the fleet would have the open sea to fight in, that is to say, instead of a narrow space which was all in the enemy's favour, a wide sea-room where their science would be of use, and where they could retreat or advance without being confined or circumscribed either when they put out or put in. In any case he was altogether opposed to their staying on where they were, and insisted on removing at once, as quickly and with as little delay as possible; and in this judgment Eurymedon agreed. Nicias however still objecting, a certain diffidence and hesitation came over them, with a suspicion that Nicias might have some further information to make him so positive.

Chapter Twenty Three

Nineteenth Year of the War–Battles in the Great Harbour–Retreat and Annihilation of the Athenian Army

WHILE THE ATHENIANS LINGERED on in this way without moving from where they were, Gylippus and Sicanus now arrived at Syracuse. Sicanus had failed to gain Agrigentum, the party friendly to the Syracusans having been driven out while he was still at Gela; but Gylippus was accompanied not only by a large number of troops raised in Sicily, but by the heavy infantry sent off in the spring from Peloponnese in the merchantmen, who had arrived at Selinus from Libya. They had been carried to Libya by a storm, and having obtained two galleys and pilots from the Cyrenians, on their voyage alongshore had taken sides with the Euesperitae and had defeated the Libyans who were besieging them, and from thence coasting on to Neapolis, a Carthaginian mart, and the nearest point to Sicily, from which it is only two days' and a night's voyage, there crossed over and came to Selinus. Immediately upon their arrival the Syracusans prepared to attack the Athenians again by land and sea at once. The Athenian generals seeing a fresh army come to the aid of the enemy, and that their own circumstances, far from improving, were becoming daily worse, and above all distressed by the sickness of the soldiers, now began to repent of not having removed before; and Nicias no longer offering the same opposition, except by urging that there should be no open voting, they gave orders as secretly as possible for all to be prepared to sail out from the camp at a given signal. All was at last ready, and they were on the point of sailing away, when an eclipse of the moon, which was then at the full, took place. Most of the Athenians, deeply impressed by this occurrence, now urged the generals to wait; and Nicias, who was somewhat over-addicted to divination and practices of that kind, refused from that moment even to take the question of departure into consideration, until they had waited the thrice nine days prescribed by the soothsayers.

The besiegers were thus condemned to stay in the country; and the Syracusans, getting wind of what had happened, became more eager than ever to press the Athenians, who had now themselves acknowledged that they were no longer their superiors either by sea or by land, as otherwise they would never have planned to sail away. Besides which the Syracusans did not wish them to settle in any other part of Sicily, where they would be more difficult to deal with, but desired to force them to fight at sea as quickly as possible, in a position favourable to themselves. Accordingly they manned their ships and practised for as many days as they thought sufficient. When the moment arrived they assaulted on the first day the Athenian lines, and upon a small force of heavy infantry and horse sallying out against them by certain gates, cut off some of the former and routed and pursued them to the lines, where, as the entrance was narrow, the Athenians lost seventy horses and some few of the heavy infantry.

Drawing off their troops for this day, on the next the Syracusans went out with a fleet of seventy-six sail, and at the same time advanced with their land forces against the lines. The Athenians put out to meet them with eighty-six ships, came to close quarters, and engaged. The Syracusans and their allies first defeated the Athenian centre, and then caught Eurymedon, the commander of the right wing, who was sailing out from the line more towards the land in order to surround the enemy, in the hollow and recess of the harbour, and killed him and destroyed the ships accompanying him; after which they now chased the whole Athenian fleet before them and drove them ashore.

Gylippus seeing the enemy's fleet defeated and carried ashore beyond their stockades and camp, ran down to the breakwater with some of his troops, in order to cut off the men as they landed and make it easier for the Syracusans to tow off the vessels by the shore being friendly ground. The Tyrrhenians who guarded this point for the Athenians, seeing them come on in disorder, advanced out against them and attacked and routed their van, hurling it into the marsh of Lysimeleia. Afterwards the Syracusan and allied troops arrived in greater numbers, and the Athenians fearing for their ships came up also to the rescue and engaged them, and defeated and pursued them to some distance and killed a few of their heavy infantry. They succeeded in rescuing most of their ships and brought them down by their camp; eighteen however were taken by the Syracusans and their allies, and all the men killed. The rest the enemy tried to burn by means of an old merchantman which they filled with faggots and pine-wood, set on fire, and let drift down the wind which blew full on the Athenians. The Athenians, however, alarmed for their ships, contrived means for stopping it and putting it out, and checking the flames and the nearer approach of the merchantman, thus escaped the danger.

After this the Syracusans set up a trophy

for the sea-fight and for the heavy infantry whom they had cut off up at the lines, where they took the horses; and the Athenians for the rout of the foot driven by the Tyrrhenians into the marsh, and for their own victory with the rest of the army.

The Syracusans had now gained a decisive victory at sea, where until now they had feared the reinforcement brought by Demosthenes, and deep, in consequence, was the despondency of the Athenians, and great their disappointment, and greater still their regret for having come on the expedition. These were the only cities that they had yet encountered, similar to their own in character, under democracies like themselves, which had ships and horses, and were of considerable magnitude. They had been unable to divide and bring them over by holding out the prospect of changes in their governments, or to crush them by their great superiority in force, but had failed in most of their attempts, and being already in perplexity, had now been defeated at sea, where defeat could never have been expected, and were thus plunged deeper in embarrassment than ever.

Meanwhile the Syracusans immediately began to sail freely along the harbour, and determined to close up its mouth, so that the Athenians might not be able to steal out in future, even if they wished. Indeed, the Syracusans no longer thought only of saving themselves, but also how to hinder the escape of the enemy; thinking, and thinking rightly, that they were now much the stronger, and that to conquer the Athenians and their allies by land and sea would win them great glory in Hellas. The rest of the Hellenes would thus immediately be either freed or released from apprehension, as the remaining forces of Athens would be henceforth unable to sustain the war that would be waged against her; while they, the Syracusans, would be regarded as the authors of this deliverance, and would be held in high admiration, not only with all men now living but also with posterity. Nor were these the only considerations that gave dignity to the struggle. They would thus conquer not only the Athenians but also their numerous allies, and conquer not alone, but with their companions in arms, commanding side by side with the Corinthians and Lacedaemonians, having offered their city to stand in the van of danger, and having been in a great measure the pioneers of naval success.

Indeed, there were never so many peoples assembled before a single city, if we except the grand total gathered together in this war under Athens and Lacedaemon. The following were the states on either side who came to Syracuse to fight for or against Sicily, to help to conquer or defend the island. Right or community of blood was not the bond of union between them, so much as interest or compulsion as the case might be. The Athenians themselves being Ionians went against the Dorians of Syracuse of their own free will; and the peoples still speaking Attic and using the Athenian laws, the Lemnians, Imbrians, and Aeginetans, that is to say the then occupants of Aegina, being their colonists, went with them. To these must be also added the Hestiaeans dwelling at Hestiaea in Euboea. Of the rest some joined in the expedition as subjects of the Athenians, others as independent allies, others as mercenaries. To the number of the subjects paying tribute belonged the Eretrians, Chalcidians, Styrians, and Carystians from Euboea; the Ceans, Andrians, and Tenians from the islands; and the Milesians, Samians, and Chians from Ionia. The Chians, however, joined as independent allies, paying no tribute, but furnishing ships. Most of these were Ionians and descended from the Athenians, except the Carystians, who are Dryopes, and although subjects and obliged to serve, were still Ionians fighting against

Dorians. Besides these there were men of Aeolic race, the Methymnians, subjects who provided ships, not tribute, and the Tenedians and Aenians who paid tribute. These Aeolians fought against their Aeolian founders, the Boeotians in the Syracusan army, because they were obliged, while the Plataeans, the only native Boeotians opposed to Boeotians, did so upon a just quarrel. Of the Rhodians and Cytherians, both Dorians, the latter, Lacedaemonian colonists, fought in the Athenian ranks against their Lacedaemonian countrymen with Gylippus; while the Rhodians, Argives by race, were compelled to bear arms against the Dorian Syracusans and their own colonists, the Geloans, serving with the Syracusans. Of the islanders round Peloponnese, the Cephallenians and Zacynthians accompanied the Athenians as independent allies, although their insular position really left them little choice in the matter, owing to the maritime supremacy of Athens, while the Corcyraeans, who were not only Dorians but Corinthians, were openly serving against Corinthians and Syracusans, although colonists of the former and of the same race as the latter, under colour of compulsion, but really out of free will through hatred of Corinth. The Messenians, as they are now called in Naupactus and from Pylos, then held by the Athenians, were taken with them to the war. There were also a few Megarian exiles, whose fate it was to be now fighting against the Megarian Selinuntines.

The engagement of the rest was more of a voluntary nature. It was less the league than hatred of the Lacedaemonians and the immediate private advantage of each individual that persuaded the Dorian Argives to join the Ionian Athenians in a war against Dorians; while the Mantineans and other Arcadian mercenaries, accustomed to go against the enemy pointed out to them at the moment, were led by interest to regard the Arcadians serving with the Corinthians as just as much their enemies as any others. The Cretans and Aetolians also served for hire, and the Cretans who had joined the Rhodians in founding Gela, thus came to consent to fight for pay against, instead of for, their colonists. There were also some Acarnanians paid to serve, although they came chiefly for love of Demosthenes and out of goodwill to the Athenians whose allies they were. These all lived on the Hellenic side of the Ionian Gulf. Of the Italiots, there were the Thurians and Metapontines, dragged into the quarrel by the stern necessities of a time of revolution; of the Siceliots, the Naxians and the Catanians; and of the barbarians, the Egestaeans, who called in the Athenians, most of the Sicels, and outside Sicily some Tyrrhenian enemies of Syracuse and Iapygian mercenaries.

Such were the peoples serving with the Athenians. Against these the Syracusans had the Camarinaeans their neighbours, the Geloans who live next to them; then passing over the neutral Agrigentines, the Selinuntines settled on the farther side of the island. These inhabit the part of Sicily looking towards Libya; the Himeraeans came from the side towards the Tyrrhenian Sea, being the only Hellenic inhabitants in that quarter, and the only people that came from thence to the aid of the Syracusans. Of the Hellenes in Sicily the above peoples joined in the war, all Dorians and independent, and of the barbarians the Sicels only, that is to say, such as did not go over to the Athenians. Of the Hellenes outside Sicily there were the Lacedaemonians, who provided a Spartan to take the command, and a force of Neodamodes or Freedmen, and of Helots; the Corinthians, who alone joined with naval and land forces, with their Leucadian and Ambraciot kinsmen; some mercenaries sent by Corinth from Arcadia; some Sicyonians forced to serve, and from outside

Peloponnese the Boeotians. In comparison, however, with these foreign auxiliaries, the great Siceliot cities furnished more in every department–numbers of heavy infantry, ships, and horses, and an immense multitude besides having been brought together; while in comparison, again, one may say, with all the rest put together, more was provided by the Syracusans themselves, both from the greatness of the city and from the fact that they were in the greatest danger.

Such were the auxiliaries brought together on either side, all of which had by this time joined, neither party experiencing any subsequent accession. It was no wonder, therefore, if the Syracusans and their allies thought that it would win them great glory if they could follow up their recent victory in the sea-fight by the capture of the whole Athenian armada, without letting it escape either by sea or by land. They began at once to close up the Great Harbour by means of boats, merchant vessels, and galleys moored broadside across its mouth, which is nearly a mile wide, and made all their other arrangements for the event of the Athenians again venturing to fight at sea. There was, in fact, nothing little either in their plans or their ideas.

The Athenians, seeing them closing up the harbour and informed of their further designs, called a council of war. The generals and colonels assembled and discussed the difficulties of the situation; the point which pressed most being that they no longer had provisions for immediate use (having sent on to Catana to tell them not to send any, in the belief that they were going away), and that they would not have any in future unless they could command the sea. They therefore determined to evacuate their upper lines, to enclose with a cross wall and garrison a small space close to the ships, only just sufficient to hold their stores and sick, and manning all the ships, seaworthy or not, with every man that could be spared from the rest of their land forces, to fight it out at sea, and, if victorious, to go to Catana, if not, to burn their vessels, form in close order, and retreat by land for the nearest friendly place they could reach, Hellenic or barbarian. This was no sooner settled than carried into effect; they descended gradually from the upper lines and manned all their vessels, compelling all to go on board who were of age to be in any way of use. They thus succeeded in manning about one hundred and ten ships in all, on board of which they embarked a number of archers and darters taken from the Acarnanians and from the other foreigners, making all other provisions allowed by the nature of their plan and by the necessities which imposed it. All was now nearly ready, and Nicias, seeing the soldiery disheartened by their unprecedented and decided defeat at sea, and by reason of the scarcity of provisions eager to fight it out as soon as possible, called them all together, and first addressed them, speaking as follows:

"Soldiers of the Athenians and of the allies, we have all an equal interest in the coming struggle, in which life and country are at stake for us quite as much as they can be for the enemy; since if our fleet wins the day, each can see his native city again, wherever that city may be. You must not lose heart, or be like men without any experience, who fail in a first essay and ever afterwards fearfully forebode a future as disastrous. But let the Athenians among you who have already had experience of many wars, and the allies who have joined us in so many expeditions, remember the surprises of war, and with the hope that fortune will not be always against us, prepare to fight again in a manner worthy of the number which you see yourselves to be.

"Now, whatever we thought would be of service against the crush of vessels in such a narrow harbour, and against the force upon the decks of the enemy, from which we suffered before, has all been considered with the helmsmen, and, as far as our means allowed, provided. A number of archers and darters will go on board, and a multitude that we should not have employed in an action in the open sea, where our science would be crippled by the weight of the vessels; but in the present land-fight that we are forced to make from shipboard all this will be useful. We have also discovered the changes in construction that we must make to meet theirs; and against the thickness of their cheeks, which did us the greatest mischief, we have provided grappling-irons, which will prevent an assailant backing water after charging, if the soldiers on deck here do their duty; since we are absolutely compelled to fight a land battle from the fleet, and it seems to be our interest neither to back water ourselves, nor to let the enemy do so, especially as the shore, except so much of it as may be held by our troops, is hostile ground.

"You must remember this and fight on as long as you can, and must not let yourselves be driven ashore, but once alongside must make up your minds not to part company until you have swept the heavy infantry from the enemy's deck. I say this more for the heavy infantry than for the seamen, as it is more the business of the men on deck; and our land forces are even now on the whole the strongest. The sailors I advise, and at the same time implore, not to be too much daunted by their misfortunes, now that we have our decks better armed and greater number of vessels. Bear in mind how well worth preserving is the pleasure felt by those of you who through your knowledge of our language and imitation of our manners were always considered Athenians, even though not so in reality, and as such were honoured throughout Hellas, and had your full share of the advantages of our empire, and more than your share in the respect of our subjects and in protection from ill treatment. You, therefore, with whom alone we freely share our empire, we now justly require not to betray that empire in its extremity, and in scorn of Corinthians, whom you have often conquered, and of Siceliots, none of whom so much as presumed to stand against us when our navy was in its prime, we ask you to repel them, and to show that even in sickness and disaster your skill is more than a match for the fortune and vigour of any other.

"For the Athenians among you I add once more this reflection: You left behind you no more such ships in your docks as these, no more heavy infantry in their flower; if you do aught but conquer, our enemies here will immediately sail thither, and those that are left of us at Athens will become unable to repel their home assailants, reinforced by these new allies. Here you will fall at once into the hands of the Syracusans–I need not remind you of the intentions with which you attacked them–and your countrymen at home will fall into those of the Lacedaemonians. Since the fate of both thus hangs upon this single battle, now, if ever, stand firm, and remember, each and all, that you who are now going on board are the army and navy of the Athenians, and all that is left of the state and the great name of Athens, in whose defence if any man has any advantage in skill or courage, now is the time for him to show it, and thus serve himself and save all."

After this address Nicias at once gave orders to man the ships. Meanwhile Gylippus and the Syracusans could perceive by the preparations which they saw going on that the Athenians meant to fight at sea. They had also notice of the grappling-irons, against which they specially provided by stretching hides over the prows and much of the upper part of their vessels, in order that the irons when thrown might slip off without taking hold. All being now ready, the generals and Gylippus addressed them in the following terms:

"Syracusans and allies, the glorious character of our past achievements and the no less glorious results at issue in the coming battle are, we think, understood by most of you, or you would never have thrown yourselves with such ardour into the struggle; and if there be any one not as fully aware of the facts as he ought to be, we will declare them to him. The Athenians came to this country first to effect the conquest of Sicily, and after that, if successful, of Peloponnese and the rest of Hellas, possessing already the greatest empire yet known, of present or former times, among the Hellenes. Here for the first time they found in you men who faced their navy which made them masters everywhere; you have already defeated them in the previous sea-fights, and will in all likelihood defeat them again now. When men are once checked in what they consider their special excellence, their whole opinion of themselves suffers more than if they had not at first believed in their superiority, the unexpected shock to their pride causing them to give way more than their real strength warrants; and this is probably now the case with the Athenians.

"With us it is different. The original estimate of ourselves which gave us courage in the days of our unskilfulness has been strengthened, while the conviction superadded to it that we must be the best seamen of the time, if we have conquered the best, has given a double measure of hope to every man among us; and, for the most part, where there is the greatest hope, there is also the greatest ardour for action. The means to combat us which they have tried to find in copying our armament are familiar to our warfare, and will be met by proper provisions; while they will never be able to have a number of heavy infantry on their decks, contrary to their custom, and a number of darters (born landsmen, one may say, Acarnanians and others, embarked afloat, who will not know how to discharge their weapons when they have to keep still), without hampering their vessels and falling all into confusion among themselves through fighting not according to their own tactics. For they will gain nothing by the number of their ships–I say this to those of you who may be alarmed by having to fight against odds–as a quantity of ships in a confined space will only be slower in executing the movements required, and most exposed to injury from our means of offence. Indeed, if you would know the plain truth, as we are credibly informed, the excess of their sufferings and the necessities of their present distress have made them desperate; they have no confidence in their force, but wish to try their fortune in the only way they can, and either to force their passage and sail out, or after this to retreat by land, it being impossible for them to be worse off than they are.

"The fortune of our greatest enemies having thus betrayed itself, and their disorder being what I have described, let us engage in anger, convinced that, as between adversaries, nothing is more legitimate than to claim to sate the whole wrath of one's soul in punishing the aggressor, and nothing more sweet, as the proverb has it, than the vengeance upon an enemy, which it will now be ours to take. That enemies they are and mortal enemies you all know, since they came here to enslave our country, and if successful had in reserve for our men all that is most dreadful, and for our children and wives all that is most dishonourable, and for the whole city the name which conveys the greatest reproach. None should therefore relent or think it gain if they go away without further danger to us. This they will do just the same, even if they get the victory; while if we succeed, as we may expect, in chastising them, and in handing down to all Sicily her ancient freedom strengthened and confirmed, we shall have achieved no mean triumph. And the rarest dangers are those in which failure brings little loss and success the greatest advantage."

After the above address to the soldiers on their side, the Syracusan generals and Gylippus now perceived that the Athenians were manning their ships, and immediately proceeded to man their own also. Meanwhile Nicias, appalled by the position of affairs, realizing the greatness and the nearness of the danger now that they were on the point of putting out from shore, and thinking, as men are apt to think in great crises, that when all has been done they have still something left to do, and when all has been said that they have not yet said enough, again called on the captains one by one, addressing each by his father's name and by his own, and by that of his tribe, and adjured them not to belie their own personal renown, or to obscure the hereditary virtues for which their ancestors were illustrious: he reminded them of their country, the freest of the free, and of the unfettered discretion allowed in it to all to live as they pleased; and added other arguments such as men would use at such a crisis, and which, with little alteration, are made to serve on all occasions alike–appeals to wives, children, and national gods–without caring whether they are thought commonplace, but loudly invoking them in the belief that they will be of use in the consternation of the moment. Having thus admonished them, not, he felt, as he would, but as he could, Nicias withdrew and led the troops to the sea, and ranged them in as long a line as he was able, in order to aid as far as possible in sustaining the courage of the men afloat; while Demosthenes, Menander, and Euthydemus, who took the command on board, put out from their own camp and sailed straight to the barrier across the mouth of the harbour and to the passage left open, to try to force their way out.

Chapter Twenty Three

The Syracusans and their allies had already put out with about the same number of ships as before, a part of which kept guard at the outlet, and the remainder all round the rest of the harbour, in order to attack the Athenians on all sides at once; while the land forces held themselves in readiness at the points at which the vessels might put into the shore. The Syracusan fleet was commanded by Sicanus and Agatharchus, who had each a wing of the whole force, with Pythen and the Corinthians in the centre. When the rest of the Athenians came up to the barrier, with the first shock of their charge they overpowered the ships stationed there, and tried to undo the fastenings; after this, as the Syracusans and allies bore down upon them from all quarters, the action spread from the barrier over the whole harbour, and was more obstinately disputed than any of the preceding ones. On either side the rowers showed great zeal in bringing up their vessels at the boatswains' orders, and the helmsmen great skill in manoeuvring, and great emulation one with another; while the ships once alongside, the soldiers on board did their best not to let the service on deck be outdone by the others; in short, every man strove to prove himself the first in his particular department. And as many ships were engaged in a small compass (for these were the largest fleets fighting in the narrowest space ever known, being together little short of two hundred), the regular attacks with the beak were few, there being no opportunity of backing water or of breaking the line; while the collisions caused by one ship chancing to run foul of another, either in flying from or attacking a third, were more frequent. So long as a vessel was coming up to the charge the men on the decks rained darts and arrows and stones upon her; but once alongside, the heavy infantry tried to board each other's vessel, fighting hand to hand. In many quarters it happened, by reason of the narrow room, that a vessel was charging an enemy on one side and being charged herself on another, and that two or sometimes more ships had perforce got entangled round one, obliging the helmsmen to attend to defence here, offence there, not to one thing at once, but to many on all sides; while the huge din caused by the number of ships crashing together not only spread terror, but made the orders of the boatswains inaudible. The boatswains on either side in the discharge of their duty and in the heat of the conflict shouted incessantly orders and appeals to their men; the Athenians they urged to force the passage out, and now if ever to show their mettle and lay hold of a safe return to their country; to the Syracusans and their allies they cried that it would be glorious to prevent the escape of the enemy, and, conquering, to exalt the countries that were theirs. The generals, moreover, on either side, if they saw any in any part of the battle backing ashore without being forced to do so, called out to the captain by name and asked him–the Athenians, whether they were retreating because they thought the thrice hostile shore more their own than that sea which had cost them so much labour to win; the Syracusans, whether they were flying from the flying Athenians, whom they well knew to be eager to escape in whatever way they could.

Meanwhile the two armies on shore, while victory hung in the balance, were a prey to the most agonizing and conflicting emotions; the natives thirsting for more glory than they had already won, while the invaders feared to find themselves in even worse plight than before. The all of the Athenians being set upon their fleet, their fear for the event was like nothing they had ever felt; while their view of the struggle was necessarily as chequered as the battle itself. Close to the scene of action and not all looking at the same point at once, some saw their friends victorious and took courage and fell to calling upon heaven not to deprive them of salvation, while others who had their eyes turned upon the losers, wailed and cried aloud, and, although spectators, were more overcome than the actual combatants. Others, again, were gazing at some spot where the battle was evenly disputed; as the strife was protracted without decision, their swaying bodies reflected the agitation of their minds, and they suffered the worst agony of all, ever just within reach of safety or just on the point of destruction. In short, in that one Athenian army as long as the sea-fight remained doubtful there was every sound to be heard at once, shrieks, cheers, "We win," "We lose," and all the other manifold exclamations that a great host would necessarily utter in great peril; and with the men in the fleet it was nearly the same; until at last the Syracusans and their allies, after the battle had lasted a long while, put the Athenians to flight, and with much shouting and cheering chased them in open rout to the shore. The naval force, one one way, one another, as many as were not taken afloat now ran ashore and rushed from on board their ships to their camp; while the army, no more divided, but carried away by one impulse, all with shrieks and groans deplored the event, and ran down, some to help the ships, others to guard what was left of their wall, while the remaining and most numerous part already began to consider how they should save themselves. Indeed, the panic of the present moment had never been surpassed. They now suffered very nearly what they had inflicted at Pylos; as then the Lacedaemonians with the loss of their fleet lost also the men who had crossed over to the island, so now the Athenians had no hope of escaping by land, without the help of some extraordinary accident.

The sea-fight having been a severe one, and many ships and lives having been lost on both sides, the victorious Syracusans and their allies now picked up their wrecks and dead, and sailed off to the city and set up a trophy. The Athenians, overwhelmed by their misfortune, never even thought of asking leave to take up their dead or wrecks, but wished to retreat that very night. Demosthenes, however, went to Nicias and gave it as his opinion that they should man the ships they had left and make another effort to force their passage out next morning; saying that they had still left more ships fit for service than the enemy, the Athenians having about sixty remaining as against less than fifty of their opponents. Nicias was quite of his mind; but when they wished to man the vessels, the sailors refused to go on board, being so utterly overcome by their defeat as no longer to believe in the possibility of success.

Accordingly they all now made up their minds to retreat by land. Meanwhile the Syracusan Hermocrates–suspecting their intention, and impressed by the danger of allowing a force of that magnitude to retire by land, establish itself in some other part of Sicily, and from thence renew the war–went and stated his views to the authorities, and pointed out to them that they ought not to let the enemy get away by night, but that all the Syracusans and their allies should at once march out and block up the roads and seize and guard the passes. The authorities were entirely of his opinion, and thought that it ought to be done, but on the other hand felt sure that the people, who had given themselves over to rejoicing, and were taking their ease after a great battle at sea, would not be easily brought to obey; besides, they were celebrating a festival, having on that day a sacrifice to Heracles, and most of them in their rapture at the victory had fallen to drinking at the festival, and would probably consent to anything sooner than to take up their arms and march out at that moment. For these reasons the thing appeared impracticable to the magistrates; and Hermocrates, finding himself unable to do anything further with them, had now recourse to the following stratagem of his own. What he feared was that the Athenians might quietly get the start of them by passing the most difficult places during the night; and he therefore sent, as soon as it was dusk, some friends of his own to the camp with some horsemen who rode up within earshot and called out to some of the men, as though they were well-wishers of the Athenians, and told them to tell Nicias (who had in fact some correspondents who informed him of what went on inside the town) not to lead off the army by night as the Syracusans were guarding the roads, but to make his preparations at his leisure and to retreat by day. After saying this they departed; and their hearers informed the Athenian generals, who put off going for that night on the strength of this message, not doubting its sincerity.

Since after all they had not set out at

once, they now determined to stay also the following day to give time to the soldiers to pack up as well as they could the most useful articles, and, leaving everything else behind, to start only with what was strictly necessary for their personal subsistence. Meanwhile the Syracusans and Gylippus marched out and blocked up the roads through the country by which the Athenians were likely to pass, and kept guard at the fords of the streams and rivers, posting themselves so as to receive them and stop the army where they thought best; while their fleet sailed up to the beach and towed off the ships of the Athenians. Some few were burned by the Athenians themselves as they had intended; the rest the Syracusans lashed on to their own at their leisure as they had been thrown up on shore, without any one trying to stop them, and conveyed to the town.

After this, Nicias and Demosthenes now thinking that enough had been done in the way of preparation, the removal of the army took place upon the second day after the sea-fight. It was a lamentable scene, not merely from the single circumstance that they were retreating after having lost all their ships, their great hopes gone, and themselves and the state in peril; but also in leaving the camp there were things most grievous for every eye and heart to contemplate. The dead lay unburied, and each man as he recognized a friend among them shuddered with grief and horror; while the living whom they were leaving behind, wounded or sick, were to the living far more shocking than the dead, and more to be pitied than those who had perished. These fell to entreating and bewailing until their friends knew not what to do, begging them to take them and loudly calling to each individual comrade or relative whom they could see, hanging upon the necks of their tent-fellows in the act of departure, and following as far as they could, and, when their bodily strength failed them, calling again and again upon heaven and shrieking aloud as they were left behind. So that the whole army being filled with tears and distracted after this fashion found it not easy to go, even from an enemy's land, where they had already suffered evils too great for tears and in the unknown future before them feared to suffer more. Dejection and self-condemnation were also rife among them. Indeed they could only be compared to a starved-out town, and that no small one, escaping; the whole multitude upon the march being not less than forty thousand men. All carried anything they could which might be of use, and the heavy infantry and troopers, contrary to their wont, while under arms carried their own victuals, in some cases for want of servants, in others through not trusting them; as they had long been deserting and now did so in greater numbers than ever. Yet even thus they did not carry enough, as there was no longer food in the camp.

Moreover their disgrace generally, and the universality of their sufferings, however to a certain extent alleviated by being borne in company, were still felt at the moment a heavy burden, especially when they contrasted the splendour and glory of their setting out with the humiliation in which it had ended. For this was by far the greatest reverse that ever befell an Hellenic army. They had come to enslave others, and were departing in fear of being enslaved themselves: they had sailed out with prayer and paeans, and now started to go back with omens directly contrary; travelling by land instead of by sea, and trusting not in their fleet but in their heavy infantry. Nevertheless the greatness of the danger still impending made all this appear tolerable.

Nicias seeing the army dejected and greatly altered, passed along the ranks and encouraged and comforted them as far as was possible under the circumstances, raising his voice still higher and higher as he went from one company to another in his earnestness, and in his anxiety that the benefit of his words might reach as many as possible:

"Athenians and allies, even in our present position we must still hope on, since men have ere now been saved from worse straits than this; and you must not condemn yourselves too severely either because of your disasters or because of your present unmerited sufferings. I myself who am not superior to any of you in strength–indeed you see how I am in my sickness–and who in the gifts of fortune am, I think, whether in private life or otherwise, the equal of any, am now exposed to the same danger as the meanest among you; and yet my life has been one of much devotion toward the gods, and of much justice and without offence toward men. I have, therefore, still a strong hope for the future, and our misfortunes do not terrify me as much as they might. Indeed we may hope that they will be lightened: our enemies have had good fortune enough; and if any of the gods was offended at our expedition, we have been already amply punished. Others before us have attacked their neighbours and have done what men will do without suffering more than they could bear; and we may now justly expect to find the gods more kind, for we have become fitter objects for their pity than their jealousy. And then look at yourselves, mark the numbers and efficiency of the heavy infantry marching in your ranks, and do not give way too much to despondency, but reflect that you are yourselves at once a city wherever you sit down, and that there is no other in Sicily that could easily resist your attack, or expel you when once established. The safety and order of the march is for yourselves to look to; the one thought of each man being that the spot on which he may be forced to fight must be conquered and held as his country and stronghold. Meanwhile we shall hasten on our way night and day alike, as our provisions are scanty; and if we can reach some friendly place of the Sicels, whom fear of the Syracusans still keeps true to us, you may forthwith consider yourselves safe. A message has been sent on to them with directions to meet us with supplies of food. To sum up, be convinced, soldiers, that you must be brave, as there is no place near for your cowardice to take refuge in, and that if you now escape from the enemy, you may all see again what your hearts desire, while those of you who are Athenians will raise up again the great power of the state, fallen though it be. Men make the city and not walls or ships without men in them."

As he made this address, Nicias went along the ranks, and brought back to their place any of the troops that he saw straggling out of the line; while Demosthenes did as much for his part of the army, addressing them in words very similar. The army marched in a hollow square, the division under Nicias leading, and that of Demosthenes following, the heavy infantry being outside and the baggage-carriers and the bulk of the army in the middle. When they arrived at the ford of the river Anapus there they found drawn up a body of the Syracusans and allies, and routing these, made good their passage and pushed on, harassed by the charges of the Syracusan horse and by the missiles of their light troops. On that day they advanced about four miles and a half, halting for the night upon a certain hill. On the next they started early and got on about two miles further, and descended into a place in the plain and there encamped, in order to procure some eatables from the houses, as the place was inhabited, and to carry on with them water from thence, as for many furlongs in front, in the direction in which they were going, it was not plentiful. The Syracusans meanwhile went on and fortified the pass in front, where there was a steep hill with a rocky ravine on each side of it, called the Acraean cliff. The next day the Athenians advancing found themselves impeded by the missiles and charges of the horse and darters, both very numerous, of the Syracusans and allies; and after fighting for a long while, at length retired to the same camp, where they had no longer provisions as before, it being impossible to leave their position by reason of the cavalry.

Early next morning they started afresh and forced their way to the hill, which had been fortified, where they found before them the enemy's infantry drawn up many shields deep to defend the fortification, the pass being narrow. The Athenians assaulted the work, but were greeted by a storm of missiles from the hill, which told with the greater effect through its being a steep one, and unable to force the passage, retreated again and rested. Meanwhile occurred some claps of thunder and rain, as often happens towards autumn, which still further disheartened the Athenians, who thought all these things to be omens of their approaching ruin. While they were resting, Gylippus and the Syracusans sent a part of their army to throw up works in their rear on the way by which they had advanced; however, the Athenians immediately sent some of their men and prevented them; after which they retreated more towards the plain and halted for the night. When they advanced the next day the Syracusans surrounded and attacked them on every side, and disabled many of them, falling back if the Athenians advanced and coming on if they retired, and in particular assaulting their rear, in the hope of routing them in detail, and thus striking a panic into the whole army. For a long while the Athenians persevered in this fashion, but after advancing for four or five furlongs halted to rest in the plain, the Syracusans also withdrawing to their own camp.

During the night Nicias and Demosthenes, seeing the wretched condition of their troops, now in want of every kind of necessary, and numbers of them disabled in the numerous attacks of the enemy, determined to light as many fires as possible, and to lead off the army, no longer by the same route as they had intended, but towards the sea in the opposite direction to that guarded by the Syracusans. The whole of this route was leading the army not to Catana but to the other side of Sicily, towards Camarina, Gela, and the other Hellenic and barbarian towns in that quarter. They accordingly lit a number of fires and set out by night. Now all armies, and the greatest most of all, are liable to fears and alarms, especially when they are marching by night through an enemy's country and with the enemy near; and the Athenians falling into one of these panics, the leading division, that of Nicias, kept together and got on a good way in front, while that of Demosthenes, comprising rather more than half the army, got separated and marched on in some disorder. By morning, however, they reached the sea, and getting into the Helorine road, pushed on in order to reach the river Cacyparis, and to follow the stream up through the interior, where they hoped to be met by the Sicels whom they had sent for. Arrived at the river, they found there also a Syracusan party engaged in barring the passage of the ford with a wall and a palisade, and forcing this guard, crossed the river and went on to another called the Erineus, according to the advice of their guides.

Meanwhile, when day came and the Syracusans and allies found that the Athenians were gone, most of them accused Gylippus of having let them escape on purpose, and hastily pursuing by the road which they had no difficulty in finding that they had taken, overtook them about dinner-time. They first came up with the troops under Demosthenes, who were behind and marching somewhat slowly and in disorder, owing to the night panic above referred to, and at once attacked and engaged them, the Syracusan horse surrounding them with more ease now that they were separated from the rest and hemming them in on one spot. The division of Nicias was five or six miles on in front, as he led them more rapidly, thinking that under the circumstances their safety lay not in staying and fighting, unless obliged, but in retreating as fast as possible, and only fighting when forced to do so. On the other hand, Demosthenes was, generally speaking, harassed more incessantly, as his post in the rear left him the first exposed to the attacks of the enemy; and now, finding that the Syracusans were in pursuit, he omitted to push on, in order to form his men for battle, and so lingered until he was surrounded by his pursuers and himself and the Athenians with him placed in the most distressing position, being huddled into an enclosure with a wall all round it, a road on this side and on that, and olive-trees in great number, where missiles were showered in upon them from every quarter. This mode of attack the Syracusans had with good reason adopted in preference to fighting at close quarters, as to risk a struggle with desperate men was now more for the advantage of the Athenians than for their own; besides, their success had now become so certain that they began to spare themselves a little in order not to be cut off in the moment of victory, thinking too that, as it was, they would be able in this way to subdue and capture the enemy.

In fact, after plying the Athenians and allies all day long from every side with missiles, they at length saw that they were worn out with their wounds and other sufferings; and Gylippus and the Syracusans and their allies made a proclamation, offering their liberty to any of the islanders who chose to come over to them; and some few cities went over. Afterwards a capitulation was agreed upon for all the rest with Demosthenes, to lay down their arms on condition that no one was to be put to death either by violence or imprisonment or want of the necessaries of life. Upon this they surrendered to the number of six thousand in all, laying down all the money in their possession, which filled the hollows of four shields, and were immediately conveyed by the Syracusans to the town.

Meanwhile Nicias with his division arrived that day at the river Erineus, crossed over, and posted his army upon some high ground upon the other side. The next day the Syracusans overtook him and told him that the troops under Demosthenes had surrendered, and invited him to follow their example. Incredulous of the fact, Nicias asked for a truce to send a horseman to see, and upon the return of the messenger with the tidings that they had surrendered, sent a herald to Gylippus and the Syracusans, saying that he was ready to agree with them on behalf of the Athenians to repay whatever money the Syracusans had spent upon the war if they would let his army go; and offered until the money was paid to give Athenians as hostages, one for every talent. The Syracusans and Gylippus rejected this proposition, and attacked this division as they had the other, standing all round and plying them with missiles until the evening. Food and necessaries were as miserably wanting to the troops of Nicias as they had been to their comrades; nevertheless they watched for the quiet of the night to resume their march. But as they were taking up their arms the Syracusans perceived it and raised their paean, upon which the Athenians, finding that they were discovered, laid them down again, except about three hundred men who forced their way through the guards and went on during the night as they were able.

As soon as it was day Nicias put his army in motion, pressed, as before, by the

Syracusans and their allies, pelted from every side by their missiles, and struck down by their javelins. The Athenians pushed on for the Assinarus, impelled by the attacks made upon them from every side by a numerous cavalry and the swarm of other arms, fancying that they should breathe more freely if once across the river, and driven on also by their exhaustion and craving for water. Once there they rushed in, and all order was at an end, each man wanting to cross first, and the attacks of the enemy making it difficult to cross at all; forced to huddle together, they fell against and trod down one another, some dying immediately upon the javelins, others getting entangled together and stumbling over the articles of baggage, without being able to rise again. Meanwhile the opposite bank, which was steep, was lined by the Syracusans, who showered missiles down upon the Athenians, most of them drinking greedily and heaped together in disorder in the hollow bed of the river. The Peloponnesians also came down and butchered them, especially those in the water, which was thus immediately spoiled, but which they went on drinking just the same, mud and all, bloody as it was, most even fighting to have it.

At last, when many dead now lay piled one upon another in the stream, and part of the army had been destroyed at the river, and the few that escaped from thence cut off by the cavalry, Nicias surrendered himself to Gylippus, whom he trusted more than he did the Syracusans, and told him and the Lacedaemonians to do what they liked with him, but to stop the slaughter of the soldiers. Gylippus, after this, immediately gave orders to make prisoners; upon which the rest were brought together alive, except a large number secreted by the soldiery, and a party was sent in pursuit of the three hundred who had got through the guard during the night, and who were now taken with the rest. The number of the enemy collected as public property was not considerable; but that secreted was very large, and all Sicily was filled with them, no convention having been made in their case as for those taken with Demosthenes. Besides this, a large portion were killed outright, the carnage being very great, and not exceeded by any in this Sicilian war. In the numerous other encounters upon the march, not a few also had fallen. Nevertheless many escaped, some at the moment, others served as slaves, and then ran away subsequently. These found refuge at Catana.

The Syracusans and their allies now mustered and took up the spoils and as many prisoners as they could, and went back to the city. The rest of their Athenian and allied captives were deposited in the quarries, this seeming the safest way of keeping them; but Nicias and Demosthenes were butchered, against the will of Gylippus, who thought that it would be the crown of his triumph if he could take the enemy's generals to Lacedaemon. One of them, as it happened, Demosthenes, was one of her greatest enemies, on account of the affair of the island and of Pylos; while the other, Nicias, was for the same reasons one of her greatest friends, owing to his exertions to procure the release of the prisoners by persuading the Athenians to make peace. For these reasons the Lacedaemonians felt kindly towards him; and it was in this that Nicias himself mainly confided when he surrendered to Gylippus. But some of the Syracusans who had been in correspondence with him were afraid, it was said, of his being put to the torture and troubling their success by his revelations; others, especially the Corinthians, of his escaping, as he was wealthy, by means of bribes, and living to do them further mischief; and these persuaded the allies and put him to death. This or the like was the cause of the death of a man who, of all the Hellenes in my time, least deserved such a fate, seeing that the whole course of his life had been regulated with strict attention to virtue.

The prisoners in the quarries were at first hardly treated by the Syracusans. Crowded in a narrow hole, without any roof to cover them, the heat of the sun and the stifling closeness of the air tormented them during the day, and then the nights, which came on autumnal and chilly, made them ill by the violence of the change; besides, as they had to do everything in the same place for want of room, and the bodies of those who died of their wounds or from the variation in the temperature, or from similar causes, were left heaped together one upon another, intolerable stenches arose; while hunger and thirst never ceased to afflict them, each man during eight months having only half a pint of water and a pint of corn given him daily. In short, no single suffering to be apprehended by men thrust into such a place was spared them. For some seventy days they thus lived all together, after which all, except the Athenians and any Siceliots or Italiots who had joined in the expedition, were sold. The total number of prisoners taken it would be difficult to state exactly, but it could not have been less than seven thousand.

This was the greatest Hellenic achievement of any in thig war, or, in my opinion, in Hellenic history; at once most glorious to the victors, and most calamitous to the conquered. They were beaten at all points and altogether; all that they suffered was great; they were destroyed, as the saying is, with a total destruction, their fleet, their army, everything was destroyed, and few out of many returned home. Such were the events in Sicily.

BOOK EIGHT

Chapter Twenty Four

Nineteenth and Twentieth Years of the War–Revolt of Ionia–Intervention of Persia–The War in Ionia

WHEN THE NEWS was brought to Athens, for a long while they disbelieved even the most respectable of the soldiers who had themselves escaped from the scene of action and clearly reported the matter, a destruction so complete not being thought credible. When the conviction was forced upon them, they were angry with the orators who had joined in promoting the expedition, just as if they had not themselves voted it, and were enraged also with the reciters of oracles and soothsayers, and all other omen-mongers of the time who had encouraged them to hope that they should conquer Sicily. Already distressed at all points and in all quarters, after what had now happened, they were seized by a fear and consternation quite without example. It was grievous enough for the state and for every man in his proper person to lose so many heavy infantry, cavalry, and able-bodied troops, and to see none left to replace them; but when they saw, also, that they had not sufficient ships in their docks, or money in the treasury, or crews for the ships, they began to despair of salvation. They thought that their enemies in Sicily would immediately sail with their fleet against Piraeus, inflamed by so signal a victory;

while their adversaries at home, redoubling all their preparations, would vigorously attack them by sea and land at once, aided by their own revolted confederates. Nevertheless, with such means as they had, it was determined to resist to the last, and to provide timber and money, and to equip a fleet as they best could, to take steps to secure their confederates and above all Euboea, to reform things in the city upon a more economical footing, and to elect a board of elders to advise upon the state of affairs as occasion should arise. In short, as is the way of a democracy, in the panic of the moment they were ready to be as prudent as possible.

These resolves were at once carried into effect. Summer was now over. The winter ensuing saw all Hellas stirring under the impression of the great Athenian disaster in Sicily. Neutrals now felt that even if uninvited they ought no longer to stand aloof from the war, but should volunteer to march against the Athenians, who, as they severally reflected, would probably have come against them if the Sicilian campaign had succeeded. Besides, they considered that the war would now be short, and that it would be creditable for them to take part in it. Meanwhile the allies of the Lacedaemonians felt all more anxious than ever to see a speedy end to their heavy labours. But above all, the subjects of the Athenians showed a readiness to revolt even beyond their ability, judging the circumstances with passion, and refusing even to hear of the Athenians being able to last out the coming summer. Beyond all this, Lacedaemon was encouraged by the near prospect of being joined in great force in the spring by her allies in Sicily, lately forced by events to acquire their navy. With these reasons for confidence in every quarter, the Lacedaemonians now resolved to throw themselves without reserve into the war, considering that, once it was happily terminated, they would be finally delivered from such dangers as that which would have threatened them from Athens, if she had become mistress of Sicily, and that the overthrow of the Athenians would leave them in quiet enjoyment of the supremacy over all Hellas.

Their king, Agis, accordingly set out at once during this winter with some troops from Decelea, and levied from the allies contributions for the fleet, and turning towards the Malian Gulf exacted a sum of money from the Oetaeans by carrying off most of their cattle in reprisal for their old hostility, and, in spite of the protests and opposition of the Thessalians, forced the Achaeans of Phthiotis and the other subjects of the Thessalians in those parts to give him money and hostages, and deposited the hostages at Corinth, and tried to bring their countrymen into the confederacy. The Lacedaemonians now issued a requisition to the cities for building a hundred ships, fixing their own quota and that of the Boeotians at twenty-five each; that of the Phocians and Locrians together at fifteen; that of the Corinthians at fifteen; that of the Arcadians, Pellenians, and Sicyonians together at ten; and that of the Megarians, Troezenians, Epidaurians, and Hermionians together at ten also; and meanwhile made every other preparation for commencing hostilities by the spring.

In the meantime the Athenians were not idle. During this same winter, as they had determined, they contributed timber and pushed on their ship-building, and fortified Sunium to enable their corn-ships to round it in safety, and evacuated the fort in Laconia which they had built on their way to Sicily; while they also, for economy, cut down any other expenses that seemed unnecessary, and above all kept a careful look-out against the revolt of their confederates.

While both parties were thus engaged, and were as intent upon preparing for the war as they had been at the outset, the Euboeans first of all sent envoys during this winter to Agis to treat of their revolting from Athens. Agis accepted their proposals, and sent for Alcamenes, son of Sthenelaidas, and Melanthus from Lacedaemon, to take the command in Euboea. These accordingly arrived with some three hundred Neodamodes, and Agis began to arrange for their crossing over. But in the meanwhile arrived some Lesbians, who also wished to revolt; and these being supported by the Boeotians, Agis was persuaded to defer acting in the matter of Euboea, and made arrangements for the revolt of the Lesbians, giving them Alcamenes, who was to have sailed to Euboea, as governor, and himself promising them ten ships, and the Boeotians the same number. All this was done without instructions from home, as Agis while at Decelea with the army that he commanded had power to send troops to whatever quarter he pleased, and to levy men and money. During this period, one might say, the allies obeyed him much more than they did the Lacedaemonians in the city, as the force he had with him made him feared at once wherever he went. While Agis was engaged with the Lesbians, the Chians and Erythraeans, who were also ready to revolt, applied, not to him but at Lacedaemon; where they arrived accompanied by an ambassador from Tissaphernes, the commander of King Darius, son of Artaxerxes, in the maritime districts, who invited the Peloponnesians to come over, and promised to maintain their army. The King had lately called upon him for the tribute from his government, for which he was in arrears, being unable to raise it from the Hellenic towns by reason of the Athenians; and he therefore calculated that by weakening the Athenians he should get the tribute better paid, and should also draw the Lacedaemonians into alliance with the King; and by this means, as the King had commanded him, take alive or dead Amorges, the bastard son of Pissuthnes, who was in rebellion on the coast of Caria.

While the Chians and Tissaphernes thus joined to effect the same object, about the same time Calligeitus, son of Laophon, a Megarian, and Timagoras, son of Athenagoras, a Cyzicene, both of them exiles from their country and living at the court of Pharnabazus, son of Pharnaces, arrived at Lacedaemon upon a mission from Pharnabazus, to procure a fleet for the Hellespont; by means of which, if possible, he might himself effect the object of Tissaphernes' ambition and cause the cities in his government to revolt from the Athenians, and so get the tribute, and by his own agency obtain for the King the alliance of the Lacedaemonians.

The emissaries of Pharnabazus and Tissaphernes treating apart, a keen competition now ensued at Lacedaemon as to whether a fleet and army should be sent first to Ionia and Chios, or to the Hellespont. The Lacedaemonians, however, decidedly favoured the Chians and Tissaphernes, who were seconded by Alcibiades, the family friend of Endius, one of the ephors for that year. Indeed, this is how their house got its Laconic name, Alcibiades being the family name of Endius. Nevertheless the Lacedaemonians first sent to Chios Phrynis, one of the Perioeci, to see whether they had as many ships as they said, and whether their city generally was as great as was reported; and upon his bringing word that they had been told the truth, immediately entered into alliance with the Chians and Erythraeans, and voted to send them forty ships, there being already, according to the statement of the Chians, not less than sixty in the island. At first the Lacedaemonians meant to send ten of these forty themselves, with Melanchridas their admiral; but afterwards, an earthquake having occurred, they sent Chalcideus instead of Melanchridas, and instead of the ten ships equipped only five in Laconia. And the winter ended, and with it ended also the nineteenth year of this war of which Thucydides is the historian.

At the beginning of the next summer the Chians were urging that the fleet should be sent off, being afraid that the Athenians, from whom all these embassies were kept a secret, might find out what was going on, and the Lacedaemonians at once sent three Spartans to Corinth to haul the ships as quickly as possible across the Isthmus from the other sea to that on the side of Athens, and to order them all to sail to Chios, those which Agis was equipping for Lesbos not excepted. The number of ships from the allied states was thirty-nine in all.

Meanwhile Calligeitus and Timagoras did not join on behalf of Pharnabazus in the expedition to Chios or give the money–twenty-five talents–which they had brought with them to help in dispatching a force, but determined to sail afterwards with another force by themselves. Agis, on the other hand, seeing the Lacedaemonians bent upon going to Chios first, himself came in to their views; and the allies assembled at Corinth and held a council, in which they decided to sail first to Chios under the command of Chalcideus, who was equipping the five vessels in Laconia, then to Lesbos, under the command of Alcamenes, the same whom Agis had fixed upon, and lastly to go to the Hellespont, where the command was given to Clearchus, son of Ramphias. Meanwhile they would take only half the ships across the Isthmus first, and let those sail off at once, in order that the Athenians might attend less to the departing squadron than to those to be taken across afterwards, as no care had been taken to keep this voyage secret through contempt of the impotence of the Athenians, who had as yet no fleet of any account upon the sea. Agreeably to this determination, twenty-one vessels were at once conveyed across the Isthmus.

They were now impatient to set sail, but the Corinthians were not willing to accompany them until they had celebrated the Isthmian festival, which fell at that time. Upon this Agis proposed to them to save their scruples about breaking the Isthmian truce by taking the expedition upon himself. The Corinthians not consenting to this, a delay ensued, during which the Athenians conceived suspicions of what was preparing at Chios, and sent Aristocrates, one of their generals, and charged them with the fact, and, upon the denial of the Chians, ordered them to send with them a contingent of ships, as faithful confederates. Seven were sent accordingly. The reason of the dispatch of the ships lay in the fact that the mass of the Chians were not privy to the negotiations, while the few who were in the secret did not wish to break with the multitude until they had something positive to lean upon, and no longer expected the Peloponnesians to arrive by reason of their delay.

In the meantime the Isthmian games took place, and the Athenians, who had been also invited, went to attend them, and now seeing more clearly into the designs of the Chians, as soon as they returned to Athens took measures to prevent the fleet putting out from Cenchreae without their knowledge. After the festival the Peloponnesians set sail with twenty-one ships for Chios, under the command of Alcamenes. The Athenians first sailed against them with an equal number, drawing off towards the open sea. The enemy, however, turning back before he had followed them far, the Athenians returned also, not trusting the seven Chian ships which formed part of their number, and afterwards manned thirty-seven vessels in all and chased him on his passage alongshore into Spiraeum, a desert Corinthian port on the edge of the Epidaurian frontier. After losing one ship out at sea, the Peloponnesians got the rest together and brought them to anchor. The Athenians now attacked not only from the sea with their fleet, but also disembarked upon the coast; and a melee ensued of the most confused and violent kind, in which the Athenians disabled most of the enemy's vessels and killed Alcamenes their commander, losing also a few of their own men.

After this they separated, and the Athenians, detaching a sufficient number of ships to blockade those of the enemy, anchored with the rest at the islet adjacent, upon which they proceeded to encamp, and sent to Athens for reinforcements; the Peloponnesians having been joined on the day after the battle by the Corinthians, who came to help the ships, and by the other inhabitants in the vicinity not long afterwards. These saw the difficulty of keeping guard in a desert place, and in their perplexity at first thought of burning the ships, but finally resolved to haul them up on shore and sit down and guard them with their land forces until a convenient opportunity for escaping should present itself. Agis also, on being informed of the disaster, sent them a Spartan of the name of Thermon. The Lacedaemonians first received the news of the fleet having put out from the Isthmus, Alcamenes having been ordered by the ephors to send off a horseman when this took place, and immediately resolved to dispatch their own five vessels under Chalcideus, and Alcibiades with him. But while they were full of this resolution came the second news of the fleet having taken refuge in Spiraeum; and disheartened at their first step in the Ionian war proving a failure, they laid aside the idea of sending the ships from their own country, and even wished to recall some that had already sailed.

Perceiving this, Alcibiades again persuaded Endius and the other ephors to persevere in the expedition, saying that the voyage would be made before the Chians heard of the fleet's misfortune, and that as soon as he set foot in Ionia, he should, by assuring them of the weakness of the Athenians and the zeal of Lacedaemon, have no difficulty in persuading the cities to revolt, as they would readily believe his testimony. He also represented to Endius himself in private that it would be glorious for him to be the means of making Ionia revolt and the King become the ally of Lacedaemon, instead of that honour being left to Agis (Agis, it must be remembered, was the enemy of Alcibiades); and Endius and his colleagues thus persuaded, he put to sea with the five ships and the Lacedaemonian Chalcideus, and made all haste upon the voyage.

About this time the sixteen Peloponnesian ships from Sicily, which had served through the war with Gylippus, were caught on their return off Leucadia and roughly handled by the twenty-seven Athenian vessels under Hippocles, son of Menippus, on the lookout for the ships from Sicily. After losing one of their number, the rest escaped from the Athenians and sailed into Corinth.

Meanwhile Chalcideus and Alcibiades seized all they met with on their voyage, to prevent news of their coming, and let them go at Corycus, the first point which they touched at in the continent. Here they were visited by some of their Chian correspondents and, being urged by them to sail up to the town without announcing their coming, arrived suddenly before Chios. The many were amazed and confounded, while the few had so arranged that the council should be sitting at the time; and after speeches from Chalcideus and Alcibiades stating that many more ships were sailing up, but saying nothing of the fleet being blockaded in Spiraeum, the Chians revolted from the Athenians, and the Erythraeans immediately afterwards. After this three vessels sailed over to Clazomenae, and made that city revolt also; and the Clazomenians immediately crossed over to the mainland and began to fortify Polichna, in order to retreat there, in case of necessity, from the island where they dwelt.

While the revolted places were all engaged in fortifying and preparing for the war, news of Chios speedily reached Athens. The Athenians thought the danger by which they were now menaced great and unmistakable, and that the rest of their allies would not consent to keep quiet after the secession of the greatest of their number. In the consternation of the moment they at once took off the penalty attaching to whoever proposed or put to the vote a proposal for using the thousand talents which they had jealously avoided touching throughout the whole war, and voted to employ them to man a large number of ships, and to send off at once under Strombichides, son of Diotimus, the eight vessels, forming part of the blockading fleet at Spiraeum, which had left the blockade and had returned after pursuing and failing to overtake the vessels with Chalcideus. These were to be followed shortly afterwards by twelve more under Thrasycles, also taken from the blockade. They also recalled the seven Chian vessels, forming part of their squadron blockading the fleet in Spiraeum, and giving the slaves on board their liberty, put the freemen in confinement, and speedily manned and sent out ten fresh ships to blockade the Peloponnesians in the place of all those that had departed, and decided to man thirty more. Zeal was not wanting, and no effort was spared to send relief to Chios.

In the meantime Strombichides with his eight ships arrived at Samos, and, taking one Samian vessel, sailed to Teos and required them to remain quiet. Chalcideus also set sail with twenty-three ships for Teos from Chios, the land forces of the Clazomenians and Erythraeans moving alongshore to support him. Informed of this in time, Strombichides put out from Teos before their arrival, and while out at sea, seeing the number of the ships from Chios, fled towards Samos, chased by the enemy. The Teians at first would not receive the land forces, but upon the flight of the Athenians took them into the town. There they waited for some time for Chalcideus to return from the pursuit, and as time went on without his appearing, began themselves to demolish the wall which the Athenians had built on the land side of the city of the Teians, being assisted by a few of the barbarians who had come up under the command of Stages, the lieutenant of Tissaphernes.

Meanwhile Chalcideus and Alcibiades, after chasing Strombichides into Samos, armed the crews of the ships from Peloponnese and left them at Chios, and filling their places with substitutes from Chios and manning twenty others, sailed off to effect the revolt of Miletus. The wish of Alcibiades, who had friends among the leading men of the Milesians, was to bring over the town before the arrival of the ships from Peloponnese, and thus, by causing the revolt of as many cities as possible with the help of the Chian power and of Chalcideus, to secure the honour for the Chians and himself and Chalcideus, and, as he had promised, for Endius who had sent them out. Not discovered until their voyage was nearly completed, they arrived a little before Strombichides and Thrasycles (who had just come with twelve ships from Athens, and had joined Strombichides in pursuing them), and occasioned the revolt of Miletus. The Athenians sailing up close on their heels with nineteen ships found Miletus closed against them, and took up their station at the adjacent island of Lade. The first alliance between the King and the Lacedaemonians was now concluded immediately upon the revolt of the Milesians, by Tissaphernes and Chalcideus, and was as follows:

The Lacedaemonians and their allies made

a treaty with the King and Tissaphernes upon the terms following:

1. Whatever country or cities the King has, or the King's ancestors had, shall be the king's: and whatever came in to the Athenians from these cities, either money or any other thing, the King and the Lacedaemonians and their allies shall jointly hinder the Athenians from receiving either money or any other thing.

2. The war with the Athenians shall be carried on jointly by the King and by the Lacedaemonians and their allies: and it shall not be lawful to make peace with the Athenians except both agree, the King on his side and the Lacedaemonians and their allies on theirs.

3. If any revolt from the King, they shall be the enemies of the Lacedaemonians and their allies. And if any revolt from the Lacedaemonians and their allies, they shall be the enemies of the King in like manner.

This was the alliance. After this the Chians

immediately manned ten more vessels and sailed for Anaia, in order to gain intelligence of those in Miletus, and also to make the cities revolt. A message, however, reaching them from Chalcideus to tell them to go back again, and that Amorges was at hand with an army by land, they sailed to the temple of Zeus, and there sighting ten more ships sailing up with which Diomedon had started from Athens after Thrasycles, fled, one ship to Ephesus, the rest to Teos. The Athenians took four of their ships empty, the men finding time to escape ashore; the rest took refuge in the city of the Teians; after which the Athenians sailed off to Samos, while the Chians put to sea with their remaining vessels, accompanied by the land forces, and caused Lebedos to revolt, and after it Erae. After this they both returned home, the fleet and the army.

About the same time the twenty ships of the Peloponnesians in Spiraeum, which we left chased to land and blockaded by an equal number of Athenians, suddenly sallied out and defeated the blockading squadron, took four of their ships, and, sailing back to Cenchreae, prepared again for the voyage to Chios and Ionia. Here they were joined by Astyochus as high admiral from Lacedaemon, henceforth invested with the supreme command at sea. The land forces now withdrawing from Teos, Tissaphernes repaired thither in person with an army and completed the demolition of anything that was left of the wall, and so departed. Not long after his departure Diomedon arrived with ten Athenian ships, and, having made a convention by which the Teians admitted him as they had the enemy, coasted along to Erae, and, failing in an attempt upon the town, sailed back again.

About this time took place the rising of the commons at Samos against the upper classes, in concert with some Athenians, who were there in three vessels. The Samian commons put to death some two hundred in all of the upper classes, and banished four hundred more, and themselves took their land and houses; after which the Athenians decreed their independence, being now sure of their fidelity, and the commons henceforth governed the city, excluding the landholders from all share in affairs, and forbidding any of the commons to give his daughter in marriage to them or to take a wife from them in future.

After this, during the same summer, the Chians, whose zeal continued as active as ever, and who even without the Peloponnesians found themselves in sufficient force to effect the revolt of the cities and also wished to have as many companions in peril as possible, made an expedition with thirteen ships of their own to Lesbos; the instructions from Lacedaemon being to go to that island next, and from thence to the Hellespont. Meanwhile the land forces of the Peloponnesians who were with the Chians and of the allies on the spot, moved alongshore for Clazomenae and Cuma, under the command of Eualas, a Spartan; while the fleet under Diniadas, one of the Perioeci, first sailed up to Methymna and caused it to revolt, and, leaving four ships there, with the rest procured the revolt of Mitylene.

In the meantime Astyochus, the Lacedaemonian admiral, set sail from Cenchreae with four ships, as he had intended, and arrived at Chios. On the third day after his arrival, the Athenian ships, twenty-five in number, sailed to Lesbos under Diomedon and Leon, who had lately arrived with a reinforcement of ten ships from Athens. Late in the same day Astyochus put to sea, and taking one Chian vessel with him sailed to Lesbos to render what assistance he could. Arrived at Pyrrha, and from thence the next day at Eresus, he there learned that Mitylene had been taken, almost without a blow, by the Athenians, who had sailed up and unexpectedly put into the harbour, had beaten the Chian ships, and landing and defeating the troops opposed to them had become masters of the city. Informed of this by the Eresians and the Chian ships, which had been left with Eubulus at Methymna, and had fled upon the capture of Mitylene, and three of which he now fell in with, one having been taken by the Athenians, Astyochus did not go on to Mitylene, but raised and armed Eresus, and, sending the heavy infantry from his own ships by land under Eteonicus to Antissa and Methymna, himself proceeded alongshore thither with the ships which he had with him and with the three Chians, in the hope that the Methymnians upon seeing them would be encouraged to persevere in their revolt. As, however, everything went against him in Lesbos, he took up his own force and sailed back to Chios; the land forces on board, which were to have gone to the Hellespont, being also conveyed back to their different cities. After this six of the allied Peloponnesian ships at Cenchreae joined the forces at Chios. The Athenians, after restoring matters to their old state in Lesbos, set sail from thence and took Polichna, the place that the Clazomenians were fortifying on the continent, and carried the inhabitants back to their town upon the island, except the authors of the revolt, who withdrew to Daphnus; and thus Clazomenae became once more Athenian.

The same summer the Athenians in the twenty ships at Lade, blockading Miletus, made a descent at Panormus in the Milesian territory, and killed Chalcideus the Lacedaemonian commander, who had come with a few men against them, and the third day after sailed over and set up a trophy, which, as they were not masters of the country, was however pulled down by the Milesians. Meanwhile Leon and Diomedon with the Athenian fleet from Lesbos issuing from the Oenussae, the isles off Chios, and from their forts of Sidussa and Pteleum in the Erythraeid, and from Lesbos, carried on the war against the Chians from the ships, having on board heavy infantry from the rolls pressed to serve as marines. Landing in Cardamyle and in Bolissus they defeated with heavy loss the Chians that took the field against them and, laying desolate the places in that neighbourhood, defeated the Chians again in another battle at Phanae, and in a third at Leuconium. After this the Chians ceased to meet them in the field, while the Athenians devastated the country, which was beautifully stocked and had remained uninjured ever since the Median wars. Indeed, after the Lacedaemonians, the Chians are the only people that I have known who knew how to be wise in prosperity, and who ordered their city the more securely the greater it grew. Nor was this revolt, in which they might seem to have erred on the side of rashness, ventured upon until they had numerous and gallant allies to share the danger with them, and until they perceived the Athenians after the Sicilian disaster themselves no longer denying the thoroughly desperate state of their affairs. And if they were thrown out by one of the surprises which upset human calculations, they found out their mistake in company with many others who believed, like them, in the speedy collapse of the Athenian power. While they were thus blockaded from the sea and plundered by land, some of the citizens undertook to bring the city over to the Athenians. Apprised of this the authorities took no action themselves, but brought Astyochus, the admiral, from Erythrae, with four ships that he had with him, and considered how they could most quietly, either by taking hostages or by some other means, put an end to the conspiracy.

While the Chians were thus engaged, a thousand Athenian heavy infantry and fifteen hundred Argives (five hundred of whom were light troops furnished with armour by the Athenians), and one thousand of the allies, towards the close of the same summer sailed from Athens in forty-eight ships, some of which were transports, under the command of Phrynichus, Onomacles, and Scironides, and putting into Samos crossed over and encamped at Miletus. Upon this the Milesians came out to the number of eight hundred heavy infantry, with the Peloponnesians who had come with Chalcideus, and some foreign mercenaries of Tissaphernes, Tissaphernes himself and his cavalry, and engaged the Athenians and their allies. While the Argives rushed forward on their own wing with the careless disdain of men advancing against Ionians who would never stand their charge, and were defeated by the Milesians with a loss little short of three hundred men, the Athenians first defeated the Peloponnesians, and driving before them the barbarians and the ruck of the army, without engaging the Milesians, who after the rout of the Argives retreated into the town upon seeing their comrades worsted, crowned their victory by grounding their arms under the very walls of Miletus. Thus, in this battle, the Ionians on both sides overcame the Dorians, the Athenians defeating the Peloponnesians opposed to them, and the Milesians the Argives. After setting up a trophy, the Athenians prepared to draw a wall round the place, which stood upon an isthmus; thinking that, if they could gain Miletus, the other towns also would easily come over to them.

Meanwhile about dusk tidings reached them that the fifty-five ships from Peloponnese and Sicily might be instantly expected. Of these the Siceliots, urged principally by the Syracusan Hermocrates to join in giving the finishing blow to the power of Athens, furnished twenty-two–twenty from Syracuse, and two from Silenus; and the ships that we left preparing in Peloponnese being now ready, both squadrons had been entrusted to Therimenes, a Lacedaemonian, to take to Astyochus, the admiral. They now put in first at Leros the island off Miletus, and from thence, discovering that the Athenians were before the town, sailed into the Iasic Gulf, in order to learn how matters stood at Miletus. Meanwhile Alcibiades came on horseback to Teichiussa in the Milesian territory, the point of the gulf at which they had put in for the night, and told them of the battle in which he had fought in person by the side of the Milesians and Tissaphernes, and advised them, if they did not wish to sacrifice Ionia and their cause, to fly to the relief of Miletus and hinder its investment.

Accordingly they resolved to relieve it the next morning. Meanwhile Phrynichus, the Athenian commander, had received precise intelligence of the fleet from Leros, and when his colleagues expressed a wish to keep the sea and fight it out, flatly refused either to stay himself or to let them or any one else do so if he could help it. Where they could hereafter contend, after full and undisturbed preparation, with an exact knowledge of the number of the enemy's fleet and of the force which they could oppose to him, he would never allow the reproach of disgrace to drive him into a risk that was unreasonable. It was no disgrace for an Athenian fleet to retreat when it suited them: put it as they would, it would be more disgraceful to be beaten, and to expose the city not only to disgrace, but to the most serious danger. After its late misfortunes it could hardly be justified in voluntarily taking the offensive even with the strongest force, except in a case of absolute necessity: much less then without compulsion could it rush upon peril of its own seeking. He told them to take up their wounded as quickly as they could and the troops and stores which they had brought with them, and leaving behind what they had taken from the enemy's country, in order to lighten the ships, to sail off to Samos, and there concentrating all their ships to attack as opportunity served. As he spoke so he acted; and thus not now more than afterwards, nor in this alone but in all that he had to do with, did Phrynichus show himself a man of sense. In this way that very evening the Athenians broke up from before Miletus, leaving their victory unfinished, and the Argives, mortified at their disaster, promptly sailed off home from Samos.

As soon as it was morning the Peloponnesians weighed from Teichiussa and put into Miletus after the departure of the Athenians; they stayed one day, and on the next took with them the Chian vessels originally chased into port with Chalcideus, and resolved to sail back for the tackle which they had put on shore at Teichiussa. Upon their arrival Tissaphernes came to them with his land forces and induced them to sail to Iasus, which was held by his enemy Amorges. Accordingly they suddenly attacked and took Iasus, whose inhabitants never imagined that the ships could be other than Athenian. The Syracusans distinguished themselves most in the action. Amorges, a bastard of Pissuthnes and a rebel from the King, was taken alive and handed over to Tissaphernes, to carry to the King, if he chose, according to his orders: Iasus was sacked by the army, who found a very great booty there, the place being wealthy from ancient date. The mercenaries serving with Amorges the Peloponnesians received and enrolled in their army without doing them any harm, since most of them came from Peloponnese, and handed over the town to Tissaphernes with all the captives, bond or free, at the stipulated price of one Doric stater a head; after which they returned to Miletus. Pedaritus, son of Leon, who had been sent by the Lacedaemonians to take the command at Chios, they dispatched by land as far as Erythrae with the mercenaries taken from Amorges; appointing Philip to remain as governor of Miletus.

Summer was now over. The winter following, Tissaphernes put Iasus in a state of defence, and passing on to Miletus distributed a month's pay to all the ships as he had promised at Lacedaemon, at the rate of an Attic drachma a day for each man. In future, however, he was resolved not to give more than three obols, until he had consulted the King; when if the King should so order he would give, he said, the full drachma. However, upon the protest of the Syracusan general Hermocrates (for as Therimenes was not admiral, but only accompanied them in order to hand over the ships to Astyochus, he made little difficulty about the pay), it was agreed that the amount of five ships' pay should be given over and above the three obols a day for each man; Tissaphernes paying thirty talents a month for fifty-five ships, and to the rest, for as many ships as they had beyond that number, at the same rate.

The same winter the Athenians in Samos, having been joined by thirty-five more vessels from home under Charminus,

Strombichides, and Euctemon, called in their squadron at Chios and all the rest, intending to blockade Miletus with their navy, and to send a fleet and an army against Chios; drawing lots for the respective services. This intention they carried into effect; Strombichides, Onamacles, and Euctemon sailing against Chios, which fell to their lot, with thirty ships and a part of the thousand heavy infantry, who had been to Miletus, in transports; while the rest remained masters of the sea with seventy-four ships at Samos, and advanced upon Miletus.

Meanwhile Astyochus, whom we left at Chios collecting the hostages required in consequence of the conspiracy, stopped upon learning that the fleet with Therimenes had arrived, and that the affairs of the league were in a more flourishing condition, and putting out to sea with ten Peloponnesian and as many Chian vessels, after a futile attack upon Pteleum, coasted on to Clazomenae, and ordered the Athenian party to remove inland to Daphnus, and to join the Peloponnesians, an order in which also joined Tamos the king's lieutenant in Ionia. This order being disregarded, Astyochus made an attack upon the town, which was unwalled, and having failed to take it was himself carried off by a strong gale to Phocaea and Cuma, while the rest of the ships put in at the islands adjacent to Clazomenae–Marathussa, Pele, and Drymussa. Here they were detained eight days by the winds, and, plundering and consuming all the property of the Clazomenians there deposited, put the rest on shipboard and sailed off to Phocaea and Cuma to join Astyochus.

While he was there, envoys arrived from the Lesbians who wished to revolt again. With Astyochus they were successful; but the Corinthians and the other allies being averse to it by reason of their former failure, he weighed anchor and set sail for Chios, where they eventually arrived from different quarters, the fleet having been scattered by a storm. After this Pedaritus, whom we left marching along the coast from Miletus, arrived at Erythrae, and thence crossed over with his army to Chios, where he found also about five hundred soldiers who had been left there by Chalcideus from the five ships with their arms. Meanwhile some Lesbians making offers to revolt, Astyochus urged upon Pedaritus and the Chians that they ought to go with their ships and effect the revolt of Lesbos, and so increase the number of their allies, or, if not successful, at all events harm the Athenians. The Chians, however, turned a deaf ear to this, and Pedaritus flatly refused to give up to him the Chian vessels.

Upon this Astyochus took five Corinthian and one Megarian vessel, with another from Hermione, and the ships which had come with him from Laconia, and set sail for Miletus to assume his command as admiral; after telling the Chians with many threats that he would certainly not come and help them if they should be in need. At Corycus in the Erythraeid he brought to for the night; the Athenian armament sailing from Samos against Chios being only separated from him by a hill, upon the other side of which it brought to; so that neither perceived the other. But a letter arriving in the night from Pedaritus to say that some liberated Erythraean prisoners had come from Samos to betray Erythrae, Astyochus at once put back to Erythrae, and so just escaped falling in with the Athenians. Here Pedaritus sailed over to join him; and after inquiry into the pretended treachery, finding that the whole story had been made up to procure the escape of the men from Samos, they acquitted them of the charge, and sailed away, Pedaritus to Chios and Astyochus to Miletus as he had intended.

Meanwhile the Athenian armament sailing round Corycus fell in with three Chian men-of-war off Arginus, and gave immediate chase. A great storm coming on, the Chians with difficulty took refuge in the harbour; the three Athenian vessels most forward in the pursuit being wrecked and thrown up near the city of Chios, and the crews slain or taken prisoners. The rest of the Athenian fleet took refuge in the harbour called Phoenicus, under Mount Mimas, and from thence afterwards put into Lesbos and prepared for the work of fortification.

The same winter the Lacedaemonian Hippocrates sailed out from Peloponnese with ten Thurian ships under the command of Dorieus, son of Diagoras, and two colleagues, one Laconian and one Syracusan vessel, and arrived at Cnidus, which had already revolted at the instigation of Tissaphernes. When their arrival was known at Miletus, orders came to them to leave half their squadron to guard Cnidus, and with the rest to cruise round Triopium and seize all the merchantmen arriving from Egypt. Triopium is a promontory of Cnidus and sacred to Apollo. This coming to the knowledge of the Athenians, they sailed from Samos and captured the six ships on the watch at Triopium, the crews escaping out of them. After this the Athenians sailed into Cnidus and made an assault upon the town, which was unfortified, and all but took it; and the next day assaulted it again, but with less effect, as the inhabitants had improved their defences during the night, and had been reinforced by the crews escaped from the ships at Triopium. The Athenians now withdrew, and after plundering the Cnidian territory sailed back to Samos.

About the same time Astyochus came to the fleet at Miletus. The Peloponnesian camp was still plentifully supplied, being in receipt of sufficient pay, and the soldiers having still in hand the large booty taken at Iasus. The Milesians also showed great ardour for the war. Nevertheless the Peloponnesians thought the first convention with Tissaphernes, made with Chalcideus, defective, and more advantageous to him than to them, and consequently while Therimenes was still there concluded another, which was as follows:

The convention of the Lacedaemonians and the allies with King Darius and the sons of the King, and with Tissaphernes for a treaty and friendship, as follows:

1. Neither the Lacedaemonians nor the allies of the Lacedaemonians shall make war against or otherwise injure any country or cities that belong to King Darius or did belong to his father or to his ancestors; neither shall the Lacedaemonians nor the allies of the Lacedaemonians exact tribute from such cities. Neither shall King Darius nor any of the subjects of the King make war against or otherwise injure the Lacedaemonians or their allies.

2. If the Lacedaemonians or their allies should require any assistance from the King, or the King from the Lacedaemonians or

their allies, whatever they both agree upon they shall be right in doing.

3. Both shall carry on jointly the war against the Athenians and their allies: and if they make peace, both shall do so jointly.

4. The expense of all troops in the King's country, sent for by the King, shall be borne by the King.

5. If any of the states comprised in this convention with the King attack the King's country, the rest shall stop them and aid the King to the best of their power. And if any in the King's country or in the countries under the King's rule attack the country of the Lacedaemonians or their allies, the King shall stop it and help them to the best of his power.

After this convention Therimenes handed over the fleet to Astyochus, sailed off in a small boat, and was lost. The Athenian armament had now crossed over from Lesbos to Chios, and being master by sea and land began to fortify Delphinium, a place naturally strong on the land side, provided with more than one harbour, and also not far from the city of Chios. Meanwhile the Chians remained inactive. Already defeated in so many battles, they were now also at discord among themselves; the execution of the party of Tydeus, son of Ion, by Pedaritus upon the charge of Atticism, followed by the forcible imposition of an oligarchy upon the rest of the city, having made them suspicious of one another; and they therefore thought neither themselves not the mercenaries under Pedaritus a match for the enemy. They sent, however, to Miletus to beg Astyochus to assist them, which he refused to do, and was accordingly denounced at Lacedaemon by Pedaritus as a traitor. Such was the state of the Athenian affairs at Chios; while their fleet at Samos kept sailing out against the enemy in Miletus, until they found that he would not accept their challenge, and then retired again to Samos and remained quiet.

In the same winter the twenty-seven

ships equipped by the Lacedaemonians for Pharnabazus through the agency of the Megarian Calligeitus, and the Cyzicene Timagoras, put out from Peloponnese and sailed for Ionia about the time of the solstice, under the command of Antisthenes, a Spartan. With them the Lacedaemonians also sent eleven Spartans as advisers to Astyochus; Lichas, son of Arcesilaus, being among the number. Arrived at Miletus, their orders were to aid in generally superintending the good conduct of the war; to send off the above ships or a greater or less number to the Hellespont to Pharnabazus, if they thought proper, appointing Clearchus, son of Ramphias, who sailed with them, to the command; and further, if they thought proper, to make Antisthenes admiral, dismissing Astyochus, whom the letters of Pedaritus had caused to be regarded with suspicion. Sailing accordingly from Malea across the open sea, the squadron touched at Melos and there fell in with ten Athenian ships, three of which they took empty and burned. After this, being afraid that the Athenian vessels escaped from Melos might, as they in fact did, give information of their approach to the Athenians at Samos, they sailed to Crete, and having lengthened their voyage by way of precaution made land at Caunus in Asia, from whence considering themselves in safety they sent a message to the fleet at Miletus for a convoy along the coast.

Meanwhile the Chians and Pedaritus, undeterred by the backwardness of Astyochus, went on sending messengers pressing him to come with all the fleet to assist them against their besiegers, and not to leave the greatest of the allied states in Ionia to be shut up by sea and overrun and pillaged by land. There were more slaves at Chios than in any one other city except Lacedaemon, and being also by reason of their numbers punished more rigorously when they offended, most of them, when they saw the Athenian armament firmly established in the island with a fortified position, immediately deserted to the enemy, and through their knowledge of the country did the greatest mischief. The Chians therefore urged upon Astyochus that it was his duty to assist them, while there was still a hope and a possibility of stopping the enemy's progress, while Delphinium was still in process of fortification and unfinished, and before the completion of a higher rampart which was being added to protect the camp and fleet of their besiegers. Astyochus now saw that the allies also wished it and prepared to go, in spite of his intention to the contrary owing to the threat already referred to.

In the meantime news came from Caunus of the arrival of the twenty-seven ships with the Lacedaemonian commissioners; and Astyochus, postponing everything to the duty of convoying a fleet of that importance, in order to be more able to command the sea, and to the safe conduct of the Lacedaemonians sent as spies over his behaviour, at once gave up going to Chios and set sail for Caunus. As he coasted along he landed at the Meropid Cos and sacked the city, which was unfortified and had been lately laid in ruins by an earthquake, by far the greatest in living memory, and, as the inhabitants had fled to the mountains, overran the country and made booty of all it contained, letting go, however, the free men. From Cos arriving in the night at Cnidus he was constrained by the representations of the Cnidians not to disembark the sailors, but to sail as he was straight against the twenty Athenian vessels, which with Charminus, one of the commanders at Samos, were on the watch for the very twenty-seven ships from Peloponnese which Astyochus was himself sailing to join; the Athenians in Samos having heard from Melos of their approach, and Charminus being on the look-out off Syme, Chalce, Rhodes, and Lycia, as he now heard that they were at Caunus.

Astyochus accordingly sailed as he was to Syme, before he was heard of, in the hope of catching the enemy somewhere out at sea. Rain, however, and foggy weather encountered him, and caused his ships to straggle and get into disorder in the dark. In the morning his fleet had parted company and was most of it still straggling round the island, and the left wing only in sight of Charminus and the Athenians, who took it for the squadron which they were watching for from Caunus, and hastily put out against it with part only of their twenty vessels, and attacking immediately sank three ships and disabled others, and had the advantage in the action until the main body of the fleet unexpectedly hove in sight, when they were surrounded on every side. Upon this they took to flight, and after losing six ships with the rest escaped to Teutlussa or Beet Island, and from thence to Halicarnassus. After this the Peloponnesians put into Cnidus and, being joined by the twenty-seven ships from Caunus, sailed all together and set up a trophy in Syme, and then returned to anchor at Cnidus.

As soon as the Athenians knew of the sea-fight, they sailed with all the ships at Samos to Syme, and, without attacking or being attacked by the fleet at Cnidus, took the ships' tackle left at Syme, and touching at Lorymi on the mainland sailed back to Samos. Meanwhile the Peloponnesian ships, being now all at Cnidus, underwent such repairs as were needed; while the eleven Lacedaemonian commissioners conferred with Tissaphernes, who had come to meet them, upon the points which did not satisfy them in the past transactions, and upon the best and mutually most advantageous manner of conducting the war in future. The severest critic of the present proceedings was Lichas, who said that neither of the treaties could stand, neither that of Chalcideus, nor that of Therimenes; it being monstrous that the King should at this date pretend to the possession of all the country formerly ruled by himself or by his ancestors–a pretension which implicitly put back under the yoke all the islands–Thessaly, Locris, and everything as far as Boeotia–and made the Lacedaemonians give to the Hellenes instead of liberty a Median master. He therefore invited Tissaphernes to conclude another and a better treaty, as they certainly would not recognize those existing and did not want any of his pay upon such conditions. This offended Tissaphernes so much that he went away in a rage without settling anything.

Chapter Twenty Five

Twentieth and Twenty-first Years of the War–Intrigues of Alcibiades–Withdrawal of the Persian Subsidies–Oligarchical Coup d'Etat at Athens–Patriotism of the Army at Samos

THE PELOPONNESIANS NOW determined to sail to Rhodes, upon the invitation of some of the principal men there, hoping to gain an island powerful by the number of its seamen and by its land forces, and also thinking that they would be able to maintain their fleet from their own confederacy, without having to ask for money from Tissaphernes. They accordingly at once set sail that same winter from Cnidus, and first put in with ninety-four ships at Camirus in the Rhodian country, to the great alarm of the mass of the inhabitants, who were not privy to the intrigue, and who consequently fled, especially as the town was unfortified. They were afterwards, however, assembled by the Lacedaemonians together with the inhabitants of the two other towns of Lindus and Ialysus; and the Rhodians were persuaded to revolt from the Athenians and the island went over to the Peloponnesians. Meanwhile the Athenians had received the alarm and set sail with the fleet from Samos to forestall them, and came within sight of the island, but being a little too late sailed off for the moment to Chalce, and from thence to Samos, and subsequently waged war against Rhodes, issuing from Chalce, Cos, and Samos.

The Peloponnesians now levied a contribution of thirty-two talents from the Rhodians, after which they hauled their ships ashore and for eighty days remained inactive. During this time, and even earlier, before they removed to Rhodes, the following intrigues took place. After the death of Chalcideus and the battle at Miletus, Alcibiades began to be suspected by the Peloponnesians; and Astyochus received from Lacedaemon an order from them to put him to death, he being the personal enemy of Agis, and in other respects thought unworthy of confidence. Alcibiades in his alarm first withdrew to Tissaphernes, and immediately began to do all he could with him to injure the Peloponnesian cause. Henceforth becoming his adviser in everything, he cut down the pay from an Attic drachma to three obols a day, and even this not paid too regularly; and told

Tissaphernes to say to the Peloponnesians that the Athenians, whose maritime experience was of an older date than their own, only gave their men three obols, not so much from poverty as to prevent their seamen being corrupted by being too well off, and injuring their condition by spending money upon enervating indulgences, and also paid their crews irregularly in order to have a security against their deserting in the arrears which they would leave behind them. He also told Tissaphernes to bribe the captains and generals of the cities, and so to obtain their connivance–an expedient which succeeded with all except the Syracusans, Hermocrates alone opposing him on behalf of the whole confederacy. Meanwhile the cities asking for money Alcibiades sent off, by roundly telling them in the name of Tissaphernes that it was great impudence in the Chians, the richest people in Hellas, not content with being defended by a foreign force, to expect others to risk not only their lives but their money as well in behalf of their freedom; while the other cities, he said, had had to pay largely to Athens before their rebellion, and could not justly refuse to contribute as much or even more now for their own selves. He also pointed out that Tissaphernes was at present carrying on the war at his own charges, and had good cause for economy, but that as soon as he received remittances from the king he would give them their pay in full and do what was reasonable for the cities.

Alcibiades further advised Tissaphernes not to be in too great a hurry to end the war, or to let himself be persuaded to bring up the Phoenician fleet which he was equipping, or to provide pay for more Hellenes, and thus put the power by land and sea into the same hands; but to leave each of the contending parties in possession of one element, thus enabling the king when he found one troublesome to call in the other. For if the command of the sea and land were united in one hand, he would not know where to turn for help to overthrow the dominant power; unless he at last chose to stand up himself, and go through with the struggle at great expense and hazard. The cheapest plan was to let the Hellenes wear each other out, at a small share of the expense and without risk to himself. Besides, he would find the Athenians the most convenient partners in empire as they did not aim at conquests on shore, and carried on the war upon principles and with a practice most advantageous to the King; being prepared to combine to conquer the sea for Athens, and for the King all the Hellenes inhabiting his country, whom the Peloponnesians, on the contrary, had come to liberate. Now it was not likely that the Lacedaemonians would free the Hellenes from the Hellenic Athenians, without freeing them also from the barbarian Mede, unless overthrown by him in the meanwhile. Alcibiades therefore urged him to wear them both out at first, and, after docking the Athenian power as much as he could, forthwith to rid the country of the Peloponnesians. In the main Tissaphernes approved of this policy, so far at least as could be conjectured from his behaviour; since he now gave his confidence to Alcibiades in recognition of his good advice, and kept the Peloponnesians short of money, and would not let them fight at sea, but ruined their cause by pretending that the Phoenician fleet would arrive, and that they would thus be enabled to contend with the odds in their favour, and so made their navy lose its efficiency, which had been very remarkable, and generally betrayed a coolness in the war that was too plain to be mistaken.

Alcibiades gave this advice to Tissaphernes and the King, with whom he then was, not merely because he thought it really the best, but because he was studying means to effect his restoration to his country, well knowing that if he did not destroy it he might one day hope to persuade the Athenians to recall him, and thinking that his best chance of persuading them lay in letting them see that he possessed the favour of Tissaphernes. The event proved him to be right. When the Athenians at Samos found that he had influence with Tissaphernes, principally of their own motion (though partly also through Alcibiades himself sending word to their chief men to tell the best men in the army that, if there were only an oligarchy in the place of the rascally democracy that had banished him, he would be glad to return to his country and to make Tissaphernes their friend), the captains and chief men in the armament at once embraced the idea of subverting the democracy.

The design was first mooted in the camp, and afterwards from thence reached the city. Some persons crossed over from Samos and had an interview with Alcibiades, who immediately offered to make first Tissaphernes, and afterwards the King, their friend, if they would give up the democracy and make it possible for the King to trust them. The higher class, who also suffered most severely from the war, now conceived great hopes of getting the government into their own hands, and of triumphing over the enemy. Upon their return to Samos the emissaries formed their partisans into a club, and openly told the mass of the armament that the King would be their friend, and would provide them with money, if Alcibiades were restored and the democracy abolished. The multitude, if at first irritated by these intrigues, were nevertheless kept quiet by the advantageous prospect of the pay from the King; and the oligarchical conspirators, after making this communication to the people, now re-examined the proposals of Alcibiades among themselves, with most of their associates. Unlike the rest, who thought them advantageous and trustworthy, Phrynichus, who was still general, by no means approved of the proposals. Alcibiades, he rightly thought, cared no more for an oligarchy than for a democracy, and only sought to change the institutions of his country in order to get himself recalled by his associates; while for themselves their one object should be to avoid civil discord. It was not the King's interest, when the Peloponnesians were now their equals at sea, and in possession of some of the chief cities in his empire, to go out of his way to side with the Athenians whom he did not trust, when he might make friends of the Peloponnesians who had never injured him. And as for the allied states to whom oligarchy was now offered, because the democracy was to be put down at Athens, he well knew that this would not make the rebels come in any the sooner, or confirm the loyal in their allegiance; as the allies would never prefer servitude with an oligarchy or democracy to freedom with the constitution which they actually enjoyed, to whichever type it belonged. Besides, the cities thought that the so-called better classes would prove just as oppressive as the commons, as being those who originated, proposed, and for the most part benefited from the acts of the commons injurious to the confederates. Indeed, if it depended on the better classes, the confederates would be put to death without trial and with violence; while the commons were their refuge and the chastiser of these men. This he positively knew that the cities had learned by experience, and that such was their opinion. The propositions of Alcibiades, and the intrigues now in progress, could therefore never meet with his approval.

However, the members of the club assembled, agreeably to their original determination, accepted what was proposed, and prepared to send Pisander and others on an embassy to Athens to treat for the restoration of Alcibiades and the abolition of the democracy in the city, and thus to make Tissaphernes the friend of the Athenians.

Phrynichus now saw that there would be a proposal to restore Alcibiades, and that the Athenians would consent to it; and fearing after what he had said against it that Alcibiades, if restored, would revenge himself upon him for his opposition, had recourse to the following expedient. He sent a secret letter to the Lacedaemonian admiral Astyochus, who was still in the neighbourhood of Miletus, to tell him that Alcibiades was ruining their cause by making Tissaphernes the friend of the Athenians, and containing an express revelation of the rest of the intrigue, desiring to be excused if he sought to harm his enemy even at the expense of the interests of his country. However, Astyochus, instead of thinking of punishing Alcibiades, who, besides, no longer ventured within his reach as formerly, went up to him and Tissaphernes at Magnesia, communicated to them the letter from Samos, and turned informer, and, if report may be trusted, became the paid creature of Tissaphernes, undertaking to inform him as to this and all other matters; which was also the reason why he did not remonstrate more strongly against the pay not being given in full. Upon this Alcibiades instantly sent to the authorities at Samos a letter against Phrynichus, stating what he had done, and requiring that he should be put to death. Phrynichus distracted, and placed in the utmost peril by the denunciation, sent again to Astyochus, reproaching him with having so ill kept the secret of his previous letter, and saying that he was now prepared to give them an opportunity of destroying the whole Athenian armament at Samos; giving a detailed account of the means which he should employ, Samos being unfortified, and pleading that, being in danger of his life on their account, he could not now be blamed for doing this or anything else to escape being destroyed by his mortal enemies. This also Astyochus revealed to Alcibiades.

Meanwhile Phrynichus having had timely

notice that he was playing him false, and that a letter on the subject was on the point of arriving from Alcibiades, himself anticipated the news, and told the army that the enemy, seeing that Samos was unfortified and the fleet not all stationed within the harbour, meant to attack the camp, that he could be certain of this intelligence, and that they must fortify Samos as quickly as possible, and generally look to their defences. It will be remembered that he was general, and had himself authority to carry out these measures. Accordingly they addressed themselves to the work of fortification, and Samos was thus fortified sooner than it would otherwise have been. Not long afterwards came the letter from Alcibiades, saying that the army was betrayed by Phrynichus, and the enemy about to attack it. Alcibiades, however, gained no credit, it being thought that he was in the secret of the enemy's designs, and had tried to fasten them upon Phrynichus, and to make out that he was their accomplice, out of hatred; and consequently far from hurting him he rather bore witness to what he had said by this intelligence.

After this Alcibiades set to work to persuade Tissaphernes to become the friend of the Athenians. Tissaphernes, although afraid of the Peloponnesians because they had more ships in Asia than the Athenians, was yet disposed to be persuaded if he could, especially after his quarrel with the Peloponnesians at Cnidus about the treaty of Therimenes. The quarrel had already taken place, as the Peloponnesians were by this time actually at Rhodes; and in it the original argument of Alcibiades touching the liberation of all the towns by the Lacedaemonians had been verified by the declaration of Lichas that it was impossible to submit to a convention which made the King master of all the states at any former time ruled by himself or by his fathers.

While Alcibiades was besieging the favour

of Tissaphernes with an earnestness proportioned to the greatness of the issue, the Athenian envoys who had been dispatched from Samos with Pisander arrived at Athens, and made a speech before the people, giving a brief summary of their views, and particularly insisting that, if Alcibiades were recalled and the democratic constitution changed, they could have the King as their ally, and would be able to overcome the Peloponnesians. A number of speakers opposed them on the question of the democracy, the enemies of Alcibiades cried out against the scandal of a restoration to be effected by a violation of the constitution, and the Eumolpidae and Ceryces protested in behalf of the mysteries, the cause of his banishment, and called upon the gods to avert his recall; when Pisander, in the midst of much opposition and abuse, came forward, and taking each of his opponents aside asked him the following question: In the face of the fact that the Peloponnesians had as many ships as their own confronting them at sea, more cities in alliance with them, and the King and Tissaphernes to supply them with money, of which the Athenians had none left, had he any hope of saving the state, unless someone could induce the King to come over to their side? Upon their replying that they had not, he then plainly said to them: "This we cannot have unless we have a more moderate form of government, and put the offices into fewer hands, and so gain the King's confidence, and forthwith restore Alcibiades, who is the only man living that can bring this about. The safety of the state, not the form of its government, is for the moment the most pressing question, as we can always change afterwards whatever we do not like."

The people were at first highly irritated at the mention of an oligarchy, but upon understanding clearly from Pisander that this was the only resource left, they took counsel of their fears, and promised themselves some day to change the government again, and gave way. They accordingly voted that Pisander should sail with ten others and make the best arrangement that they could with Tissaphernes and Alcibiades. At the same time the people, upon a false accusation of Pisander, dismissed Phrynichus from his post together with his colleague Scironides, sending Diomedon and Leon to replace them in the command of the fleet. The accusation was that Phrynichus had betrayed Iasus and Amorges; and Pisander brought it because he thought him a man unfit for the business now in hand with Alcibiades. Pisander also went the round of all the clubs already existing in the city for help in lawsuits and elections, and urged them to draw together and to unite their efforts for the overthrow of the democracy; and after taking all other measures required by the circumstances, so that no time might be lost, set off with his ten companions on his voyage to Tissaphernes.

In the same winter Leon and Diomedon, who had by this time joined the fleet, made an attack upon Rhodes. The ships of the Peloponnesians they found hauled up on shore, and, after making a descent upon the coast and defeating the Rhodians who appeared in the field against them, withdrew to Chalce and made that place their base of operations instead of Cos, as they could better observe from thence if the Peloponnesian fleet put out to sea. Meanwhile Xenophantes, a Laconian, came to Rhodes from Pedaritus at Chios, with the news that the fortification of the Athenians was now finished, and that, unless the whole Peloponnesian fleet came to the rescue, the cause in Chios must be lost. Upon this they resolved to go to his relief. In the meantime Pedaritus, with the mercenaries that he had with him and the whole force of the Chians, made an assault upon the work round the Athenian ships and took a portion of it, and got possession of some vessels that were hauled up on shore, when the Athenians sallied out to the rescue, and first routing the Chians, next defeated the remainder of the force round Pedaritus, who was himself killed, with many of the Chians, a great number of arms being also taken.

After this the Chians were besieged even more straitly than before by land and sea, and the famine in the place was great. Meanwhile the Athenian envoys with Pisander arrived at the court of Tissaphernes, and conferred with him about the proposed agreement. However, Alcibiades, not being altogether sure of Tissaphernes (who feared the Peloponnesians more than the Athenians, and besides wished to wear out both parties, as Alcibiades himself had recommended), had recourse to the following stratagem to make the treaty between the Athenians and Tissaphernes miscarry by reason of the magnitude of his demands. In my opinion Tissaphernes desired this result, fear being his motive; while Alcibiades, who now saw that Tissaphernes was determined not to treat on any terms, wished the Athenians to think, not that he was unable to persuade Tissaphernes, but that after the latter had been persuaded and was willing to join them, they had not conceded enough to him. For the demands of Alcibiades, speaking for Tissaphernes, who was present, were so extravagant that the Athenians, although for a long while they agreed to whatever he asked, yet had to bear the blame of failure: he required the cession of the whole of Ionia, next of the islands adjacent, besides other concessions, and these passed without opposition; at last, in the third interview, Alcibiades, who now feared a complete discovery of his inability, required them to allow the King to build ships and sail along his own coast wherever and with as many as he pleased. Upon this the Athenians would yield no further, and concluding that there was nothing to be done, but that they had been deceived by Alcibiades, went away in a passion and proceeded to Samos.

Tissaphernes immediately after this, in the same winter, proceeded along shore to Caunus, desiring to bring the Peloponnesian fleet back to Miletus, and to supply them with pay, making a fresh convention upon such terms as he could get, in order not to bring matters to an absolute breach between them. He was afraid that if many of their ships were left without pay they would be compelled to engage and be defeated, or that their vessels being left without hands the Athenians would attain their objects without his assistance. Still more he feared that the Peloponnesians might ravage the continent in search of supplies. Having calculated and considered all this, agreeably to his plan of keeping the two sides equal, he now sent for the Peloponnesians and gave them pay, and concluded with them a third treaty in words following:

In the thirteenth year of the reign of Darius,

while Alexippidas was ephor at Lacedaemon, a convention was concluded in the plain of the Maeander by the Lacedaemonians and their allies with Tissaphernes, Hieramenes, and the sons of Pharnaces, concerning the affairs of the King and of the Lacedaemonians and their allies.

1. The country of the King in Asia shall be the King's, and the King shall treat his own country as he pleases.

2. The Lacedaemonians and their allies shall not invade or injure the King's country: neither shall the King invade or injure that of the Lacedaemonians or of their allies. If any of the Lacedaemonians or of their allies invade or injure the King's country, the Lacedaemonians and their allies shall prevent it: and if any from the King's country invade or injure the country of the Lacedaemonians or of their allies, the King shall prevent it.

3. Tissaphernes shall provide pay for the ships now present, according to the

agreement, until the arrival of the King's vessels: but after the arrival of the King's vessels the Lacedaemonians and their allies may pay their own ships if they wish it. If, however, they choose to receive the pay from Tissaphernes, Tissaphernes shall furnish it: and the Lacedaemonians and their allies shall repay him at the end of the war such moneys as they shall have received.

4. After the vessels have arrived, the ships of the Lacedaemonians and of their allies and those of the King shall carry on the war jointly, according as Tissaphernes and the Lacedaemonians and their allies shall think best. If they wish to make peace with the Athenians, they shall make peace also jointly.

This was the treaty. After this Tissaphernes prepared to bring up the Phoenician fleet according to agreement, and to make good his other promises, or at all events wished to make it appear that he was so preparing.

Winter was now drawing towards its

close, when the Boeotians took Oropus by treachery, though held by an Athenian garrison. Their accomplices in this were some of the Eretrians and of the Oropians themselves, who were plotting the revolt of Euboea, as the place was exactly opposite Eretria, and while in Athenian hands was necessarily a source of great annoyance to Eretria and the rest of Euboea. Oropus being in their hands, the Eretrians now came to Rhodes to invite the Peloponnesians into Euboea. The latter, however, were rather bent on the relief of the distressed Chians, and accordingly put out to sea and sailed with all their ships from Rhodes. Off Triopium they sighted the Athenian fleet out at sea sailing from Chalce, and, neither attacking the other, arrived, the latter at Samos, the Peloponnesians at Miletus, seeing that it was no longer possible to relieve Chios without a battle. And this winter ended, and with it ended the twentieth year of this war of which Thucydides is the historian.

Early in the spring of the summer following, Dercyllidas, a Spartan, was sent with a small force by land to the Hellespont to effect the revolt of Abydos, which is a Milesian colony; and the Chians, while Astyochus was at a loss how to help them, were compelled to fight at sea by the pressure of the siege. While Astyochus was still at Rhodes they had received from Miletus, as their commander after the death of Pedaritus, a Spartan named Leon, who had come out with Antisthenes, and twelve vessels which had been on guard at Miletus, five of which were Thurian, four Syracusans, one from Anaia, one Milesian, and one Leon's own. Accordingly the Chians marched out in mass and took up a strong position, while thirty-six of their ships put out and engaged thirty-two of the Athenians; and after a tough fight, in which the Chians and their allies had rather the best of it, as it was now late, retired to their city.

Immediately after this Dercyllidas arrived by land from Miletus; and Abydos in the Hellespont revolted to him and Pharnabazus, and Lampsacus two days later. Upon receipt of this news Strombichides hastily sailed from Chios with twenty-four Athenian ships, some transports carrying heavy infantry being of the number, and defeating the Lampsacenes who came out against him, took Lampsacus, which was unfortified, at the first assault, and making prize of the slaves and goods restored the freemen to their homes, and went on to Abydos. The inhabitants, however, refusing to capitulate, and his assaults failing to take the place, he sailed over to the coast opposite, and appointed Sestos, the town in the Chersonese held by the Medes at a former period in this history, as the centre for the defence of the whole Hellespont.

In the meantime the Chians commanded the sea more than before; and the Peloponnesians at Miletus and Astyochus, hearing of the sea-fight and of the departure of the squadron with Strombichides, took fresh courage. Coasting along with two vessels to Chios, Astyochus took the ships from that place, and now moved with the whole fleet upon Samos, from whence, however, he sailed back to Miletus, as the Athenians did not put out against him, owing to their suspicions of one another. For it was about this time, or even before, that the democracy was put down at Athens. When Pisander and the envoys returned from Tissaphernes to Samos they at once strengthened still further their interest in the army itself, and instigated the upper class in Samos to join them in establishing an oligarchy, the very form of government which a party of them had lately risen to avoid. At the same time the Athenians at Samos, after a consultation among themselves, determined to let Alcibiades alone, since he refused to join them, and besides was not the man for an oligarchy; and now that they were once embarked, to see for themselves how they could best prevent the ruin of their cause, and meanwhile to sustain the war, and to contribute without stint money and all else that might be required from their own private estates, as they would henceforth labour for themselves alone.

After encouraging each other in these resolutions, they now at once sent off half the envoys and Pisander to do what was necessary at Athens (with instructions to establish oligarchies on their way in all the subject cities which they might touch at), and dispatched the other half in different directions to the other dependencies. Diitrephes also, who was in the neighbourhood of Chios, and had been elected to the command of the Thracian towns, was sent off to his government, and arriving at Thasos abolished the democracy there. Two months, however, had not elapsed after his departure before the Thasians began to fortify their town, being already tired of an aristocracy with Athens, and in daily expectation of freedom from Lacedaemon. Indeed there was a party of them (whom the Athenians had banished), with the Peloponnesians, who with their friends in the town were already making every exertion to bring a squadron, and to effect the revolt of Thasos; and this party thus saw exactly what they most wanted done, that is to say, the reformation of the government without risk, and the abolition of the democracy which would have opposed them. Things at Thasos thus turned out just the contrary to what the oligarchical conspirators at Athens expected; and the same in my opinion was the case in many of the other dependencies; as the cities no sooner got a moderate government and liberty of action, than they went on to absolute freedom without being at all seduced by the show of reform offered by the Athenians.

Pisander and his colleagues on their voyage alongshore abolished, as had been determined, the democracies in the cities, and also took some heavy infantry from certain places as their allies, and so came to Athens. Here they found most of the work already done by their associates. Some of the younger men had banded together, and secretly assassinated one Androcles, the chief leader of the commons, and mainly responsible for the banishment of Alcibiades; Androcles being singled out both because he was a popular leader and because they sought by his death to recommend themselves to Alcibiades, who was, as they supposed, to be recalled, and to make Tissaphernes their friend. There were also some other obnoxious persons whom they secretly did away with in the same manner. Meanwhile their cry in public was that no pay should be given except to persons serving in the war, and that not more than five thousand should share in the government, and those such as were most able to serve the state in person and in purse.

But this was a mere catchword for the multitude, as the authors of the revolution were really to govern. However, the Assembly and the Council of the Bean still met notwithstanding, although they discussed nothing that was not approved of by the conspirators, who both supplied the speakers and reviewed in advance what they were to say. Fear, and the sight of the numbers of the conspirators, closed the mouths of the rest; or if any ventured to rise in opposition, he was presently put to death in some convenient way, and there was neither search for the murderers nor justice to be had against them if suspected; but the people remained motionless, being so thoroughly cowed that men thought themselves lucky to escape violence, even when they held their tongues. An exaggerated belief in the numbers of the conspirators also demoralized the people, rendered helpless by the magnitude of the city, and by their want of intelligence with each other, and being without means of finding out what those numbers really were. For the same reason it was impossible for any one to open his grief to a neighbour and to concert measures to defend himself, as he would have had to speak either to one whom he did not know, or whom he knew but did not trust. Indeed all the popular party approached each other with suspicion, each thinking his neighbour concerned in what was going on, the conspirators having in their ranks persons whom no one could ever have believed capable of joining an oligarchy; and these it was who made the many so suspicious, and so helped to procure impunity for the few, by confirming the commons in their mistrust of one another.

At this juncture arrived Pisander and his colleagues, who lost no time in doing the rest. First they assembled the people, and moved to elect ten commissioners with full powers to frame a constitution, and that when this was done they should on an appointed day lay before the people their opinion as to the best mode of governing the city. Afterwards, when the day arrived, the conspirators enclosed the assembly in Colonus, a temple of Poseidon, a little more than a mile outside the city; when the commissioners simply brought forward this single motion, that any Athenian might propose with impunity whatever measure he pleased, heavy penalties being imposed upon any who should indict for illegality, or otherwise molest him for so doing. The way thus cleared, it was now plainly declared that all tenure of office and receipt of pay under the existing institutions were at an end, and that five men must be elected as presidents, who should in their turn elect one hundred, and each of the hundred three apiece; and that this body thus made up to four hundred should enter the council chamber with full powers and govern as they judged best, and should convene the five thousand whenever they pleased.

The man who moved this resolution was Pisander, who was throughout the chief ostensible agent in putting down the democracy. But he who concerted the whole affair, and prepared the way for the catastrophe, and who had given the greatest thought to the matter, was Antiphon, one of the best men of his day in Athens; who, with a head to contrive measures and a tongue to recommend them, did not willingly come forward in the assembly or upon any public scene, being ill looked upon by the multitude owing to his reputation for talent; and who yet was the one man best able to aid in the courts, or before the assembly, the suitors who required his opinion. Indeed, when he was afterwards himself tried for his life on the charge of having been concerned in setting up this very government, when the Four Hundred were overthrown and hardly dealt with by the commons, he made what would seem to be the best defence of any known up to my time. Phrynichus also went beyond all others in his zeal for the oligarchy. Afraid of Alcibiades, and assured that he was no stranger to his intrigues with Astyochus at

Samos, he held that no oligarchy was ever likely to restore him, and once embarked in the enterprise, proved, where danger was to be faced, by far the staunchest of them all. Theramenes, son of Hagnon, was also one of the foremost of the subverters of the democracy–a man as able in council as in debate. Conducted by so many and by such sagacious heads, the enterprise, great as it was, not unnaturally went forward; although it was no light matter to deprive the Athenian people of its freedom, almost a hundred years after the deposition of the tyrants, when it had been not only not subject to any during the whole of that period, but accustomed during more than half of it to rule over subjects of its own.

The assembly ratified the proposed constitution, without a single opposing voice, and was then dissolved; after which the Four Hundred were brought into the council chamber in the following way. On account of the enemy at Decelea, all the Athenians were constantly on the wall or in the ranks at the various military posts. On that day the persons not in the secret were allowed to go home as usual, while orders were given to the accomplices of the conspirators to hang about, without making any demonstration, at some little distance from the posts, and in case of any opposition to what was being done, to seize the arms and put it down. There were also some Andrians and Tenians, three hundred Carystians, and some of the settlers in Aegina come with their own arms for this very purpose, who had received similar instructions. These dispositions completed, the Four Hundred went, each with a dagger concealed about his person, accompanied by one hundred and twenty Hellenic youths, whom they employed wherever violence was needed, and appeared before the Councillors of the Bean in the council chamber, and told them to take their pay and be gone; themselves bringing it for the whole of the residue of their term of office, and giving it to them as they went out.

Upon the Council withdrawing in this way without venturing any objection, and the rest of the citizens making no movement, the Four Hundred entered the council chamber, and for the present contented themselves with drawing lots for their Prytanes, and making their prayers and sacrifices to the gods upon entering office, but afterwards departed widely from the democratic system of government, and except that on account of Alcibiades they did not recall the exiles, ruled the city by force; putting to death some men, though not many, whom they thought it convenient to remove, and imprisoning and banishing others. They also sent to Agis, the Lacedaemonian king, at Decelea, to say that they desired to make peace, and that he might reasonably be more disposed to treat now that he had them to deal with instead of the inconstant commons.

Agis, however, did not believe in the

tranquillity of the city, or that the commons would thus in a moment give up their ancient liberty, but thought that the sight of a large Lacedaemonian force would be sufficient to excite them if they were not already in commotion, of which he was by no means certain. He accordingly gave to the envoys of the Four Hundred an answer which held out no hopes of an accommodation, and sending for large reinforcements from Peloponnese, not long afterwards, with these and his garrison from Decelea, descended to the very walls of Athens; hoping either that civil disturbances might help to subdue them to his terms, or that, in the confusion to be expected within and without the city, they might even surrender without a blow being struck; at all events he thought he would succeed in seizing the Long Walls, bared of their defenders. However, the Athenians saw him come close up, without making the least disturbance within the city; and sending out their cavalry, and a number of their heavy infantry, light troops, and archers, shot down some of his soldiers who approached too near, and got possession of some arms and dead. Upon this Agis, at last convinced, led his army back again and, remaining with his own troops in the old position at Decelea, sent the reinforcement back home, after a few days' stay in Attica. After this the Four Hundred persevering sent another embassy to Agis, and now meeting with a better reception, at his suggestion dispatched envoys to Lacedaemon to negotiate a treaty, being desirous of making peace.

They also sent ten men to Samos to reassure the army, and to explain that the oligarchy was not established for the hurt of the city or the citizens, but for the salvation of the country at large; and that there were five thousand, not four hundred only, concerned; although, what with their expeditions and employments abroad, the Athenians had never yet assembled to discuss a question important enough to bring five thousand of them together. The emissaries were also told what to say upon all other points, and were so sent off immediately after the establishment of the new government, which feared, as it turned out justly, that the mass of seamen would not be willing to remain under the oligarchical constitution, and, the evil beginning there, might be the means of their overthrow.

Indeed at Samos the question of the oligarchy had already entered upon a new phase, the following events having taken place just at the time that the Four Hundred were conspiring. That part of the Samian population which has been mentioned as rising against the upper class, and as being the democratic party, had now turned round, and yielding to the solicitations of Pisander during his visit, and of the Athenians in the conspiracy at Samos, had bound themselves by oaths to the number of three hundred, and were about to fall upon the rest of their fellow citizens, whom they now in their turn regarded as the democratic party. Meanwhile they put to death one Hyperbolus, an Athenian, a pestilent fellow that had been ostracized, not from fear of his influence or position, but because he was a rascal and a disgrace to the city; being aided in this by Charminus, one of the generals, and by some of the Athenians with them, to whom they had sworn friendship, and with whom they perpetrated other acts of the kind, and now determined to attack the people. The latter got wind of what was coming, and told two of the generals, Leon and Diomedon, who, on account of the credit which they enjoyed with the commons, were unwilling supporters of the oligarchy; and also Thrasybulus and Thrasyllus, the former a captain of a galley, the latter serving with the heavy infantry, besides certain others who had ever been thought most opposed to the conspirators, entreating them not to look on and see them destroyed, and Samos, the sole remaining stay of their empire, lost to the Athenians. Upon hearing this, the persons whom they addressed now went round the soldiers one by one, and urged them to resist, especially the crew of the Paralus, which was made up entirely of Athenians and freemen, and had from time out of mind been enemies of oligarchy, even when there was no such thing existing; and Leon and Diomedon left behind some ships for their protection in case of their sailing away anywhere themselves. Accordingly, when the Three Hundred attacked the people, all these came to the rescue, and foremost of all the crew of the Paralus; and the Samian commons gained the victory, and putting to death some thirty of the Three Hundred, and banishing three others of the ringleaders, accorded an amnesty to the rest, and lived together under a democratic government for the future.

The ship Paralus, with Chaereas, son of Archestratus, on board, an Athenian who had taken an active part in the revolution, was now without loss of time sent off by the Samians and the army to Athens to report what had occurred; the fact that the Four Hundred were in power not being yet known. When they sailed into harbour the Four Hundred immediately arrested two or three of the Parali and, taking the vessel from the rest, shifted them into a troopship and set them to keep guard round Euboea. Chaereas, however, managed to secrete himself as soon as he saw how things stood, and returning to Samos, drew a picture to the soldiers of the horrors enacting at Athens, in which everything was exaggerated; saying that all were punished with stripes, that no one could say a word against the holders of power, that the soldiers' wives and children were outraged, and that it was intended to seize and shut up the relatives of all in the army at Samos who were not of the government's way of thinking, to be put to death in case of their disobedience; besides a host of other injurious inventions.

On hearing this the first thought of the army was to fall upon the chief authors of the oligarchy and upon all the rest concerned. Eventually, however, they desisted from this idea upon the men of moderate views opposing it and warning them against ruining their cause, with the enemy close at hand and ready for battle. After this, Thrasybulus, son of Lycus, and Thrasyllus, the chief leaders in the revolution, now wishing in the most public manner to change the government at Samos to a democracy, bound all the soldiers by the most tremendous oaths, and those of the oligarchical party more than any, to accept a democratic government, to be united, to prosecute actively the war with the Peloponnesians, and to be enemies of the Four Hundred, and to hold no communication with them. The same oath was also taken by all the Samians of full age; and the soldiers associated the Samians in all their affairs and in the fruits of their dangers, having the conviction that there was no way of escape for themselves or for them, but that the success of the Four Hundred or of the enemy at Miletus must be their ruin.

The struggle now was between the army trying to force a democracy upon the city, and the Four Hundred an oligarchy upon the camp. Meanwhile the soldiers forthwith held an assembly, in which they deposed the former generals and any of the captains whom they suspected, and chose new captains and generals to replace them, besides Thrasybulus and Thrasyllus, whom they had already. They also stood up and encouraged one another, and among other things urged that they ought not to lose heart because the city had revolted from them, as the party seceding was smaller and in every way poorer in resources than themselves. They had the whole fleet with which to compel the other cities in their empire to give them money just as if they had their base in the capital, having a city in Samos which, so far from wanting strength, had when at war been within an ace of depriving the Athenians of the command of the sea, while as far as the enemy was concerned they had the same base of operations as before. Indeed, with the fleet in their hands, they were better able to provide themselves with supplies than the government at home. It was their advanced position at Samos which had throughout enabled the home authorities to command the entrance into Piraeus; and if they refused to give them back the constitution, they would now find that the army was more in a position to exclude them from the sea than they were to exclude the army. Besides, the city was of little or no use towards enabling them to overcome the enemy; and they had lost nothing in losing those who had no longer either money to send them (the soldiers having to find this for themselves), or good counsel, which entitles cities to direct armies. On the contrary, even in this the home government had done wrong in abolishing the institutions of their ancestors, while the army maintained the said institutions, and would try to force the home government to do so likewise. So that even in point of good counsel the camp had as good counsellors as the city. Moreover, they had but to grant him security for his person and his recall, and Alcibiades would be only too glad to procure them the alliance of the King. And above all if they failed altogether, with the navy which they possessed, they had numbers of places to retire to in which they would find cities and lands.

Debating together and comforting themselves after this manner, they pushed on their war measures as actively as ever; and the ten envoys sent to Samos by the Four Hundred, learning how matters stood while they were still at Delos, stayed quiet there. About this time a cry arose a Peloponnesian fleet at Miletus that

Astyochus and Tissaphernes were ruining their cause. Astyochus had not been willing to fight at sea–either before, while they were still in full vigour and the fleet of the Athenians small, or now, when the enemy was, as they were informed, in a state of sedition and his ships not yet united–but kept them waiting for the Phoenician fleet from Tissaphernes, which had only a nominal existence, at the risk of wasting away in inactivity. While Tissaphernes not only did not bring up the fleet in question, but was ruining their navy by payments made irregularly, and even then not made in full. They must therefore, they insisted, delay no longer, but fight a decisive naval engagement. The Syracusans were the most urgent of any.

The confederates and Astyochus, aware of these murmurs, had already decided in council to fight a decisive battle; and when the news reached them of the disturbance at Samos, they put to sea with all their ships, one hundred and ten in number, and, ordering the Milesians to move by land upon Mycale, set sail thither. The Athenians with the eighty-two ships from Samos were at the moment lying at Glauce in Mycale, a point where Samos approaches near to the continent; and, seeing the Peloponnesian fleet sailing against them, retired into Samos, not thinking themselves numerically strong enough to stake their all upon a battle. Besides, they had notice from Miletus of the wish of the enemy to engage, and were expecting to be joined from the Hellespont by Strombichides, to whom a messenger had been already dispatched, with the ships that had gone from Chios to Abydos. The Athenians accordingly withdrew to Samos, and the Peloponnesians put in at Mycale, and encamped with the land forces of the Milesians and the people of the neighbourhood. The next day they were about to sail against Samos, when tidings reached them of the arrival of Strombichides with the squadron from the Hellespont, upon which they immediately sailed back to Miletus. The Athenians, thus reinforced, now in their turn sailed against Miletus with a hundred and eight ships, wishing to fight a decisive battle, but, as no one put out to meet them, sailed back to Samos.

Chapter Twenty Six

Twenty-first Year of the War–Recall of Alcibiades to Samos–Revolt of Euboea and Downfall of the Four Hundred–Battle of Cynossema

IN THE SAME SUMMER, immediately after this, the Peloponnesians having refused to fight with their fleet united, through not thinking themselves a match for the enemy, and being at a loss where to look for money for such a number of ships, especially as Tissaphernes proved so bad a paymaster, sent off Clearchus, son of Ramphias, with forty ships to Pharnabazus, agreeably to the original instructions from Peloponnese; Pharnabazus inviting them and being prepared to furnish pay, and Byzantium besides sending offers to revolt to them. These Peloponnesian ships accordingly put out into the open sea, in order to escape the observation of the Athenians, and being overtaken by a storm, the majority with Clearchus got into Delos, and afterwards returned to Miletus, whence Clearchus proceeded by land to the Hellespont to take the command: ten, however, of their number, under the Megarian Helixus, made good their passage to the Hellespont, and effected the revolt of Byzantium. After this, the commanders at Samos were informed of it, and sent a squadron against them to guard the Hellespont; and an encounter took place before Byzantium between eight vessels on either side.

Meanwhile the chiefs at Samos, and especially Thrasybulus, who from the moment that he had changed the government had remained firmly resolved to recall Alcibiades, at last in an assembly brought over the mass of the soldiery, and upon their voting for his recall and amnesty, sailed over to Tissaphernes and brought Alcibiades to Samos, being convinced that their only chance of salvation lay in his bringing over Tissaphernes from the Peloponnesians to themselves. An assembly was then held in which Alcibiades complained of and deplored his private misfortune in having been banished, and speaking at great length upon public affairs, highly incited their hopes for the future, and extravagantly magnified his own influence with Tissaphernes. His object in this was to make the oligarchical government at Athens afraid of him, to hasten the dissolution of the clubs, to increase his credit with the army at

Samos and heighten their own confidence, and lastly to prejudice the enemy as strongly as possible against Tissaphernes, and blast the hopes which they entertained. Alcibiades accordingly held out to the army such extravagant promises as the following: that Tissaphernes had solemnly assured him that if he could only trust the Athenians they should never want for supplies while he had anything left, no, not even if he should have to coin his own silver couch, and that he would bring the Phoenician fleet now at Aspendus to the Athenians instead of to the Peloponnesians; but that he could only trust the Athenians if Alcibiades were recalled to be his security for them.

Upon hearing this and much more besides, the Athenians at once elected him general together with the former ones, and put all their affairs into his hands. There was now not a man in the army who would have exchanged his present hopes of safety and vengeance upon the Four Hundred for any consideration whatever; and after what they had been told they were now inclined to disdain the enemy before them, and to sail at once for Piraeus. To the plan of sailing for Piraeus, leaving their more immediate enemies behind them, Alcibiades opposed the most positive refusal, in spite of the numbers that insisted upon it, saying that now that he had been elected general he would first sail to Tissaphernes and concert with him measures for carrying on the war. Accordingly, upon leaving this assembly, he immediately took his departure in order to have it thought that there was an entire confidence between them, and also wishing to increase his consideration with Tissaphernes, and to show that he had now been elected general and was in a position to do him good or evil as he chose; thus managing to frighten the Athenians with Tissaphernes and Tissaphernes with the Athenians.

Meanwhile the Peloponnesians at Miletus

heard of the recall of Alcibiades and, already distrustful of Tissaphernes, now became far more disgusted with him than ever. Indeed after their refusal to go out and give battle to the Athenians when they appeared before Miletus, Tissaphernes had grown slacker than ever in his payments; and even before this, on account of Alcibiades, his unpopularity had been on the increase. Gathering together, just as before, the soldiers and some persons of consideration besides the soldiery began to reckon up how they had never yet received their pay in full; that what they did receive was small in quantity, and even that paid irregularly, and that unless they fought a decisive battle or removed to some station where they could get supplies, the ships' crews would desert; and that it was all the fault of Astyochus, who humoured Tissaphernes for his own private advantage.

The army was engaged in these reflections, when the following disturbance took place about the person of Astyochus. Most of the Syracusan and Thurian sailors were freemen, and these the freest crews in the armament were likewise the boldest in setting upon Astyochus and demanding their pay. The latter answered somewhat stiffly and threatened them, and when Dorieus spoke up for his own sailors even went so far as to lift his baton against him; upon seeing which the mass of men, in sailor fashion, rushed in a fury to strike Astyochus. He, however, saw them in time and fled for refuge to an altar; and they were thus parted without his being struck. Meanwhile the fort built by Tissaphernes in Miletus was surprised and taken by the Milesians, and the garrison in it turned out–an act which met with the approval of the rest of the allies, and in particular of the Syracusans, but which found no favour with Lichas, who said moreover that the Milesians and the rest in the King's country ought to show a reasonable submission to Tissaphernes and to pay him court, until the war should be happily settled. The Milesians were angry with him for this and for other things of the kind, and upon his afterwards dying of sickness, would not allow him to be buried where the Lacedaemonians with the army desired.

The discontent of the army with Astyochus and Tissaphernes had reached this pitch, when Mindarus arrived from Lacedaemon to succeed Astyochus as admiral, and assumed the command. Astyochus now set sail for home; and Tissaphernes sent with him one of his confidants, Gaulites, a Carian, who spoke the two languages, to complain of the Milesians for the affair of the fort, and at the same time to defend himself against the Milesians, who were, as he was aware, on their way to Sparta chiefly to denounce his conduct, and had with them Hermocrates, who was to accuse Tissaphernes of joining with Alcibiades to ruin the Peloponnesian cause and of playing a double game. Indeed Hermocrates had always been at enmity with him about the pay not being restored in full; and eventually when he was banished from Syracuse, and new commanders–Potamis, Myscon, and Demarchus–had come out to Miletus to the ships of the Syracusans, Tissaphernes, pressed harder than ever upon him in his exile, and among other charges against him accused him of having once asked him for money, and then given himself out as his enemy because he failed to obtain it.

While Astyochus and the Milesians and Hermocrates made sail for Lacedaemon, Alcibiades had now crossed back from Tissaphernes to Samos. After his return the envoys of the Four Hundred sent, as has been mentioned above, to pacify and explain matters to the forces at Samos, arrived from Delos; and an assembly was held in which they attempted to speak. The soldiers at first would not hear them, and cried out to put to death the subverters of the democracy, but at last, after some difficulty, calmed down and gave them a hearing. Upon this the envoys proceeded to inform them that the recent change had been made to save the city, and not to ruin it or to deliver it over to the enemy, for they had already had an opportunity of doing this when he invaded the country during their government; that all the Five Thousand would have their proper share in the government; and that their hearers' relatives had neither outrage, as Chaereas had slanderously reported, nor other ill treatment to complain of, but were all in undisturbed enjoyment of their property just as they had left them. Besides these they made a number of other statements which had no better success with their angry auditors; and amid a host of different opinions the one which found most favour was that of sailing to Piraeus. Now it was that Alcibiades for the first time did the state a service, and one of the most signal kind.

For when the Athenians at Samos were bent upon sailing against their countrymen, in which case Ionia and the Hellespont would most certainly at once have passed into possession of the enemy, Alcibiades it was who prevented them. At that moment, when no other man would have been able to hold back the multitude, he put a stop to the intended expedition, and rebuked and turned aside the resentment felt, on personal grounds, against the envoys; he dismissed them with an answer from himself, to the effect that he did not object to the government of the Five Thousand, but insisted that the Four Hundred should be deposed and the Council of Five Hundred reinstated in power: meanwhile any retrenchments for economy, by which pay might be better found for the armament, met with his entire approval. Generally, he bade them hold out and show a bold face to the enemy, since if the city were saved there was good hope that the two parties might some day be reconciled, whereas if either were once destroyed, that at Samos, or that at Athens, there would no longer be any one to be reconciled to. Meanwhile arrived envoys from the Argives, with offers of support to the Athenian commons at Samos: these were thanked by Alcibiades, and dismissed with a request to come when called upon. The Argives were accompanied by the crew of the Paralus, whom we left placed in a troopship by the Four Hundred with orders to cruise round Euboea, and who being employed to carry to Lacedaemon some Athenian envoys sent by the Four Hundred–Laespodias, Aristophon, and Melesias–as they sailed by Argos laid hands upon the envoys, and delivering them over to the Argives as the chief subverters of the democracy, themselves, instead of returning to Athens, took the Argive envoys on board, and came to Samos in the galley which had been confided to them.

The same summer at the time that the return of Alcibiades coupled with the general conduct of Tissaphernes had carried to its height the discontent of the Peloponnesians, who no longer entertained any doubt of his having joined the Athenians, Tissaphernes wishing, it would seem, to clear himself to them of these charges, prepared to go after the Phoenician fleet to Aspendus, and invited Lichas to go with him; saying that he would appoint Tamos as his lieutenant to provide pay for the armament during his own absence. Accounts differ, and it is not easy to ascertain with what intention he went to Aspendus, and did not bring the fleet after all. That one hundred and forty-seven Phoenician ships came as far as Aspendus is certain; but why they did not come on has been variously accounted for. Some think that he went away in pursuance of his plan of wasting the Peloponnesian resources, since at any rate Tamos, his lieutenant, far from being any better, proved a worse paymaster than himself: others that he brought the Phoenicians to Aspendus to exact money from them for their discharge, having never intended to employ them: others again that it was in view of the outcry against him at Lacedaemon, in order that it might be said that he was not in fault, but that the ships were really manned and that he had certainly gone to fetch them. To myself it seems only too evident that he did not bring up the fleet because he wished to wear out and paralyse the Hellenic forces, that is, to waste their strength by the time lost during his journey to Aspendus, and to keep them evenly balanced by not throwing his weight into either scale. Had he wished to finish the war, he could have done so, assuming of course that he made his appearance in a way which left no room for doubt; as by bringing up the fleet he would in all probability have given the victory to the Lacedaemonians, whose navy, even as it was, faced the Athenian more as an equal than as an inferior. But what convicts him most clearly, is the excuse which he put forward for not bringing the ships. He said that the number assembled was less than the King had ordered; but surely it would only have enhanced his credit if he spent little of the King's money and effected the same end at less cost. In any case, whatever was his intention, Tissaphernes went to Aspendus and saw the Phoenicians; and the Peloponnesians at his desire sent a Lacedaemonian called Philip with two galleys to fetch the fleet.

Alcibiades finding that Tissaphernes had gone to Aspendus, himself sailed thither with thirteen ships, promising to do a great and certain service to the Athenians at Samos, as he would either bring the Phoenician fleet to the Athenians, or at all events prevent its joining the Peloponnesians. In all probability he had long known that Tissaphernes never meant to bring the fleet at all, and wished to compromise him as much as possible in the eyes of the Peloponnesians through his apparent friendship for himself and the Athenians, and thus in a manner to oblige him to join their side.

While Alcibiades weighed anchor and sailed eastward straight for Phaselis and Caunus, the envoys sent by the Four Hundred to Samos arrived at Athens. Upon their delivering the message from Alcibiades, telling them to hold out and to show a firm front to the enemy, and saying that he had great hopes of reconciling them with the army and of overcoming the Peloponnesians, the majority of the members of the oligarchy, who were already discontented and only too much inclined to be quit of the business in any safe way that they could, were at once greatly strengthened in their resolve. These now banded together and strongly criticized the administration, their leaders being some of the principal generals and men in office under the oligarchy, such as

Theramenes, son of Hagnon, Aristocrates, son of Scellias, and others; who, although among the most prominent members of the government (being afraid, as they said, of the army at Samos, and most especially of Alcibiades, and also lest the envoys whom they had sent to Lacedaemon might do the state some harm without the authority of the people), without insisting on objections to the excessive concentration of power in a few hands, yet urged that the Five Thousand must be shown to exist not merely in name but in reality, and the constitution placed upon a fairer basis. But this was merely their political cry; most of them being driven by private ambition into the line of conduct so surely fatal to oligarchies that arise out of democracies. For all at once pretend to be not only equals but each the chief and master of his fellows; while under a democracy a disappointed candidate accepts his defeat more easily, because he has not the humiliation of being beaten by his equals. But what most clearly encouraged the malcontents was the power of Alcibiades at Samos, and their own disbelief in the stability of the oligarchy; and it was now a race between them as to which should first become the leader of the commons.

Meanwhile the leaders and members of the Four Hundred most opposed to a democratic form of government–Phrynichus who had had the quarrel with Alcibiades during his command at Samos, Aristarchus the bitter and inveterate enemy of the commons, and Pisander and Antiphon and others of the chiefs who already as soon as they entered upon power, and again when the army at Samos seceded from them and declared for a democracy, had sent envoys from their own body to Lacedaemon and made every effort for peace, and had built the wall in Eetionia–now redoubled their exertions when their envoys returned from Samos, and they saw not only the people but their own most trusted associates turning against them. Alarmed at the state of things at Athens as at Samos, they now sent off in haste Antiphon and Phrynichus and ten others with injunctions to make peace with Lacedaemon upon any terms, no matter what, that should be at all tolerable. Meanwhile they pushed on more actively than ever with the wall in Eetionia. Now the meaning of this wall, according to Theramenes and his supporters, was not so much to keep out the army of Samos, in case of its trying to force its way into Piraeus, as to be able to let in, at pleasure, the fleet and army of the enemy. For Eetionia is a mole of Piraeus, close alongside of the entrance of the harbour, and was now fortified in connection with the wall already existing on the land side, so that a few men placed in it might be able to command the entrance; the old wall on the land side and the new one now being built within on the side of the sea, both ending in one of the two towers standing at the narrow mouth of the harbour. They also walled off the largest porch in Piraeus which was in immediate connection with this wall, and kept it in their own hands, compelling all to unload there the corn that came into the harbour, and what they had in stock, and to take it out from thence when they sold it.

These measures had long provoked the murmurs of Theramenes, and when the envoys returned from Lacedaemon without having effected any general pacification, he affirmed that this wall was like to prove the ruin of the state. At this moment forty-two ships from Peloponnese, including some Siceliot and Italiot vessels from Locri and Tarentum, had been invited over by the Euboeans and were already riding off Las in Laconia preparing for the voyage to Euboea, under the command of Agesandridas, son of Agesander, a Spartan. Theramenes now affirmed that this squadron was destined not so much to aid Euboea as the party fortifying Eetionia, and that unless precautions were speedily taken the city would be surprised and lost. This was no mere calumny, there being really some such plan entertained by the accused. Their first wish was to have the oligarchy without giving up the empire; failing this to keep their ships and walls and be independent; while, if this also were denied them, sooner than be the first victims of the restored democracy, they were resolved to call in the enemy and make peace, give up their walls and ships, and at all costs retain possession of the government, if their lives were only assured to them.

For this reason they pushed forward the construction of their work with posterns and entrances and means of introducing the enemy, being eager to have it finished in time. Meanwhile the murmurs against them were at first confined to a few persons and went on in secret, until Phrynichus, after his return from the embassy to Lacedaemon, was laid wait for and stabbed in full market by one of the Peripoli, falling down dead before he had gone far from the council chamber. The assassin escaped; but his accomplice, an Argive, was taken and put to the torture by the Four Hundred, without their being able to extract from him the name of his employer, or anything further than that he knew of many men who used to assemble at the house of the commander of the Peripoli and at other houses. Here the matter was allowed to drop. This so emboldened Theramenes and Aristocrates and the rest of their partisans in the Four Hundred and out of doors, that they now resolved to act. For by this time the ships had sailed round from Las, and anchoring at Epidaurus had overrun Aegina; and Theramenes asserted that, being bound for Euboea, they would never have sailed in to Aegina and come back to anchor at Epidaurus, unless they had been invited to come to aid in the designs of which he had always accused the government. Further inaction had therefore now become impossible. In the end, after a great many seditious harangues and suspicions, they set to work in real earnest. The heavy infantry in Piraeus building the wall in Eetionia, among whom was Aristocrates, a colonel, with his own tribe, laid hands upon Alexicles, a general under the oligarchy and the devoted adherent of the cabal, and took him into a house and confined him there. In this they were assisted by one Hermon, commander of the Peripoli in Munychia, and others, and above all had with them the great bulk of the heavy infantry. As soon as the news reached the Four Hundred, who happened to be sitting in the council chamber, all except the disaffected wished at once to go to the posts where the arms were, and menaced Theramenes and his party. Theramenes defended himself, and said that he was ready immediately to go and help to rescue Alexicles; and taking with him one of the generals belonging to his party, went down to Piraeus, followed by Aristarchus and some young men of the cavalry. All was now panic and confusion. Those in the city imagined that Piraeus was already taken and the prisoner put to death, while those in Piraeus expected every moment to be attacked by the party in the city. The older men, however, stopped the persons running up and down the town and making for the stands of arms; and Thucydides the Pharsalian, proxenus of the city, came forward and threw himself in the way of the rival factions, and appealed to them not to ruin the state, while the enemy was still at hand waiting for his opportunity, and so at length succeeded in quieting them and in keeping their hands off each other. Meanwhile Theramenes came down to Piraeus, being himself one of the generals, and raged and stormed against the heavy infantry, while Aristarchus and the adversaries of the people were angry in right earnest. Most of the heavy infantry, however, went on with the business without faltering, and asked Theramenes if he thought the wall had been constructed for any good purpose, and whether it would not be better that it should be pulled down. To this he answered that if they thought it best to pull it down, he for his part agreed with them. Upon this the heavy infantry and a number of the people in Piraeus immediately got up on the fortification and began to demolish it. Now their cry to the multitude was that all should join in the work who wished the Five Thousand to govern instead of the Four Hundred. For instead of saying in so many words "all who wished the commons to govern," they still disguised themselves under the name of the Five Thousand; being afraid that these might really exist, and that they might be speaking to one of their number and get into trouble through ignorance. Indeed this was why the Four Hundred neither wished the Five Thousand to exist, nor to have it known that they did not exist; being of opinion that to give themselves so many partners in empire would be downright democracy, while the mystery in question would make the people afraid of one another.

The next day the Four Hundred, although alarmed, nevertheless assembled in the council chamber, while the heavy infantry in Piraeus, after having released their prisoner Alexicles and pulled down the fortification, went with their arms to the theatre of Dionysus, close to Munychia, and there held an assembly in which they decided to march into the city, and setting forth accordingly halted in the Anaceum. Here they were joined by some delegates from the Four Hundred, who reasoned with them one by one, and persuaded those whom they saw to be the most moderate to remain quiet themselves, and to keep in the rest; saying that they would make known the Five Thousand, and have the Four Hundred chosen from them in rotation, as should be decided by the Five Thousand, and meanwhile entreated them not to ruin the state or drive it into the arms of the enemy. After a great many had spoken and had been spoken to, the whole body of heavy infantry became calmer than before, absorbed by their fears for the country at large, and now agreed to hold upon an appointed day an assembly in the theatre of Dionysus for the restoration of concord.

When the day came for the assembly in the theatre, and they were upon the point of assembling, news arrived that the forty-two ships under Agesandridas were sailing from Megara along the coast of Salamis. The people to a man now thought that it was just what Theramenes and his party had so often said, that the ships were sailing to the fortification, and concluded that they had done well to demolish it. But though it may possibly have been by appointment that Agesandridas hovered about Epidaurus and the neighbourhood, he would also naturally be kept there by the hope of an opportunity arising out of the troubles in the town. In any case the Athenians, on receipt of the news immediately ran down in mass to Piraeus, seeing themselves threatened by the enemy with a worse war than their war among themselves, not at a distance, but close to the harbour of Athens. Some went on board the ships already afloat, while others launched fresh vessels, or ran to defend the walls and the mouth of the harbour.

Meanwhile the Peloponnesian vessels sailed by, and rounding Sunium anchored between Thoricus and Prasiae, and afterwards arrived at Oropus. The Athenians, with revolution in the city, and unwilling to lose a moment in going to the relief of their most important possession (for Euboea was everything to them now that they were shut out from Attica), were compelled to put to sea in haste and with untrained crews, and sent Thymochares with some vessels to Eretria. These upon their arrival, with the ships already in Euboea, made up a total of thirty-six vessels, and were immediately forced to engage. For Agesandridas, after his crews had dined, put out from Oropus, which is about seven miles from Eretria by sea; and the Athenians, seeing him sailing up, immediately began to man their vessels. The sailors, however, instead of being by their ships, as they supposed, were gone away to purchase provisions for their dinner in the houses in the outskirts of the town; the Eretrians having so arranged that there should be nothing on sale in the marketplace, in order that the Athenians might be a long time in manning their ships, and, the enemy's attack taking them by surprise, might be compelled to put to sea just as they were. A signal also was raised in Eretria to give them notice in Oropus when to put to sea. The Athenians, forced to put out so poorly prepared, engaged off the harbour of Eretria, and after holding their own for some little while notwithstanding, were at length put to flight and chased to the shore. Such of their number as took refuge in Eretria, which they presumed to be friendly to them, found their fate in that city, being butchered by the inhabitants; while those who fled to the Athenian fort in the Eretrian territory, and the vessels which got to Chalcis, were saved. The Peloponnesians, after taking twenty-two Athenian ships, and killing or making prisoners of the crews, set up a trophy, and not long afterwards effected the revolt of the whole of Euboea (except Oreus, which was held by the Athenians themselves), and made a general settlement of the affairs of the island.

When the news of what had happened in Euboea reached Athens, a panic ensued such as they had never before known. Neither the disaster in Sicily, great as it seemed at the time, nor any other had ever so much alarmed them. The camp at Samos was in revolt; they had no more ships or men to man them; they were at discord among themselves and might at any moment come to blows; and a disaster of this magnitude coming on the top of all, by which they lost their fleet, and worst of all Euboea, which was of more value to them than Attica, could not occur without throwing them into the deepest despondency. Meanwhile their greatest and most immediate trouble was the possibility that the enemy, emboldened by his victory, might make straight for them and sail against Piraeus, which they had no longer ships to defend; and every moment they expected him to arrive. This, with a little more courage, he might easily have done, in which case he would either have increased the dissensions of the city by his presence, or, if he had stayed to besiege it, have compelled the fleet from Ionia, although the enemy of the oligarchy, to come to the rescue of their country and of their relatives, and in the meantime would have become master of the Hellespont, Ionia, the islands, and of everything as far as Euboea, or, to speak roundly, of the whole Athenian empire. But here, as on so many other occasions, the Lacedaemonians proved the most convenient people in the world for the Athenians to be at war with. The wide difference between the two characters, the slowness and want of energy of the Lacedaemonians as contrasted with the dash and enterprise of their opponents, proved of the greatest service, especially to a maritime empire like Athens. Indeed this was shown by the Syracusans, who were most like the Athenians in character, and also most successful in combating them.

Nevertheless, upon receipt of the news, the Athenians manned twenty ships and called immediately a first assembly in the Pnyx, where they had been used to meet formerly, and deposed the Four Hundred and voted to hand over the government to the Five Thousand, of which body all who furnished a suit of armour were to be members, decreeing also that no one should receive pay for the discharge of any office, or if he did should be held accursed. Many other assemblies were held afterwards, in which law-makers were elected and all other measures taken to form a constitution. It was during the first period of this constitution that the Athenians appear to have enjoyed the best government that they ever did, at least in my time. For the fusion of the high and the low was effected with judgment, and this was what first enabled the state to raise up her head after her manifold disasters. They also voted for the recall of Alcibiades and of other exiles, and sent to him and to the camp at Samos, and urged them to devote themselves vigorously to the war.

Upon this revolution taking place, the party of Pisander and Alexicles and the chiefs of the oligarchs immediately withdrew to Decelea, with the single exception of Aristarchus, one of the generals, who hastily took some of the most barbarian of the archers and marched to Oenoe. This was a fort of the Athenians upon the Boeotian border, at that moment besieged by the Corinthians, irritated by the loss of a party returning from Decelea, who had been cut off by the garrison. The Corinthians had volunteered for this service, and had called upon the Boeotians to assist them. After communicating with them, Aristarchus deceived the garrison in Oenoe by telling them that their countrymen in the city had compounded with the Lacedaemonians, and that one of the terms of the capitulation was that they must surrender the place to the Boeotians. The garrison believed him as he was general, and besides knew nothing of what had occurred owing to the siege, and so evacuated the fort under truce. In this way the Boeotians gained possession of Oenoe, and the oligarchy and the troubles at Athens ended.

To return to the Peloponnesians in Miletus. No pay was forthcoming from any of the agents deputed by Tissaphernes for that purpose upon his departure for Aspendus; neither the Phoenician fleet nor Tissaphernes showed any signs of appearing, and Philip, who had been sent with him, and another Spartan, Hippocrates, who was at Phaselis, wrote word to Mindarus, the admiral, that the ships were not coming at all, and that they were being grossly abused by Tissaphernes. Meanwhile Pharnabazus was inviting them to come, and making every effort to get the fleet and, like Tissaphernes, to cause the revolt of the cities in his government still subject to Athens, founding great hopes on his success; until at length, at about the period of the summer which we have now reached, Mindarus yielded to his importunities, and, with great order and at a moment's notice, in order to elude the enemy at Samos, weighed anchor with seventy-three ships from Miletus and set sail for the Hellespont. Thither sixteen vessels had already preceded him in the same summer, and had overrun part of the Chersonese. Being caught in a storm, Mindarus was compelled to run in to Icarus and, after being detained five or six days there by stress of weather, arrived at Chios.

Meanwhile Thrasyllus had heard of his having put out from Miletus, and immediately set sail with fifty-five ships from Samos, in haste to arrive before him in the Hellespont. But learning that he was at Chios, and expecting that he would stay there, he posted scouts in Lesbos and on the continent opposite to prevent the fleet moving without his knowing it, and himself coasted along to Methymna, and gave orders to prepare meal and other necessaries, in order to attack them from Lesbos in the event of their remaining for any length of time at Chios. Meanwhile he resolved to sail against Eresus, a town in Lesbos which had revolted, and, if he could, to take it. For some of the principal Methymnian exiles had carried over about fifty heavy infantry, their sworn associates, from Cuma, and hiring others from the continent, so as to make up three hundred in all, chose Anaxander, a

Theban, to command them, on account of the community of blood existing between the Thebans and the Lesbians, and first attacked Methymna. Balked in this attempt by the advance of the Athenian guards from Mitylene, and repulsed a second time in a battle outside the city, they then crossed the mountain and effected the revolt of Eresus. Thrasyllus accordingly determined to go there with all his ships and to attack the place. Meanwhile Thrasybulus had preceded him thither with five ships from Samos, as soon as he heard that the exiles had crossed over, and coming too late to save Eresus, went on and anchored before the town. Here they were joined also by two vessels on their way home from the Hellespont, and by the ships of the Methymnians, making a grand total of sixty-seven vessels; and the forces on board now made ready with engines and every other means available to do their utmost to storm Eresus.

Chapter Twenty Six

In the meantime Mindarus and the Peloponnesian fleet at Chios, after taking provisions for two days and receiving three Chian pieces of money for each man from the Chians, on the third day put out in haste from the island; in order to avoid falling in with the ships at Eresus, they did not make for the open sea, but keeping Lesbos on their left, sailed for the continent. After touching at the port of Carteria, in the Phocaeid, and dining, they went on along the Cumaean coast and supped at Arginusae, on the continent over against Mitylene. From thence they continued their voyage along the coast, although it was late in the night, and arriving at Harmatus on the continent opposite Methymna, dined there; and swiftly passing Lectum, Larisa, Hamaxitus, and the neighbouring towns, arrived a little before midnight at Rhoeteum. Here they were now in the Hellespont. Some of the ships also put in at Sigeum and at other places in the neighbourhood.

Meanwhile the warnings of the fire signals and the sudden increase in the number of fires on the enemy's shore informed the eighteen Athenian ships at Sestos of the approach of the Peloponnesian fleet. That very night they set sail in haste just as they were, and, hugging the shore of the Chersonese, coasted along to Elaeus, in order to sail out into the open sea away from the fleet of the enemy.

After passing unobserved the sixteen ships at Abydos, which had nevertheless been warned by their approaching friends to be on the alert to prevent their sailing out, at dawn they sighted the fleet of Mindarus, which immediately gave chase. All had not time to get away; the greater number however escaped to Imbros and Lemnos, while four of the hindmost were overtaken off Elaeus. One of these was stranded opposite to the temple of Protesilaus and taken with its crew, two others without their crews; the fourth was abandoned on the shore of Imbros and burned by the enemy.

After this the Peloponnesians were joined by the squadron from Abydos, which made up their fleet to a grand total of eighty-six vessels; they spent the day in unsuccessfully besieging Elaeus, and then sailed back to Abydos. Meanwhile the Athenians, deceived by their scouts, and never dreaming of the enemy's fleet getting by undetected, were tranquilly besieging Eresus. As soon as they heard the news they instantly abandoned Eresus, and made with all speed for the Hellespont, and after taking two of the Peloponnesian ships which had been carried out too far into the open sea in the ardour of the pursuit and now fell in their way, the next day dropped anchor at Elaeus, and, bringing back the ships that had taken refuge at Imbros, during five days prepared for the coming engagement.

After this they engaged in the following way. The Athenians formed in column and sailed close alongshore to Sestos; upon perceiving which the Peloponnesians put out from Abydos to meet them. Realizing that a battle was now imminent, both combatants extended their flank; the Athenians along the Chersonese from Idacus to Arrhiani with seventy-six ships; the Peloponnesians from Abydos to Dardanus with eighty-six. The Peloponnesian right wing was occupied by the Syracusans, their left by Mindarus in person with the best sailers in the navy; the Athenian left by Thrasyllus, their right by Thrasybulus, the other commanders being in different parts of the fleet. The Peloponnesians hastened to engage first, and outflanking with their left the Athenian right sought to cut them off, if possible, from sailing out of the straits, and to drive their centre upon the shore, which was not far off. The Athenians perceiving their intention extended their own wing and outsailed them, while their left had by this time passed the point of Cynossema. This, however, obliged them to thin and weaken their centre, especially as they had fewer ships than the enemy, and as the coast round Point Cynossema formed a sharp angle which prevented their seeing what was going on on the other side of it.

The Peloponnesians now attacked their centre and drove ashore the ships of the Athenians, and disembarked to follow up their victory. No help could be given to the centre either by the squadron of Thrasybulus on the right, on account of the number of ships attacking him, or by that of Thrasyllus on the left, from whom the point of Cynossema hid what was going on, and who was also hindered by his Syracusan and other opponents, whose numbers were fully equal to his own. At length, however, the Peloponnesians in the confidence of victory began to scatter in pursuit of the ships of the enemy, and allowed a considerable part of their fleet to get into disorder. On seeing this the squadron of Thrasybulus discontinued their lateral movement and, facing about, attacked and routed the ships opposed to them, and next fell roughly upon the scattered vessels of the victorious Peloponnesian division, and put most of them to flight without a blow. The Syracusans also had by this time given way before the squadron of Thrasyllus, and now openly took to flight upon seeing the flight of their comrades.

The rout was now complete. Most of the Peloponnesians fled for refuge first to the river Midius, and afterwards to Abydos. Only a few ships were taken by the Athenians; as owing to the narrowness of the Hellespont the enemy had not far to go to be in safety. Nevertheless nothing could have been more opportune for them than this victory. Up to this time they had feared the Peloponnesian fleet, owing to a number of petty losses and to the disaster in Sicily; but they now ceased to mistrust themselves or any longer to think their enemies good for anything at sea. Meanwhile they took from the enemy eight Chian vessels, five Corinthian, two Ambraciot, two Boeotian, one Leucadian, Lacedaemonian, Syracusan, and Pellenian, losing fifteen of their own. After setting up a trophy upon Point Cynossema, securing the wrecks, and restoring to the enemy his dead under truce, they sent off a galley to Athens with the news of their victory. The arrival of this vessel with its unhoped-for good news, after the recent disasters of Euboea, and in the revolution at Athens, gave fresh courage to the Athenians, and caused them to believe that if they put their shoulders to the wheel their cause might yet prevail.

On the fourth day after the sea-fight the Athenians in Sestos having hastily refitted their ships sailed against Cyzicus, which had revolted. Off Harpagium and Priapus they sighted at anchor the eight vessels from Byzantium, and, sailing up and routing the troops on shore, took the ships, and then went on and recovered the town of Cyzicus, which was unfortified, and levied money from the citizens. In the meantime the Peloponnesians sailed from Abydos to Elaeus, and recovered such of their captured galleys as were still uninjured, the rest having been burned by the Elaeusians, and sent Hippocrates and Epicles to Euboea to fetch the squadron from that island.

About the same time Alcibiades returned with his thirteen ships from Caunus and Phaselis to Samos, bringing word that he had prevented the Phoenician fleet from joining the Peloponnesians, and had made Tissaphernes more friendly to the Athenians than before. Alcibiades now manned nine more ships, and levied large sums of money from the Halicarnassians, and fortified Cos. After doing this and placing a governor in Cos, he sailed back to Samos, autumn being now at hand. Meanwhile Tissaphernes, upon hearing that the Peloponnesian fleet had sailed from Miletus to the Hellespont, set off again back from Aspendus, and made all sail for Ionia. While the Peloponnesians were in the Hellespont, the Antandrians, a people of Aeolic extraction, conveyed by land across Mount Ida some heavy infantry from Abydos, and introduced them into the town; having been ill-treated by Arsaces, the Persian lieutenant of Tissaphernes. This same Arsaces had, upon pretence of a secret quarrel, invited the chief men of the Delians to undertake military service (these were Delians who had settled at Atramyttium after having been driven from their homes by the Athenians for the sake of purifying Delos); and after drawing them out from their town as his friends and allies, had laid wait for them at dinner, and surrounded them and caused them to be shot down by his soldiers. This deed made the Antandrians fear that he might some day do them some mischief; and as he also laid upon them burdens too heavy for them to bear, they expelled his garrison from their citadel.

Tissaphernes, upon hearing of this act of the Peloponnesians in addition to what had occurred at Miletus and Cnidus, where his garrisons had been also expelled, now saw that the breach between them was serious; and fearing further injury from them, and being also vexed to think that Pharnabazus should receive them, and in less time and at less cost perhaps succeed better against Athens than he had done, determined to rejoin them in the Hellespont, in order to complain of the events at Antandros and excuse himself as best he could in the matter of the Phoenician fleet and of the other charges against him. Accordingly he went first to Ephesus and offered sacrifice to Artemis....

[When the winter after this summer is over the twenty-first year of this war will be completed.]

THE END

www.ingramcontent.com/pod-product-compliance
Lightning Source LLC
Chambersburg PA
CBHW020919310726

48980CB00011B/953/J
* 9 7 8 1 8 3 4 1 2 4 1 8 6 *